LIVING WITH THE AFTERMATH
Trauma, nostalgia and grief in post-war Australia

This very powerful and moving book on the shifting patterns of mourning and grief focuses on the experiences of Australian women who lost their husbands during the Second World War and the wars in Korea and Vietnam, and those who suffered when their men came home. The book makes use of extensive oral testimonies to illustrate how widows internalised and absorbed the traumas of their husbands' war experiences. Damousi is able to demonstrate that a significant shift in attitudes towards grieving and loss came about between the mid and the later part of the twentieth century. In charting the memory of grief and its expression, she discerns a move away from the denial and silence which shaped attitudes in the 1950s towards a much fuller expression of grief and mourning and perhaps a new way of understanding death and loss at the beginning of the new century.

Joy Damousi is an Associate Professor in the Department of History at the University of Melbourne. She is the author of *Women Come Rally: Socialism, Communism and Gender in Australia, 1890–1955* (Oxford, 1994), *Depraved and Disorderly: Female Convicts, Sexuality and Gender in Colonial Australia* (1997), *The Labour of Loss: Mourning, Memory and Wartime Bereavement in Australia* (1999), which was shortlisted for the NSW Premier's Australian History Prize in 2000, and co-editor (with Marilyn Lake) of *Gender and War: Australians at War in the Twentieth Century* (1995) (all published by Cambridge University Press). Joy Damousi is also a contributor to *The Oxford Companion to Australian History* (1998) and *The Oxford Companion to Australian Feminism* (1998).

For my father, George

LIVING WITH THE AFTERMATH

Trauma, nostalgia and grief in post-war Australia

JOY DAMOUSI
University of Melbourne

PUBLISHED BY THE PRESS SYNDICATE OF THE UNIVERSITY OF CAMBRIDGE
The Pitt Building, Trumpington Street, Cambridge, United Kingdom

CAMBRIDGE UNIVERSITY PRESS
The Edinburgh Building, Cambridge CB2 2RU, UK
40 West 20th Street, New York, NY 10011–4211, USA
10 Stamford Road, Oakleigh, VIC 3166, Australia
Ruiz de Alarcón 13, 28014 Madrid, Spain
Dock House, The Waterfront, Cape Town 8001, South Africa

http://www.cambridge.org

First published 2001

Printed in Australia by Brown Prior Anderson

Typeface Times (*Adobe*) 11/13 pt.   *System* QuarkXPress®   [BC]

A catalogue record for this book is available from the British Library

National Library of Australia Cataloguing in Publication data
Damousi, Joy, 1961–   .
Living with the aftermath: trauma, nostalgia and grief in
post-war Australia.
Bibliography.
Includes index.
ISBN 0 521 80218 0.
1. World War, 1914–1918 – Social aspects – Australia.
2. World War, 1914–1918 – Psychological aspects.
3. World War, 1939–1945 – Social aspects – Australia.
4. Grief – Psychological aspects. 5. World War, 1939–1945 –
Psychological aspects. 6. Bereavement – Psychological
aspects. I. Title.
155.9370994

ISBN 0 521 80218 0 hardback

Contents

Acknowledgements

My foremost debt is to the war widows who gave so generously and fully of their intimate experiences. Although I have not directly cited material from all of the interviews we conducted, each of the interviews was of invaluable assistance to me in the development of this book. I am most grateful to them all for their enthusiasm and commitment to the project, without which this book would not have been possible. I also wish to acknowledge the assistance of the War Widows' Guild of Australia and the War Widows' and Widowed Mothers' Association who kindly helped with arranging interviews and contacting widows.

I was also privileged to work with Katherine Ellinghaus, whose organisational skills, initiative and professionalism expanded the possibilities and scope of this research. Without her considerable support, her foresight, and meticulous attention to detail, this work would have been impossible to undertake, let alone to complete. Financial assistance was provided by the Australian Research Council which eased the task of interviewing.

Others kindly and freely gave their suggestions and ideas. Stuart Macintyre provided much needed direction on several drafts, and many of the arguments in this book have evolved and developed through his considerable input. Emma Grahame applied her formidable editorial skills to the manuscript during the early stages of writing. Robert Reynolds and Charles Zika engaged thoughtfully and generously with my ideas as they formed. Ann Turner read the manuscript, offered incisive comments and gave constant encouragement for which I am greatly indebted.

At Cambridge University Press, Peter Debus lent ongoing support and assistance and maintained faith in the project. Paul Watt contributed invaluable suggestions and wise advice, while Carla Taines was a skilled and deft editor who made a significant contribution to the book in its evolution to completion.

My academic and administrative colleagues in the history department at the University of Melbourne continue to provide a nurturing environment within which to research and write. This has provided a crucial impetus for my ongoing historical inquiry and I thank them all for their generosity and collegiate support.

Friends continued to engage me in many different ways. I wish to thank Bain Attwood, Verity Burgmann, Barbara Caine, Georgine Clarsen, Paul Collins, Ann Curthoys, John Dillane, Sarah Ferber, Esther Faye, Patricia Grimshaw, Phillip Harvey, Lucy Healey, Katie Holmes, Diane Kirkby, Rose Lucas, Marilyn Lake, Carmel Reilly, Suzanne Rickard, Judith Smart, Charles Sowerwine, Marion K. Stell, Shurlee Swain, Christina Twomey and Julie Wells.

Finally, I have dedicated this book to my father who did not live to see its completion, but whose life experiences inspired me to explore the themes of family, identity, grief and courage, which I pursue in the following pages.

CHAPTER ONE

INTRODUCTION

'I am a war widow' explains Pat Medaris, whose husband, Jack had served in the Korean and Vietnam wars.

> I think it fills me in with Jack because he was away so much at Vietnam and Korea, Malaysia, but I feel I'm part of that, you know what I mean? Part of his thing, by being a war widow … By association I feel that I'm actually a war widow through him, so therefore what I am is part of him. It keeps me connected with him.[1]

The role of this connection between the past and the present in shaping identity is one of the key concerns of this book. Through an analysis of seventy interviews conducted with war widows, my aim is to explore how memory and identity are linked. What does it mean to be a war widow? How have memories shaped that identity? How do women convey their life histories?

This study is based on interviews conducted with Australian war widows whose husbands died either during wartime, or afterwards because of a war-related injury. Using oral testimonies as the basis for a study of war widows opens up possibilities that official sources do not allow in the same way, for the emotional detail of widows' experiences is not documented in such material. Rather than consider war widows primarily as welfare recipients – as others have done – I shift the attention to the emotional experience of widowhood during the post-war period.

Using interviews, this work extends the themes covered in my previous study, *The Labour of Loss*, and introduces other issues through the use of oral testimonies. In the earlier book, I considered the ways that mothers, fathers and widows dealt with grief immediately after each of the two world wars. I used letters, diaries and newsletters to reconstruct the world of the wartime bereaved, and explore the ways in which grief and mourning mobilised these people.

Unlike these written sources, the interview is the *means* by which a narrative takes shape, in the interaction between the interviewer and interviewee.[2] It is in that relationship that historical memory is formed in a shape which is specific to time and place. The interviews conducted for this book were primarily arranged through advertisement in war widows' newsletters and through organisations such as the War Widows' Guild and the War Widows' and Widowed Mothers' Association. While the selection of widows may have be skewed in this way, the stories presented here cover a diverse range of experiences. Each interview was between one and two hours in length, and conducted in the home of the interviewee. In most cases, the widows are referred to by their names, but pseudonyms have been used if widows requested that their names be changed. Although informants were asked specific questions, the interview invariably became free-ranging and wider in scope as the conversation developed. It is also important to remember that these exchanges are informed by what people can tell us about their lives, and what they perceive their audience wishes to hear.[3] An interview then is shaped by both participants, but, as Luisa Passerini points out, the narrative of memory is inescapably drawn from pre-existing 'ways of telling stories'.[4]

The use of these sources raises the question of how oral testimonies should be read. Oral history has been celebrated for allowing marginalised groups to find a voice. It has been seen as a means of retrieving those experiences of women that are eliminated from official documentation.[5] The enterprise of oral history has often been conflated with women's history and the two have informed each other in retrieving women's untold stories.[6] Oral history does however, offer more than a mere supplementation of the historical record. Historians have long claimed that its value lies not in 'revealing facts and events',[7] but rather, in showing how the 'facts' are in the 'memory itself'.[8] Portelli has argued it can tell us 'less about events as such than about their meaning',[9] for 'it is always a work in progress, in which narrators revise the image of their past as they go along'.[10] A life story has a life of its own. Yet these are fragmentary tales, for memory is not spoken as a coherent, organised whole.[11] In his autobiography, the writer Graham Greene reflected how 'memory is like a long broken night … the fragments remain fragments, the complete story always escapes'.[12]

Each oral testimony conveys only one of the many possible ways of telling a life history.[13] We have 'only one life', observes the French analyst J.B. Pontalis, 'but we have innumerable ways of recounting that life to ourselves'.[14] In oral testimonies we make meaning from our experiences, but that meaning is under constant revision.[15] What is remembered is a highly selective process, as experience is organised to contextualise a sense of oneself.[16] Memory is not simply a selective, interpretive exercise of what we remember.[17] It also involves a method of forgetting, of disavowal of that which is undesirable.[18] We remake our past by remembering and forgetting – it is not simply events which we recall, for the past we recreate becomes a repository of our defences, emotions, desires, and fantasies.[19] The 'ambivalences, absences and inconsistencies' in oral accounts draw the listener to these aspects of the 'unexpressed story'.[20]

In attempting to address these issues, my concerns in this book are threefold. First, I consider how widows internalised and absorbed the traumas of their husband's war experience through an examination of their memories of war, marriage and their husband's death. Trauma, grief and loss are not experienced as frozen, timeless emotional states. These emotions have a history, and are ever-changing as they are rewritten from the perspective of the present.

Second, I reflect on how attitudes towards, and experiences of, death and grieving have changed from the mid to the late twentieth century. These two themes are related, for the ways that widows dealt with loss, grief and domestic trauma in post-war Australia were predicated, to some extent, on the culturally acceptable ways they could publicly express these emotions. These interviews suggest a significant shift from a mid-twentieth-century sense that grieving was not spoken of in the community and was restrained by obligation and duty, to a late twentieth-century consensus that we can articulate grief, that it is desirable and necessary to do so and that we *need* to grieve.[21] The women in this book have lived through these changes in the ways emotions are dealt with, and have been affected by them. They articulate a grief in the late twentieth century that did not find expression earlier in their lives.

The changing nature of attitudes towards death has generated debate among historians. The pathbreaking scholarship of Philippe Airès – which has since been contested and challenged[22] – still offers insights which enhance our understandings of the experience of mourning by war widows. Airès argues that throughout the twentieth century 'death has been banished',[23] and mourning has become 'an extension of modesty'.[24] Death has been accompanied by a 'system of constraints and controls' which has 'unified mass society against death'.[25] Others like John Dollimore argue that the implication in Airès' work – that earlier cultures accepted death better and were therefore more fully integrated – is a dubious and questionable proposition.[26]

The memories of war widows documented in this book confirm that a denial of death informed the experiences of widows during the immediate post-war period. Many widows who lost their husbands in war believe that their mourning and grief was not allowed full expression. I argue that there has been a discernible shift at the end of the twentieth century towards an openness, and a return to a nineteenth-century frankness in mourning and grief.[27] Others have conceptualised this shift in terms of an emergence of a 'pathological public sphere' in the late twentieth century, where individual and collective trauma and loss have found increasing expression and legitimacy in the public arena, exposed through media such as television.[28]

Another dimension of this historical shift is the increasingly secular nature of Australian society. The influence of institutional religion has diminished as more Australians have chosen not to follow the rituals of denominational religion.[29] While there may be a more open expression of grief, there has been no revival of the heavily ritualised practices of the nineteenth century which characterised public mourning.[30] Nineteenth-century practices which have been relinquished by death-denying generations cannot be revived because the religious underpinnings which sustained these rituals have also disappeared. In recent years, the collapse of the distinction between the public and the private in the expression of loss and grief – most notably reflected in public testimonies – has characterised contemporary expressions of grief.

Third, these oral testimonies challenge a sharp periodisation of the war and post-war period. In many historical accounts of the Second World War, the lasting psychological impact of war on wives and children is only beginning to emerge. These interviews dramatically challenge the stereotype of the post-war period as an idyllic time when Australians became entrenched in the suburbs. While Australian studies have concentrated on the experiences of returned soldiers, the trauma that others endured remains unexamined. Accounts of the home-front have concentrated on protesters or domestic responses to particular wars, and on women's participation in protest movements or home-front activities, such as munitions industries. 'Public' rather than 'private' events continue to dominate in the narratives of war. The memoirs told in this book take the story into the private, domestic realm, offering another perspective to collective, national memories.[31] In attempting to 'publicize rather than privatize' these memories, this work seeks to move beyond a single version of war experience.[32]

One of the striking themes that emerges from this oral material is how the psychological impact of war remains well after the event, not just for soldiers, but also for those around them who also have to absorb the legacy of war. While this has been the focus of clinical studies, few historians have contemplated the implications of this for understanding historical change.[33] Stephen Garton, Judith Allen and Joan Beaumont have discussed the phenomenon, but it is deserving of closer interrogation.[34] I have considered the ways that these oral testimonies can make us reassess our understanding of the impact of war, and how its history is written. Just as the inter-war years cannot be understood without reference to the long shadow cast by the First World War, so too the post-war years need to be reassessed in light of the unexamined psychological impact of the Second World War. The schematic and stereotyped periodisation between war and post-war periods, and the tendency to prioritise public sacrifices over private griefs have denied war widows a legitimate voice and presence in post-war narratives. This study is also a part of the ongoing reassessment by historians of the post-war period as one which was unstable, uncertain and permeated by anxieties. As John Murphy has eloquently argued, these years were 'more contrary and more dynamic than our contemporary imaginings of a flat, complacent and largely uneventful period'.[35]

The use of oral narratives marks this research in distinctive ways. Oral history has been widely used in Australian history across a range of themes and topics,[36] yet there have been surprisingly few oral history accounts of the spouses of servicemen.[37] Alistair Thomson applied the insights of oral history to offer new perspectives on the impact of the Anzac mythology on the memories of ex-soldiers after the First World War.[38] John Barrett drew on questionnaires in his examination of soldiers who returned from the Second World War.[39] Kate Darian-Smith interviewed women to explore how they romanticised memories of the home-front during the Second World War.[40] In other oral histories of women and war, grief and loss have not been the focus of these interviews, nor of how aspects of grief have shaped women's subjectivity.[41]

The relationship between war, memory and oral history has been more comprehensively examined in relation to the impact of the colonial wars. It is by examining the 'narrative strategies' of Aboriginal people, argues Heather Goodall, that we can 'trace out the shape of change, resistance and conflict' in Australia's colonial past.[42] Oral accounts of the impact of the cultural decimation of Aboriginal communities, and of the lingering legacy of colonialism, are a reminder of the grief and loss which continues to haunt Australia's history.[43] Beyond Australia, the literature which most exhaustively explores the relationship between war, loss and oral histories is that of the Holocaust, which despite ever-growing attention, defies our powers of understanding.[44]

This book is organised according to the different experiences of war widows. In attempting to capture the diversity of their experience I have used a range of life stories, rather than focusing on a few interviews from which to create a narrative of the testimonies. This is to stress that there cannot be one experience of war widowhood: widowhoods are many and varied. Indeed, the term 'war widow' became a contested category among the war widows themselves. What constitutes a 'war widow' is disputed, with those who lost husbands in wartime claiming exclusive ownership, and those whose husbands have died since arguing for a more inclusive category. This difference is mirrored in the significance a widow attached to the war in explaining her husband's behaviour.

Chapter 2 considers the mobilisation of war widows during the immediate post-war period, when they organised themselves against what they perceived to be a lack of remuneration and a denial of justice. The emphasis is on the ways in which women maintained their memories of their husbands after the war, and how they attempted to articulate grief through anger, thereby challenging the prevailing image of war widows as passive victims. In particular, this chapter considers the role of two leading organisations, the War Widows' Guild of Australia and the War Widows' and Widowed Mothers' Association, which both campaigned for better provisions for widows. The trauma of death in war was expressed through ritual and memory, which shaped a sense of community and cohesion around the identity of 'war widow'. Despite the growth of services provided by social workers and psychiatrists at this time, war widows were of the generation that sought comfort for loss in community networks rather than through the new professionals.

Chapter 3 examines how women remembered the absence of their husbands during the wars. One of the powerful themes to emerge from these testimonies is that women internalised the sacrifices of their husbands. A slight on the behaviour of their husbands is a comment on their own sacrifice. They perceived themselves as contributing to the wars their husbands fought. Absence becomes an important motif in these narratives, and the women's views on war shape their senses of themselves as soldiers' wives. Their 'waiting' was never an empty exercise: they established networks, reared children, and entered paid employment. The different wars created particular circumstances which produced a range of experiences between widows of the Second World War and the wars in Korea and Vietnam. Given the magnitude of total war, the Second World War provided more avenues than later wars through which women could become part of support networks. In retelling these experiences, women convey the message that their own sacrifices are undermined when their husbands' contribution remain unrecognised.

The shock of losing a husband at the time of war is explored in chapter 4. The women who experienced this pain retell their stories in nostalgic terms. Their narratives are shaped around ideas of romance, lost opportunities and perfect love. A memory expressed through nostalgia allows them to explain why they did not remarry and why it was not possible to do so. In some instances, their stories are a response to trauma caused by an inability to mourn completely, and with that repression, a denial of death and grief.

Chapter 5 looks at the silences that faced women when their husbands returned from war. Silence has been a motif in many accounts of war and this chapter explores how it often defined relationships between returned soldiers and their wives. Such silences symbolised the denial of the impact of war, and also of grief, since what is remembered is the suppression of grieving. The wives, too, maintained a silence of what they experienced, as cultural mores negated an expression of *their* trauma. Paradoxically, a plethora of recent memoirs by returned soldiers has finally broken this silence. It is significant that these accounts have emerged in the late twentieth century when discussion of grief and death has become less constrained.

Chapter 6 examines the ways that women witnessed and experienced the trauma around them. It reflects on how they relate their experience trauma and, in some cases, internalised their husband's survivor guilt. The shadow cast by the war over the post-war period is clearest in this chapter: the narratives women tell do not fit easily into the familiar representation of the 1950s as a period of domestic tranquillity.

In chapter 7 I consider similar themes in relation to the Korean and Vietnam wars. Portrayed as 'forgotten' wars and overshadowed by the greater conflict of recent total war, memories of Korea and Vietnam and their aftermaths are conveyed very differently. But they reveal further that women absorbed their husband's anguish and angst, so that it became a part of their own identity. This chapter shows that the effect of remembering 'smaller wars' was no less profound on the wives and children of returned servicemen. The 'battler' motif which emerges is suggestive of the cultural emphasis on moving on and not dwelling on grief, let alone expressing it in public.

Finally, chapter 8 considers recent widowhood. Here, I argue that, in recent times, an understanding has developed that the full expression of the anguish and pain that results from death is necessary for a resolution of grief. This understanding that a release of grief, rather than its denial, is necessary, marks an important shift in late twentieth-century perceptions and practices.

This book attempts to correct the absence of war widows from Australian history. Through their memories, I explore the ways in which they absorbed their husbands' traumas and attempted to maintain a connectedness with the past. This can be seen through their need to sustain their memories; through their feelings of being slighted when their husbands have been attacked or forgotten; in the trauma of the denial of death and a retreat into nostalgia; in the effect of absorbing the anguish of silence; in dealing with domestic violence and carrying survivor guilt; and in experiencing the loss of the man they once knew. In admitting to these experiences, we can come to a new understanding of the legacy of war beyond the public arena, and of women's place – long neglected – within national narratives about war. Oral testimonies powerfully challenge conceptions of the post-war period, and show how the legacy of loss unsettled post-war calm in a period long assumed to be untainted by the lingering presence of psychological disturbance and anguish. In charting the memory of grief and its expression, we can also discern a shift away from the denial and silence which shaped attitudes towards death during the mid-twentieth century towards a much fuller expression of grief and mourning and, perhaps, a new way of dealing with death and loss, at the beginning of a new century.

CHAPTER TWO

WAR WIDOWS REMEMBER

> [T]he husband has given his life for his country and that wife has given her husband so I don't think she really should have to be burdened with anything to do with money. I think anything she gets she deserves.[1]

In 1954, the Melbourne branch of the War Widows' Guild of Australia broke with the tradition and custom of the day, and took the radical step of organising a Remembrance Day service exclusively for war widows. This dramatic gesture was a protest against the dismissive treatment it believed war widows had received on a number of public occasions earlier that year. Jessie Vasey, the Guild's founder and president, asserted that war widows had no choice but to organise a ceremony which would be inclusive of their mourning and their grief. They decided to hold:

> a service in praise of and thankfulness for our own men's sacrifice, with a few words of comfort and advice to us in our problems and sorrows, would bring help and satisfaction to many war widows, bereaved mothers and other bereaved relatives because I think we should ask all bereaved folk to share the service with us.[2]

Vasey was motivated by events during the Royal Visit to Melbourne in 1954, when the Queen had delivered a dedication to fallen soldiers at the Shrine of Remembrance, the iconographic war memorial in Melbourne. The slight they had received at this event had became a source of anguish for some war widows:

> I think few things more hurtful have been done to the war widow or the bereaved relatives. On that day there were two groups of

widows; those who had a distant view of the ceremony and could
hear a little of it and so felt they had taken part ... and those heart-
broken widows and mothers who were pushed round to the east
steps and could neither hear nor see and who felt as they watched
the hundreds of people massed on the steps and around the Queen
that to suggest the service was in honour of the fallen was a
mockery.[3]

The feeling of public humiliation on this and on other occasions made
these war widows believe that they 'have no alternative but to make
it clear that if the Anzac Day Service gives you any personal help
you should go to it'. However, to those for whom it was 'hurtful', and
'to the thousands of you who never go near it', Mrs Vasey proposed
'an alternative':[4] their own independent Remembrance Day commemoration, which would provide them and their dead husbands with
due acknowledgement and recognition.

Why had war widows become so incensed? How was their
agitation received and what does their public outcry suggest about the
place of public expressions of grief in post-war Australia? In this
chapter I consider the climate within which war widows attempted to
grieve publicly, and suggest that during the immediate post-war period
a culture of reserve limited the extent to which they could articulate
their loss.

THE DISTINCTIVE SACRIFICE

During the 1950s, the war widows felt extremely slighted at being
marginalised from the significance and ritual of Anzac Day ceremonies.
They became angry because not one officer of the Guild received an
invitation to the Anzac Day Service; those in the Guild had difficulty
accepting that survivors had priority over the widows of victims. This
marginalisation undermined the particular and distinctive sacrifice of
these widows. The slight was expressed symbolically through their
placement on the reserve, when they were 'steadily being pushed away
from the centre to the side until last year we were placed on the side'.
Vasey made a plea for the relatives of the men: 'If Anzac Day is to be
anything but a mockery to our way of thinking, the relatives of the dead
who are their only relatives should sit in the seats of honour'. It was
her honour and pride that were so dramatically threatened. Vasey experienced pain, hurt and anger when she had 'the pleasure of watching
my husband's juniors and barrack soldiers and their wives sailing with
much aplomb into seats ahead of us'.[5]

The wreath-laying ritual was reduced to a farce as participants clamoured to lay down their sacred mementos. In Vasey's view, the event became a disgraceful public spectacle. The jostling and wrestling which ensued was 'too painful to go over'. Some of those who attempted to lay wreaths out-manoeuvred those doing the same, while other participants pushed off wreaths which had already been laid, moved them to the ground and then placed their wreaths on top.[6] The sacredness of the event had been violated. What was meant to be a solemn and respectful procession turned into a combative and belligerent display. The public expression of respect by war widows had been stifled.

Wreath laying, the observance of silences and other rituals of the Anzac tradition mimicked the rituals of death and became almost like a public, secular funeral.[7] Anzac Day became the occasion when memories of war continued into civilian life, symbolising the grief of the living and allowing for its expression. It was, according to Ken Inglis, the 'principal occasion for public remembering of the war'. Valorising Anzac Day was specific to Australia and New Zealand, as most other countries had 'chosen for their principal wartime anniversary the day the killing stopped'.[8] Wreaths, both from individuals and from institutions, were laid at every war memorial. Processions and marches became more common after the mid-1920s, and the 'number of participants and spectators increas[ed] as state governments made Anzac Day ... a sacred and industrial holiday'. At these ceremonies, 'flowers were placed, speeches made, hymns sung, prayers and secular statements spoken, and heads bowed in a silence enclosed by Last Post and Reveille'. A correct, formal procedure characterised these rituals which 'displayed a sometimes intricate pattern of harmony, tension and accommodation, as the parties worked to create an occasion that reconciled commitments to churches, to the freemasonry of old soldiers, and the civic community'.[9]

It is not surprising that given Anzac Day's symbolic and emotional significance, wreath-laying ceremonies were often the point where controversy arose. Official recognition at the ceremony was important. In Hobart in April 1954, it was noted that the War Widows' Guild was not invited to lay a wreath during the Service.[10] In 1955 a member of the Tasmanian branch did lay a wreath, but there was 'no official recognition as the representative of the Guild', and the branch resolved that the president and honorary secretary would 'arrange an interview with the RSL re this matter'.[11] Again, in April 1957, a wreath was laid during the Service of Remembrance and 'the President expressed concern at the manner in which War Widows were treated as far as recognition and suitable seating area was concerned'.[12] In the following year, they were pleased to report that, 'our guild was officially recognised at the wreath-laying ceremony on Anzac Day'.[13]

The same feeling of humiliation was often expressed about ceremonies at the unveiling of war monuments. In one instance, in Papua New Guinea in 1953, the complainant said she 'would assume that bereaved would have priority over the Secretaries of our Federal Parliamentarians'. But 'why it was necessary for these people to take their secretaries to the unveiling, is beyond our comprehension, when over 100 applications were received by the Government from the Next-Of-Kin of those [to] whom the memorials had been erected'.[14] The Pacific region resonated with a particular significance as a place of memorials and wreath laying. Few new memorials were established after the Second World War, but most of these were in the territories of Papua and New Guinea, where more Australians fought and died than anywhere else in the Pacific.[15]

The unveiling of a war monument was a time of 'spectacle and music as well as words'. As Inglis describes it, 'unveiling day' incorporated elements of ceremony from a range of other rituals. These occasions shared 'elements with a service of religious worship or an army church parade'. The dead were eulogised in words inscribed and spoken, and 'the ritual of unveiling resembles ceremonies of "secondary burial" described by anthropologists, in which mortal body and soul are both deemed to be finally at rest'. As one of the few public expressions of grief, widows expressed their discontent openly when made to feel marginal on such occasions.[16]

Indeed, widows claimed that their grief was not accepted as a part of this public, collective memory. In denying them a revered place in the central occasion of public grieving, widows felt they were not given an opportunity to express their anguish. Challenging the conventions of the day, they asserted their right to express it themselves on Remembrance Day, Sunday, 7 November 1954, when Guild widows went ahead with their own service at midday at the Melbourne Shrine. 'We feel we need a special kind of service', Vasey reiterated.[17] It was significant that Vasey should select Remembrance Day as the day to voice her protest. The Guild observed a less elaborate ritual with the most striking characteristic being two minutes of silence at 11 o'clock. Although it did not carry the symbolic weight of Anzac Day, Remembrance Day occupied a revered place in the cultural memory. By the end of the Second World War, it had assumed a status different from its earlier configuration, one reserved more for actual combatants.[18] Some have argued that in Britain, for instance, the contribution of civilians during the Second World War was so taken-for-granted that the sacrifices of mothers and widows did not need to be highlighted in public commemorations like Remembrance Day. Celebrations, therefore, could focus on the achievements of returned soldiers, rather than on those of civilians. The level of sacrifice between soldiers and civilians, 'was apparently sufficiently balanced', argues Gregory, 'to allow Remembrance Sunday during the post-war years to concentrate its symbolism on the veterans of the armed forces'.[19]

During the 1950s in Australia, though, Mrs Vasey insisted that the contribution of civilians should not be taken-for-granted, especially that of widows, who continued to endure grief. She was optimistic that her alternative service would become a leisurely meeting between widows and their children, to be followed by a walk to the Botanic Gardens after the service. She told her members that it was 'an obligation to help your Guild to make this Service worthwhile'. Vasey believed women should be able to express their grief in a supportive environment and displayed foresight when she alerted widows to the danger of psychological stress. She urged women to boldly 'accept their burdens and face them [and they will be] the ones who escape the nervous breakdowns and all the attendant ills which afflict so many of our people'.[20] Although not promoting an excessive outpouring of emotions, Vasey nonetheless pointed out that 'every authority we have consulted has said that if we can express occasionally some of the grief felt by so many of us we will relieve that grief to a tremendous extent'.[21]

The first meeting of the alternative ceremony organised by the Guild was held in 'torrential rain'. Despite these conditions, 'some hundreds' of the Guild 'braved the elements and many came from quite long distances'. It was a simple service, conducted by Sir Sydney Rowell, and 'most inspiring', as he 'spoke beautifully and about us and our problems as well as in praise of our men'.[22] Vasey challenged the stereotyped view of war widows as passive victims, who should remain silent mourners. She insisted that women be allowed to express their loss publicly and distinctively. In doing so, she defied the practice of the day to contain or channel rather than express grief. In holding an alternative event in defiance of conventional celebrations, these war widows were attempting to assert the importance of their memory, their identity and their history. They were forcing the boundaries of the meanings of sacrifice and the legacy of war in claiming a place for their own grief.

Vasey's protestations caused considerable controversy. Other widows did not agree with her vocal interventions and believed Anzac Day was inclusive. The president of the Soldiers', Sailors' and Airmen's Widows' Association, which consisted mainly of First World War widows, asserted that current practices served her members' needs well:

> It seems that these 200 women are losing sight of the fact that the Anzac Day ceremony is held in memory of their own husbands. We hold Anzac Day as our sacred day. It has been one of our consolations and pleasures to attend these Shrine ceremonies where we have always been given an honoured place by the RSL [Returned Services League].[23]

It would be impossible to give everybody a front seat, she claimed, and asserted that in her experience, the Shrine Trustees had always 'treated widows with the greatest consideration'.[24]

The president of the War Widows' and Widowed Mothers' Association (WWWMA), Mrs M. Ebeling, agreed. She claimed that 'her members considered the paying of a tribute at the Shrine on Anzac Day was above personal discomfort or inconvenience'.[25]

Despite Ebeling's personal disapproval, other members of the WWWMA sided with Vasey. The executive had a different view of the Queen's wreath-laying and attendant proceedings in 1954. 'This gathering of Ex-Servicemen, Ex-Service women and the War Bereaved at the MCG [Melbourne Cricket Ground] grounds', it was reported, 'was a wonderful sight, and so many of our members had the opportunity of seeing the Queen and her Husband'. But two questions were raised:

> (a) Who represented the War Bereaved?
> (b) Do we Bereaved have the support or sympathy of those hundreds of people who clamoured to get tickets for this rally? I believe if we had the support of these men and women, our position would be different.[26]

It was reported that the Forecourt Dedication Ceremony was another occasion when the:

> War Bereaved were 'Overlooked', or should I say 'Hurt'. The Ceremony was Sacred to we women, and our only thoughts were of the Men and Women to whom the Forecourt was being dedicated ... those men and Women who had made the Supreme Sacrifice.[27]

Local branches of WWWMA were dismayed by this marginalisation. In March 1954, the Box Hill branch reported that:

> members expressed indignation at the slight given to the War Bereaved at both the Rally and The Dedication Ceremony of the Forecourt at the Shrine. Our members feel there should be some united effort when other functions are to be held, to see that we are not overlooked. We do not favour any slight to the Anzac Day service. This is one day we pay homage to our dead.[28]

Anzac Day had been considered a day that resonated with a sacredness too precious to be disturbed with protest or claims of discrimination. In April 1938 a group of women in Melbourne had attempted to join the march, much to the chagrin of soldiers' organisations.[29] During the 1950s, the Guild stressed that it remained loyal and patriotic and did not see its role to be critical of patriotic groups. Indeed, in attempting to uphold the memory of war and the achievements of their husbands, Guild members believed they were more patriotic than supporters in most other groups.

In April 1954, Ebeling sought to clarify her attitude to the boycott, writing to WWWMA members:

> Some of you will have read in the papers or heard over the air that I did not agree with boycotting Anzac Day by not attending the service at the Shrine. It was my personal opinion, but I felt you would support me, and the splendid attendance on that occasion proved your loyalty. However much we felt the slight shown to the bereaved during the Queen's visit, both on the Rally Day and at the Shrine Dedication by not having a representative of the bereaved on the dais, Anzac Day is too sacred and the Shrine too holy a place to show any grievances.[30]

The Executive reported that:

> Again this year through the Press there is a lot of controversy regarding this day. This time a section of War Widows are suggesting the boycotting of the Commemoration Service. No matter in what way the day is held in the future, we sincerely hope the powers that be will never do away with that Service at the Shrine of Remembrance. I know our members would never want to see the day when our War dead would be forgotten.[31]

War widows did have public support, but it was more forthcoming when widows were viewed as passive and helpless victims of tragic circumstances. In October 1945, the Melbourne *Herald* had highlighted the problem facing war widows. The wives of men who served 'had every right to look forward to many years of happiness and companionship after five or six years of sacrifice and separation'. But now women had to struggle without their menfolk, and do their best to rear and educate their children from whatever income they could earn themselves.[32] In March 1955, the Melbourne *Argus* launched a public appeal to provide material and financial assistance to war widows. The dilemma of the war widow was epitomised by Joy Howard, mother of three children aged eight, five, and three and a half years of age. She expressed her own personal difficulty in these terms:

> I was faced with the awful dilemma of going out to work to add to our slender income or staying at home and battling to make ends meet. I stayed at home. Whatever happens, my children will not be denied a mother's care when they most need it.[33]

The report noted that with 'quiet determination', Mrs Howard went about her 'daily work'.[34] An editorial the following day commented that Howard had 'wisely and nobly … decided to devote all her time and her efforts to her family, in preference to supplementing her income by going to work'. In making this choice, however, she was 'condemned to an austere existence, with no opportunities of saving for a few small luxuries'.[35] This assessment would have reflected the views of most Australians on the issue. Following the war, married and single women increasingly joined the paid workforce, predominantly on a part-time basis.[36] But, as John Murphy has observed, Australians believed that the primary role of women with children was to rear the children, and so they favoured married women without children participating in the workforce.[37]

Several tales of hardship were reported in the press. The *Herald* claimed in July 1947, in horror, that some war widows 'had to work to help support themselves and their children'.[38] One widow was reported as saying that she wanted 'a pension that will enable me to raise my children as my husband and I had planned until they are old enough to support themselves'.[39] The image of the war widow, enduring sacrifice quietly with her children, was in contrast to the defiant style adopted by Vasey.

Some war widows attempted to claim the right to an expression of their grief at a time when it was deemed unacceptable for mourning to be so forcefully articulated in public. Loss in war remained with many women during the post-war period. Their need to sustain certain memories reveals that, for them, there was no sharp break between the war and what came after it. During the post-war period, in a predominantly white, Anglo-Saxon Australian community, grief was believed best expressed in private. In a pamphlet published by the Roman Catholic order of Christian Brothers and entitled *When We Are Bereaved*, T. Howard Crago typified the ethos of the day. It was wrong to 'imagine that to weep is unmanly – a sign of hysteria or weakness'. Indeed, tears 'are the safety valves of emotions ... Never can they relieve us more than when we are suffering the pain of pent-up grief'. But this outpouring of emotion was not meant to be conducted in the public arena:

> That is not to say that we need to make a public exhibition of our grief. But to weep – perhaps behind the closed door – can help us to purge our emotions and express the sense of unutterable loss we feel ... Don't be afraid to weep. Let the tears flow unchecked ... then wash away the evidence of tears and go out bravely to face the world. We can weep.[40]

A similar message was conveyed in a pamphlet written by the American Granger E. Westberg, published in 1966 in Melbourne by the Church Education Press. Westberg argued that grief should be expressed; although to:

> some people it may sound strange in a day of scientific objectivity and coldness that we should encourage the expression of emotions ... Emotion is essential to man [*sic*] and [to] try to repress it is to make him less than a man [*sic*].

It was important not to dwell on such matters; we 'must not, however, wallow in our gloom, for it will only prolong our grief work'.[41] The actions of the Guild challenged these assumptions, however decorously.

The Guild's view on their right to recognition became inseparable from demands for remuneration. The Guild declared, as early as 1946, that war widows could not live on the present pensions and that they should take action to improve their predicament.

> We ourselves feel, and many of the public with us, that the price of our soldiers' lives should include decent living conditions for the families they left behind them. Without these men's sacrifices there would be no standard of living for anyone in this community.[42]

Women were encouraged to protest if their pay was not sufficient because 'improvement in your treatment is your responsibility'.[43]

The Guild's annual report for 1950–51 observed bitterly that the war widow was expected to deny her grief, to:

> overlook her sorrow, her hopes for the future, her lost social
> position, lack of security for her children, and to set out on another
> plane of living to be father and mother too. Mothers today think
> they have a hard job. Most fathers would say theirs is a full time
> one. How is it that we expect one sad and broken woman to do
> both jobs?[44]

The obstacle most widows faced as heads of households was the
problem of 'the male dominance in Australia'. She could do 'father's
job but she won't get father's pay, yet she must pay male rates and
taxes and expenses'. She finds that there is no 'planning' in the community for special needs of the bereaved family. War widows should
be treated with respect and some be granted further reward:

> It might well be thought that any human being who is expected to
> combine the wage-earning capacity of the male and the home
> making capacity of the female would be regarded as a very special
> person, but to the War Widow's staggered surprise she finds that
> she rates at something below normal. She is not supposed to have
> ordinary human drives and needs.[45]

Widows were treated in a patronising manner and told what was
good for them, and this had a damaging effect on their shrinking self-
confidence and self-respect. Vasey was appalled at the lowly view
people had of war widows. She agreed that all:

> changes in social thinking come slowly, but how terribly slow we
> are in recognising that the families of our war dead should not be
> mercilessly punished for the sacrifice made by husband and father
> in the country's service, but rewarded and honoured.[46]

Vasey saw that provisions of pensions and housing were crucial to 'the
special needs of the bereaved family, who would if this were done, be
able to preserve their self-respect and standing as independent units
in the community'.[47]

In a letter to the press, Vasey stressed that 'any service in honour
of the fallen which discounts the wives and mothers of these men is a
mockery of the suffering and sacrifice of our beloved dead'. It was a
disgrace that 'most war widows and mothers were pushed behind walls
away from their allotted place, out of hearing and out of sight of the
service, and the seats of honour in our original space were given to
people (no doubt fine citizens) who had subscribed money to the Shrine
Appeal'.[48] The sacrifice of the widows, she inferred, had not been taken
into account: 'Our men gave their lives, and could no longer subscribe
money. We have given our own and our children's happiness and

security'. Cynically, she concluded, that 'surely on this day the trustees need not have used the memory of our dead to pay off their financial obligations'.[49]

Widows had experienced a sense of abandonment on Anzac Day services and in the public ceremony before the Royal Visit in 1954. In 1953, the Anzac Day march 'from the war widows point of view met with almost universal disapproval'. All 'the rest of our members informed us that the day as celebrated was hurtful and a great majority have asked the Guild to organise a service of our own'.[50] Guild women felt being asked to place crosses on a piece of turf was 'cruel and thoughtless'.[51] They made it clear that widows were not asking 'for prestige for themselves as persons but they felt the honour supposedly paid to their husband's memories was farcical when the widows of those same men were so pointedly ignored'.[52]

A COMMUNITY TO SUSTAIN THE GRIEVING

Why were these events so important? The bitterness and resentment expressed by Vasey drew war widows into a particularly close community. The sense of belonging to a community that shared its grief and loss was very important to many Guild members. It provided a supportive framework within which women could sustain a continuity with the past and with change over time.[53] Many former war widows – those who had remarried –

> ask us if they might still receive the circular, particularly because they want to keep in touch with all the help that may be given for their children but also because, as one of them said, 'I will never quite lose my feeling of belonging'.[54]

Despite the growth of psychiatry and social work during the immediate post-war period, and the increasing role psychiatrists and social workers played in treating social problems, war widows relied on pre-war networks through a model of community support and collectivism,[55] and the Guild was such a network for many.

It has been argued that 'belonging' is one crucial aspect of the purpose of commemoration. Not only does commemoration affirm individual identity as part of a group, it also produces a collapse of boundary between the past and the present, between the mourner and the one being mourned. Identity is sharpened at such events, as the past shapes a sense of self, and provides structure and a meaning.[56] Rituals such as commemorations provide coherence and an anchor for those who evoke and relive traumatic events.[57] These events legitimise the emotion expressed and participants experience, witness, and connect with others who are also engaged with it.[58] They 'give value and meaning' to those who perform them.[59] In forming both individual and collective identities, commemorations demarcate time and establish 'temporal continuity', for another purpose of commemoration is to order and to structure time. The purpose of such events is to create a space for the sharing of emotions in order to deal with them and to establish further bonds with the deceased.[60]

Commemorations shape what is remembered and why it is remembered. They suit the identities of participants and the construction of one memory may not be shared by others.[61] Nostalgia plays a central part in such recollections and rituals as identity and self-cohesion are derived from a projection of the past.[62] As Donna Bassin remarks, nostalgia is suggestive of 'incomplete mourning' and a quest for 'an object that can never be found'.[63]

These themes of commemoration, nostalgia and belonging are drawn together in this book and can be found expressed explicitly in the two organisations widows formed – the Guild and the Association. A close look at their activities show how the war continued to affect war widows, but also points to how they addressed the same questions differently. In insisting on their rights during peace, war widows dissolved the sharp line some were attempting to draw between the war and the post-war period. They adopted a particular identity by keeping alive the memory of their husbands, and thus challenged the image of the war widow as an emotionally passive and helpless figure. Furthermore, they insisted on a public expression of war widows' grief, by keeping this at the forefront of their campaigns, against a prevailing culture of restraint and reserve.

The War Widows' Guild

There can be no consideration of war widows during the post-war period without a discussion of Jessie Vasey and the organisation she formed to assist them. While the history of the War Widows' Guild has been documented elsewhere,[64] it is worth summarising some of the main aspects of its history. What is notable about the histories of the Guild and the Association was how they both developed a system of support based on pre-war models of assistance from community and family.[65]

Vasey, the wife of General George Vasey, was the driving force behind the Guild. Her endeavour to assist widows became a life-long crusade and she demanded the right to a certain measure of comfort and dignity – 'not merely a pension sufficient to keep their heads just above water'.[66] The War Widows' Guild was formed on 21 February 1946. The Australian Imperial Force (AIF) Women's Association provided premises on the top floor of its building in Collins Street, so that weaving classes could be held, while the Red Cross organised a nursery nearby to care for the children of war widows.[67] Vasey soon made this into a national organisation. In 1946, she established branches throughout Victoria, NSW, South Australia, Western Australia, Tasmania and then, in early 1947, in Queensland. The organisation of the Guild was based on a three-tier structure. The sub-branches or clubs were the centre of social activities. The state branches co-ordinated the activities of clubs and formulated issues to be presented at the national council. The role of the national council was to liaise with the Commonwealth government.

Vasey used the Guild to impress on the authorities that the task of the war widow was supreme. It was to:

> make up to our children, as far as is humanly possible, the very terrible lack in their lives which the loss of their fathers had caused. If we as mothers blind ourselves to the fact that there is this lack in their lives, I think we are failing in our first and paramount duty.[68]

Vasey believed that in the community a widow was often regarded as a 'half-wit', and it was important to point out 'to the less sympathetic members of the community that you are only asking that the nation pay for the life it used'. The argument 'we are working on … is that life has a value and that if the nation wants to use a man's life that nation must be honest enough to assume his responsibilities'.[69] The 'slur of charity' had to be removed and the idea of handouts had to be challenged because these destroyed any notions of self respect and self-reliance, 'qualities we must preserve if our children are to be worthy of their fathers'. The burdens on war widows as mothers were real. '"Responsibility, planning, management": these are sobering influences; these are the marks of a good wife and mother; these are the things our widows could and should bring to the discussion of their needs and those of their children.'[70] War widows needed to dispel the belief that women would cope, regardless. 'We all have to struggle against a man's idea that a woman can always manage.'[71]

One way in which the state honoured the memory of its war dead was through remuneration of the women who were left to carry the financial and cultural burdens of wartime remembrance without a breadwinner. Historically, the war widow has been a highly ambivalent figure, at once financially dependent on the state, and yet undermining its social and cultural value system because of her ambiguous marital status.[72] Object of both pity and anxiety, the citizenship of war widows was shaped in relation to men. As Jill Roe has argued, notions of citizenship were dependent on the male as a worker until the First World War and then on the soldier after the war.[73]

The war widows' pension was paid on the assumption that the widow should be compensated for the loss of a breadwinner. Between 1914 and 1916, a widow lost her entitlement on remarriage; in 1916, amendments were introduced to allow a de jure widow to continue to receive a pension for the two years after remarriage, and to allow a pension for a de facto widow or wife.[74] The right of a widow to receive a pension for two years after her remarriage was abolished in 1931, with the onset of the Depression.[75] It was assumed that on remarriage, she would be supported by her new husband, not the state.[76]

Although politicians were unanimous about the need for the war widows' pension, there was much debate about its terms. A discussion surrounding the *Social Security Act* of 1947 reflected the value system which governed the payment of the pension. Politicians who supported the cause of war widows used the familiar arguments of the need to ensure the woman's role as family nurturer and as a substitute father-figure in the home. Senator Brand, from Victoria, declared in May 1947 that the:

> lack of a father is a terrible hardship. There is no one to advise and control young children. In addition, she has to do or leave undone many necessary things about the house that her husband would have done. It is wrong that a widow with children should have to go out working at all. The correct upbringing of the children is most important. Denied a father's guiding hand they tend to drift into undesirable ways of life.[77]

The war widow was entitled to expect more from society given the sacrifices she made, because 'she struggled along cheerfully while her husband was away. She looked forward to easier times when the war was over and the head of the family was earning much more than her war-time allotments.'[78] Anxiety about the future of the family was central to arguments over the level of assistance to widows. 'I hold no brief for the young widow without children', claimed Brand:

> She can supplement her pension considerably in many walks of life … Nor do I hold any brief for the widow who is in comfortable

circumstances. It is the 60 or 65 per cent of other war widows with whom I am concerned. How can they be assisted? Would it be better to increase the allowance for the children or increase the widows' pensions?[79]

Brand identified the core of the problem 'where the mother has not sufficient time and energy after a day's work to [the children's] well-being'.[80]

War widows, some politicians argued, had a precarious status. Mrs Doris Blackburn, the left-wing Labor member for Bourke, argued in May 1947 that 'one widow she knew of was refused residency at one hostel on the grounds that she was an unmarried woman'.[81] There was an anomaly in the law, because widows 'believe that, as their husbands might well be considered totally and permanently incapacitated as far as maintaining their families is concerned, those families should receive the same consideration as that given to the families of in-capacitated men'.[82] The Joint Committee made the first interim report in September 1941 noting that in 'caring for their children, widows are performing a national service, and are entitled to community assist-ance'.[83] There were three classes of widows' pensions, including de facto as well as legal widows. Roe argues that war widows 'headed the hierarchy of women welfare recipients until the 1960s'.[84] Politicians who supported the pension attained it by claiming that widows needed to be kept in a state of reliance, at the same time as Vasey argued for them to eschew dependency.

It was not until 1943 that the war widows' pension was increased to the same level as the 'partially incapacitated ex-servicemen'. Yet the pension was 'still only a little more than half the basic wage'.[85] Post-war inflation devalued the increase, so that by 1947 the basic wage had risen to £5 9s a week, while the war widows' pension remained at £2 12s per week. Many war widows were in desperate financial straits. In 1947, it was announced that their pension would be increased by 5s. Efforts by the Guild to have their pension tied to the basic wage created tensions between Legacy, the other organisation which offered sub-stantial support to widows and the Guild. Mark Lyons has argued that these differences arose because of personality clashes, but they occurred also because of the abhorrence Vasey and the Guild had to receiving 'charity'. Vasey argued that as long as Legacy supplemented the income of widows, and 'refused to campaign to have their pensions tied to the basic wage, governments could continue to ignore their res-ponsibilities to war widows'. This issue created tensions with other ex-service organisations, especially with the Returned Services League.[86]

The Guild did more than lobby politicians. From its earliest beginnings, it provided a centre of social and cultural activity for war widows. Widows sought solace and comfort from each other rather than from medical or psychological professionals.[87] The skills women learned through the Guild, such as millinery, basket weaving and glove making, 'proved a joy to all those who have taken part in them and in many cases widows have found that renovating hats for friends and relations can be most remunerative'.[88] In Adelaide, Marjory Miller remembers fondly the feeling of community and belonging; the Guild was an important part of her adjustment after the death of her husband, Rex. She joined the Guild after the war and did a course in weaving 'which was most most interesting'. The circle used to 'meet every month to each other's homes … We had some lovely years'. She joined the basket classes and the dress-making classes. In this community, 'we sort of needed each other'. 'We had some lovely times at the Guild and through our weaving we used to sell the goods and we'd go out to the country and … display our goods and sell. We did very well.'[89] The Guild was progressive for its day in promoting these skills as legitimate forms of wage-earning activity.

A further aim was to give pleasure to widows by 'getting to know the other widows in their districts'.[90] Holiday homes were another way of assisting war widows. In 1948, the Guild hoped to obtain 'some land for the erection of cottages suitable for holidays and permanent housing'.[91] The attempt to bond widows together was made explicit. In August 1949, the King's Empire Day message was quoted: 'We all belong to each other. We all need each other. It is in serving each other and in sacrificing for our common good that we are finding our true life.'[92] Women in country areas were especially targeted, and it was felt that 'now that we know one another, the friendliness of our meetings gives that happy feeling that, as the king says, we all belong to each other and we all need each other'.[93] This King's message was seen to be the motive behind all Guild work.[94] Indeed, when the King died in 1952, the Guild claimed that 'his devotion to duty and service to his country, typified for many of us the spirit of service which animated our husbands'. They felt special affinity with the Queen 'in her widowhood'.

Providing housing for women was part of the attempt to build a community among the widows, which was favoured over support that entailed far more individualistic solutions. War widows preferred flats to houses, both for companionship and for rearing their children.[95] In 1954, the Guild opened its first home for war widows, which was a two-storey house converted into nine self-contained flats. There were

over 200 applicants for the homes, and the successful applicants were
all elderly war widows from the First World War. These were not
homes with 'dull uniformity … Some have wide windows with views
of Parramatta River, others open on to the garden, and the furnishings
range from Victorian to contemporary'.[96] It was claimed in 1949 that
the aim was to establish a 'housing community, where widows would
have their own flatlet and while being independent, can still receive
help and companionship for the other widows in the group'.[97] Vasey
undertook the development of housing for war widows, especially
those who were ill or elderly. Initially, funding was sought from the
Commonwealth government, with assistance from Legacy and the
RSL, but when these bodies could not agree, Vasey went alone, seeking
money from her friends, and through public fund-raising. In 1954, the
Commonwealth government introduced the *Aged Persons' Homes Act*,
whereby it undertook to match the money spent by eligible voluntary
agencies pound for pound. In 1958, Vasey formed the Vasey Housing
Auxiliary as a company. She was its managing director. By 1965, 250
widows were housed under this scheme. But it caused divisions, and
the Guild separated its functions from those of the Housing Auxiliary
in 1968.[98]

Two underlying purposes of the Guild were to make women self-
sufficient, and to help them collectively sustain the memory of their
husbands' heroism and by implication, their own. The first annual
report of the NSW branch identified its purpose with that of their
husbands: 'the Guild is fulfilling a noble purpose. Animated by the
spirit that inspired your husbands, you are striving to be more self-
reliant and you are succeeding', members were told in September
1947.[99] Vasey articulated this theme in terms of women giving to the
community: 'The women had given a commodity – their husbands – to
the community'.[100] The sacrifices the war widows had made were
similar to those of their husbands. Vasey argued that 'the war widows
have the greatest stake in this country since they helped to buy it at a
great price'. Their remuneration should be higher because 'the monies
widows receive in pensions were bought with their men's blood'.[101]
Women should challenge the view that they could manage on less and
remain passive. 'Women are always expected to manage on less than
men in salaries, wages and pensions', Vasey claimed to the second
annual meeting of the NSW branch, 'and widows are very nearly state-
owned'. Women 'must banish the attitude that because we are women,
we can manage on low pensions. Our children should not be objects
of charity, but able to stand on their own feet.'[102] Vasey argued that war

widows were marginalised and ill-treated, ostracised and harassed. They had become 'foreigners' in their own country, she claimed, 'because of the special physical and mental stresses to which they were subjected'.

More radically, Vasey claimed that 'women need companionship among themselves, and a co-operative effort for rearing their children. This is more easily managed in flats.'[103] There was, however, to be no room for 'disgruntlement' among widows, for they should not look at themselves as martyrs. The balance must be right between 'forcing our woes on the community and getting our just dues'.[104] The battle ahead for war widows was similar to the ones experienced by their husbands. 'Our husbands fought against hopeless odds and overcame them', declared Vasey, and 'we can do the same, for from their sacrifice will come our strength. It rests with us, the war widows, to make our Guild a power in the land.'[105]

Comparing themselves with their husbands sustained a connection that helped war widows to perpetuate their husbands' memory after the war. In July 1947, Vasey declared with great resentment that:

> Australia's wealth and future were paid for in blood and sweat and tears. The cruellest price of all was that of blood. The war widow had paid the greatest price. Her husband was worth to her at least what he could earn. If a man gave his life the nation called him a hero. But it gave his widow a shoddy badge and ruined her and her family financially ... I do not regard it as a pension – but as the country's debt to the men who died in its defence.[106]

The war widow also became the victim of 'careless and muddling thinking', Vasey claimed. In 1947 she argued that the 'nation's freedom was the lives of our men. The community still ignores this debt, ignores the pitiful helplessness of the dead'.[107] Drawing on the language of war, these were 'battles' still to be fought, she claimed. In the early 1950s, there were 'bitter battles' fought, and 'we have done a very great deal to improve the lot of the war widow, but there are still cruel anomalies and injustices to overcome, the chief of which is the pension'.[108] Others continued the comparison of the widows, and especially Vasey, with soldiers. Opening the annual meeting of the War Widows' Guild, Lieutenant-General Woodward declared that 'Mrs Vasey will now give you her annual call to arms'.[109]

This was Vasey's favoured way of defending war widows: to compare their plight to their husbands' sacrifice and to merge their experiences and make the difficulties they faced into part of their husbands' history. The Guild argued for special privileges on this basis. In a letter to the editor of the *Sydney Morning Herald*, a 'War Widow' wrote asking 'the Government to recognise the claims of the dead and the unsung by granting to their dependants privileges equivalent to those about to be lavished on our returned men and women in the name of rehabilitation'.[110]

As its members aged, the priorities of the Guild shifted. The issue of aged women, with the consequent need to promote a sense of community, was a major preoccupation and concern of the Guild from early in the Guild's history. In May 1950, the Council announced that:

> We are deeply concerned in regard to our elderly war widows, who need assistance and companionship. Some of these, we know, are without relatives and friends. One of our ambitions is to obtain a home which could be run by the Guild where these women may live in a communal atmosphere.[111]

The Guild discussed individual cases of hardship and attempted to alleviate women's despair, especially during the immediate post-war period when housing was in short supply.[112] In the late 1950s, an emergency fund aimed to assist war widows with housing difficulties. The Guild served as a welfare group at a time when the family and community was the principal form of aged care. Despite the expanded social security system after the war, and the increase in welfare spending by the Chifley Labor government, the means test meant that social security 'was not a universal right in Australia and recipients were still the subject of inspection'.[113] Assistance from friends and neighbours was commonplace in sustaining those struggling financially.[114] In 1957 the Executive Committee reported the case of Mrs B. Whittle of Bondi, a World War One widow who was 'living in a room under very difficult conditions as landlady is old … her relations will not do anything for her. She has to be cared for and nursed by the tenants'. Another woman, Mrs I. Jackson, of Burwood, was 'being persecuted to leave her accommodation', because of a 'change of ownership'.[115] At the annual public meeting in 1960, Vasey argued that she would like:

> to see the Guild one day afford to employ a team of research officers who could offer practical advice to young widows from the time of their immediate bereavement until they were able to establish themselves with some security … We must encourage this spirit of self-help.[116]

The resentment of charity became a central argument in the claims of war widows: 'people needed rights, not charity, and they needed most of all the opportunity of standing on their own feet'.[117]

The relationship between the Guild and Legacy was at times strained. The Guild consisted of the wives and children of ex-servicemen who died on active service, and Legacy was also concerned with the welfare of wives and children of ex-servicemen who died after the war. The Guild aimed to restrict the term 'war widow' to its 'specific clientele', a point which distinguished it from other organisations like Legacy and the WWWMA. The Guild claimed that Legacy insulted it by assuming that a widow needed the assistance and advice of a man in bringing up her children. The history of the relationship between Legacy and the Guild was marked by continuing tension and dispute over who should represent the widows' interests. It escalated in 1947 when two organisations competed for funds from the Services Canteens Trust Fund. The Guild pressured Legacy to cease its wide definition of the term 'war widow'. In 1949 Vasey sent letters to the Legacy Clubs objecting to their definition of 'war widow' and asking them to comply with the Guild's and to consult the Guild before giving any assistance to war widows. Relations remained cool. In 1949, Legacy decided to end all relations with the Guild at a national level. The ban lasted a year.[118]

War Widows' and Widowed Mothers' Association

Another group which catered for war widows was the War Widows'and Widowed Mothers' Association. Formed in 1922, it 'aimed to improve conditions for the bereaved' and continues that aim today. All war widows are accepted as members, whether their husbands had served abroad or locally. Like the Guild, it began as a specifically Melbourne group, but did not become a nationwide organisation. The Association remained a Victorian group with twenty-five branches in suburbs and country areas.[119]

The First World War produced a plethora of organisations which attempted to alleviate the plight of war widows and mothers. Most of these organisations did not survive to the next war, but were active in promoting the cause of war widows. The Sailors and Soldiers' Mothers, Wives and Widows' Association was one of the leading groups during the inter-war years. The RSL also had auxiliary groups: the Friendly Union of Soldiers' Wives; Soldiers' Mothers' Association and the Friendly Union of Sailors' Wives.

The WWWMA was less militant than the Guild, although it did take political action. It protested to government officials about the level of the war widows' pension and other benefits to which war widows were entitled. In August 1953, the secretary of the Association, A.E. McCutchan, argued that the war widows' pension should be brought into line with the benefits for totally and permanently incapacitated ex-servicemen.[120] In 1951, the Association declared that:

> our main interest has been centred on getting a better pension for the dependents of our deceased servicemen and though the last rise of 20/- for the war widow was better than the previous 5/-, it is still not comparable with the high cost of living, so we must keep on fighting.[121]

Throughout its history, the Association attempted to obtain a range of concessions and benefits for widows. At its annual conference in March 1953 it demanded an increase in pension, free ambulance service for war widows and widowed mothers, abolition of the means test for war widows and widowed mothers and for cancer to be accepted as a war disability.[122]

Over the ensuing years, there were variations on these demands. During the early 1960s, there were requests for a reduction in television and wireless licences; for more flats to be built at reasonable rates for war widows; for heart disease as well as cancer to be accepted as due to war service; for yearly rental of telephones to be covered for war widows or widowed mothers who lived alone, and, perhaps more radically, for the widow of any person who served in the forces in time of war to be regarded as a war widow for the purposes of repatriation benefits whether the death was due to war service or not.[123] As more and more returned men died of heart-related diseases and cancer, the Association became insistent about the role of the war in inducing heart-related diseases and causing cancer. The Association's annual conference in 1970, resolved that:

> all Widows over 60 years of age, whose husbands served in the Forces and whose Health suffered by War Service and had to be nursed by their Wives, But died of Heart. Which is not accepted: be granted a full War Pension. And that all Heart cases be accepted as due to War Service by the Repatriation.[124]

The general purpose of the organisation remained consistent throughout its history. It aimed for the 'betterment of pensions, amenities and concessions, the promotion of fellowship, interest and co-operation among members with help and advice wherever possible to the bereaved'.[125] A strong stalwart, longstanding secretary and then president of the Association, Mrs McCutchan, ensured the Association kept its requests reasonable and within the realm of possibility. She asked that:

members not ask for anything absurd … the repatriation do the best
they can but they cannot exceed their limits. This Association does
the best it can for the unaccepted widow in making every possible
endeavour on her behalf + widowed mother.[126]

Unlike the Guild, it records only once in its minutes the tragedy of loss
and grief – it was through their actions, they insisted, that the repercussions of war would be recognised. The one instance was in response
to a visitor's talk to the Association. At the 1965 annual meeting,
Matron Sage commended the women on the:

ways in which they had taken up the threads of their lives after the
anguish of the loss of their dear ones … Even after a woman's
helpmate is taken she still has to fight. The important thing is the
longing – you feel that you are not wanted anymore. And that
is where an organisation such as war widows is the finest thing a
woman could belong to … you are taking care of one another …

The president, Mrs Ebeling, said that these words:

took her back 40 years – how she suffered – she was in France at
the time + she felt there was nothing left in life – finally she
decided to return home + could think of nothing better to do than
join the war widows.

Mrs McCutchan agreed 'with Mrs Ebeling's remarks and she felt
Matron Sage understood just what each one of us had gone through'.[127]
In many respects, the Association represented another model of dealing
with grief, one more consistent with the general attitude towards grief
and its public expression than the more militant position of Vasey and
the Guild.

The organisation has enjoyed longevity with many thriving
branches throughout Victoria continuing to attract large numbers to
meetings. In the early 1950s, local meetings attracted between 75
and 90 members.[128] The Association offered a variety of support for
widows, including visits to hospitals and several social occasions
for members each week.[129] Although the organisation attempted to cast
its membership net widely, it was particular about who could join and
of the responsibilities of membership. Badges carried with them particular responsibilities. In May 1967, the General Meeting noted that
'some past members who no longer pay their dues will still wear the
badge of this Association claming they are members'. This was a unacceptable and the return of the badge was most important.[130] This was
a longstanding issue – in July 1949, the president, Mrs Ebeling, had
asked members to 'realise that our badges were our identification as
members of an Association and to care for them as such. Some of these

badges having been lost, [and] worn by people who were not war widows'.[131] The badge was the property of the Association at all times, and an 'appeal is made to the families of deceased members to see that the badge is returned to the secretary and that it does not fall into the hands of a person not eligible to wear it'.[132] Despite the fact that the Association accepted widows of all who served, when the Australian government introduced conscription shortly before it joined the Vietnam War, the subject of eligibility arose, in regard to widows of conscripts and widows of those who volunteered for active service.[133]

Like the Guild, the Association identified housing as an important issue, both as a material necessity and as a way of fostering community co-operation. In 1951, the General Meeting voted that the 'housing commission be asked to build flats of one room and community kitchens for war widows'.[134] In February 1953, a 'letter had been received from the commission saying 2 houses were allotted to W. Widows and that 1 unit flats were to be built for widows with no family at Ascot Vale'.[135] In 1959 the Association supported the resolution passed by the RSL that the League 'continue to press for an amendment to the War Service Homes Act to allow single and widowed returned servicewomen to become eligible for loans whether or not they have dependents'.[136] Holiday homes had been purchased at Olinda and Clematis for use by war widows.[137] Information provided by the Association had allowed widows to receive further payments.[138] A welfare officer was appointed, and reported cases of widows under duress back to the Association. In 1957, she reported that:

> pensions are the biggest problem. These applications do not increase as the years go on. Much success has been achieved in having cases accepted as due to war service. I am pleased to report on the number of second dependants' pensions granted to widowed mothers or aged fathers.

She also reported a 'busy year' in 'finding suitable homes for the widows, particularly country widows who have been left with farms … previously carried on by their late husband'. There were also a 'distressing number of war bereaved who are placed in mental hospitals', not because they are mentally ill, but 'because of the effects of old age'. It was suggested that some kind of home should be established to cater for aged people.[139]

Pensions

Some of the problems war widows experienced were endured by widows in general. During the post-war period, war widows and civilian widows generally maintained harmonious relations and assisted each other where they shared similar concerns, but there were tensions, particularly because the war widows' pension was not means tested.[140] As a result, war widows were sometimes much better off, and often appeared to occupy a more privileged place in welfare hierarchies.

The social stigma attached to all widows shaped the experiences of civilian widows throughout the nineteenth and twentieth centuries.[141] Civilian widows, like their war-widow counterparts, organised themselves into lobby groups. The Civilian Widows' Association, formed in NSW on 8 November 1949 was one of the most prominent. Under the auspices of the United Associations of Women, led by the well-known feminist and social justice campaigner, Jessie Street, the organisation tried to get women together to 'raise their voices as one to say they should have fair play'.[142] Ivy Kent was the major force behind this civilian widows group and attempted to improve their conditions and their entitlements. The Civilian Widows' Association aimed to raise the status of civilian widows; to improve their living standards; to educate widows on their legal status and to raise the means test threshold.[143] In 1955, the Perth *Daily News* identified a group of poverty-stricken widows, 'bereft of fathers and husbands'.[144] Throughout its history, the War Widows' Guild offered support to civilian widows.[145] In March 1950 it agreed to 'furnish any information requested' and resolved that the president and secretary of the organisations should speak to the office bearers of the Guild.[146] Vasey and Kent shared a similar vision and there was no antagonism between them, although war widows were offered more remuneration than civilian widows.[147] The Civilian Widows' Association also highlighted the needs of Aboriginal women and worked to assist them.[148]

While war widows believed they should be entitled to a payment, they did not assume that civilian widows could claim the same privilege. The NSW state government was the first to pay the pension to civilian widows in 1926. Premier Jack Lang explained as he introduced the Widows' Pensions Bill to the NSW parliament in 1925 that it was a 'simple recognition of the fact that the State owes a duty to the mothers and the children of the State'.[149] The aim of the pension was to prepare the future citizens of the country and provide the best environment for those who have been 'bereft of their father – the bread-winner for the home'. In what became a widespread belief among many ex-servicemen's groups. Lang echoed the belief of many ex-servicemen's groups when he insisted that the state should take on the role of breadwinner:

if the state steps in, and says it will keep the home together while
the children are at such an age that they must have a mother's care
and attention ... It will have helped them in every possible way.[150]

Widows found it difficult to escape these assumptions. Victoria
had no provision for widows' support during the 1920s and 1930s, and
it was only with the introduction of the *Widowed Mothers Act* of 1937
that the question of widows' poverty was considered in parliamentary
legislation.[151] Discussion about the pensions was revived in 1942,
when the Commonwealth government finally introduced provisions for
widows. Imbued with the welfare reformist zeal of the day, the Interim
Report of the Joint Committee on Social Security, issued in September
1941, enunciated the responsibility of the state to protect those who
could not protect themselves:

> More modern opinion is that poverty is mostly not the fault of the
> individual but of the environment in which he [*sic*] lives. Social
> services were developed largely because of the conviction that it is
> misfortune, not inherent evil, which brings people into want, and
> therefore it is the duty of the community to mitigate the worst
> effects of that want.[152]

While various financial restrictions were introduced during the
Second World War the Committee agreed that particular welfare services should not be reduced because of the war effort. The need to
protect the family was an important priority and the payment of the
pension to widows was believed to be a form of protecting children.
The Committee noted with alarm that in the majority of cases, widows
are without 'private means and must therefore work for a living in
default of outside assistance'. In doing so, they 'deprive their children
of essential parental care and supervision'. The role widows performed
was a 'national service', and they were therefore entitled to community
assistance.

The Committee differentiated between those with and those without children. Widows without children were not in the same 'invidious
position', except when they were over 50 years of age. All widows,
however, needed to prove their disability, and so a widow was subject
to 'a residence, a means and a character test'.[153] It was decided that the
pension of 'one pound one shilling per week for widows and 10s per
week for one dependent child under the age of sixteen years not
covered by child endowment' be raised to 'all widows with dependent
children, widows over 50 years, widows in ill health, widows in
destitute circumstances immediately after the death of their husbands,

deserted wives and wives whose husbands are inmates of mental hospitals'.[154] There was an acute awareness that these provisions should also create a stable climate for peace. 'It has been said', concluded the Committee, 'that the Allies won the Great War and lost the peace; this time we must win both. If we are to do that we must have ready a complete plan of social security'.[155]

Although the Committee decided that it was not necessary to grant the pension to widows under 50 years of age without dependent children, it did stipulate that 'temporary assistance should sometimes be granted to widows under 50 years of age ... to enable them to adjust themselves to the changed conditions that followed upon the death of the husband'.[156] The Commonwealth *Pensions Act* stipulated three groups of widows: A; those who have at least one child under the age of 16 years; B; widows without dependent children, over 50 years; and C; widows under 50 years of age without dependent children who, upon the death of their husbands, find themselves in 'necessitous circumstances'. Within these categories, 'widow' was given a wide definition because the *Widows Pension Act* stipulated that 'widow' included a de facto widow; a deserted wife who had been deserted by her husband for not less than 6 months; a divorced woman who had not remarried; and a woman whose husband had been in a hospital for the insane. The term 'deserted' wife did not include a deserted de facto wife.[157]

The conditions of eligibility which applied to all three classes of widows included the moralism that all widows be required to be of 'good character and deserving of a pension' and the racial imperative, common at that time, that 'aliens', 'natives' of Africa, New Zealand, Pacific Islands and Australian Aborigines were excluded.[158] There was a different cultural understanding of widows, whereby the widow with children performed a 'national' role, but the widow of a soldier represented a blood sacrifice. In 1961, the highest pension rate a war widow could receive in Sydney was £20 19s 6d per week while the highest a civilian widow could be given was £8 6s.[159] These differences accentuated tensions between widows and war widows, although they did work together and co-operate with the widows' associations.[160]

In demanding that governments take their claims seriously, the Guild and the Association were insisting the authorities acknowledge the legacy of war on war widows, and the terms of their sacrifice. As this chapter has suggested, the onset of peace did not eradicate the financial, psychological and social burdens many war widows endured. As war receded, the feeling of obligation became more tenuous. War widows of this generation were less likely to seek professional assistance for their grief. Rather, they channelled it through organisations like the Guild and the Association, seeking solace in familial models of community. These organisations offered contrasting models of grieving. Vasey and the Guild were vocal and insistent that the grief of widows be acknowledged, while the Association, more restrained in its public pronouncements of grief and mourning, was more aligned with the practices of the day.

This chapter has explored the expression of grief in the public arena during the immediate post-war period as a way of contexualising the oral testimonies that follow. The ways in which the various wars have been understood and remembered since this time are analysed in the next chapter.

CHAPTER THREE

THE WARS

> Memory can ... be expressed ... not consciously but through symbolic ... condensation and displacement.[1]

In histories of war, women's roles have been understood through a series of familiar images and stereotypes. Most retrospective accounts of the Second World War are by women who remember a time of youth, exuberance and romance, or of a heightened sense of involvement through their 'input' in the war effort.[2] In contrast, women remain invisible in narratives of the Korean War, reflecting the fate of that war in collective memory. Different again is the place of women in the Vietnam War which has, for the most part, been understood through the history of the protest and anti-war movements, framed as memories of youth, and to a lesser extent through recollections of female entertainers and nurses.[3]

In contrast to these selective stories of women in wartime, those whose husbands were serving abroad remember war as a time of absence and loss. For women with men at the front, absence was a major theme in their memories of the home-front, although these were often imbued with either a tragic or romantic hue. Histories of women's activism in wartime have focused on women involved in industrial labour, the implication being that this 'activism' should be the focus of study over other activities. Women's place in war narratives continues to be understood in terms of their relationship to the public domain, which has been deemed more relevant to the public memory of war than their private experience.[4]

Oral testimonies by women whose experience falls outside these commonly known areas give expression to another dimension of

36

women's war experience. Wives of servicemen are one such group. They present wars in their narratives in ways drawn from present-day understandings which have evolved over time through an amalgam of public and private commemorations. The Second World War has become the 'Just War'; the Korean War, the 'Forgotten War' and Vietnam, the 'Dirty War'. Wives of servicemen frame their accounts around these popular representations as a way of understanding their private experiences and presenting their memories of them. But while they accept these images of each of the wars, they also challenge them. Memories of the Second World War include bitterness about the strain it placed on their relationships and the impact of absent fathers on children. The comparative silence surrounding the Korean War belittles both the contribution of the husbands and by association, the wives' sacrifices. The perceived silence and neglect in the present is projected onto memories of the past. This projection is also true of the controversial response to the Vietnam War. Each time women recalled the ways in which they believed protesters challenged the actions of their men, they also, by association, felt undermined and slighted as soldiers' wives and as war widows. The subsequent re-writing of war has become the memory of war at the time.

This chapter looks at how women remember their roles as wives of servicemen while their husbands were serving abroad. They are the stories of women whose husbands did return from the war. Absence is a central motif in their memories; enduring the absence of their husbands, it is argued, was a part of wives' contribution to war. Furthermore, women internalised the feeling of loss experienced by their husbands when they returned, and this added a distinctive aspect to their experience and to their memories of war. The memory of a lack of recognition of their husbands' contribution is conflated with a sense that their own sacrifices have also been unacknowledged.

THE SECOND WORLD WAR: 'ABSENCE' – TRAGIC AND ROMANTIC

In contrast to the popular reactions to other wars, there was little overt resistance to Australia's involvement in the Second World War. Australia entered the war in close alliance with the British forces. Despite the lingering memories of the earlier world war, the need to defend democracy and freedom was perceived to be so immediate and urgent that after June 1940 support for total mobilisation was almost unconditional.[5] With the bombing of Pearl Harbor in December 1941 and the fall of Singapore in February 1942, support for the war increased further. As Stuart Macintyre notes, the memory of these events is tainted by a sense of betrayal by the British forces.[6] Some widows recall this time with a resentment of another kind – that the war created a profound absence in their marriage and within their families.

Widows remember the Second World War through a prism of both tragic and romantic absence, a reminiscence which is inevitably shaped by subsequent events. Lorna Higgenbotham's husband William was in the army before they met in 1937 and served in Borneo and New Guinea. He had joined as a bandsman, playing the double bass. She was 21 when they met and 23 when they married. In retrospect, she recalled the war years as a period of:

> sadness of having six years taken out of your marriage, life that you think you could have had six years together. When you think of that … you think well I could have had six more years if that war hadn't been running and been perhaps [in] better health … it is a big bite … right out of your life that you can never put back.[7]

The anxiety of that time alone came back to her with terror as she recalled the fear of receiving news of death:

> your heart was always in your mouth when you saw a telegram boy coming down the street, coming down your street, you'd think, 'I hope he's not coming to me' … you were always on tenter-hooks, you were always really het up in a certain way waiting that you were for sadness all the time …

Higgenbotham confessed that she continued to recall the death of her husband, who died in 1984, and she spoke of the difficulties of being on her own as a widow. When linking the past with the present, she merges the absence that forms her present solitude with the absence that she felt during the war years: the past and the present come together around the absence, and in her identity of being a war widow.

During the Second World War women continued to be sustained by female networks, which gave them particular support while men were absent. Mary Hopper, whose first husband Arthur died in the Second World War, describes how there was no news of her husband for three and a half years. He was in the army from 1940, and as 'the war was getting worse he said, "ah, he was a pacifist at heart, but he said I can't stand back"… so he joined the army'. During this time, she was fortunate to have the support of her family, and 'of course you're not the only one … the wives of the men … used to meet up in Melbourne and I used to go up and [get any news]'.[8] Hopper subsequently

remarried, and spoke with less vulnerability of her experiences and
indeed of her absences than did Higgenbotham. Although bereft by the
death of her husband at the time, her remarriage has, since the war,
allayed the feeling of absence as has remarriage for some of the other
widows.

Women with children felt wartime absence acutely. During the
war, there was a general fear about children being raised without the
parental guidance of the father. The absence of fathers created anxiety
about the extent to which discipline and order in the family could be
maintained. The *Sydney Morning Herald* played on these anxieties
when it reported in 1944 that among 'the social consequences of wartime conditions in Sydney, the breakdown of home relationships in the
absence of the father with the armed forces must be regarded as one
of the most disastrous'. The cases of 'uncontrollable children' where
'boys ... fall into a life of petty crime and girls ... seeking glamour,
find a life of drunkenness and vice', were increasing at a disturbing
rate, confirming that:

> a woman left alone to worry about her husband in the Army
> becomes less fitted to discharge the functions of a mother. Her
> emotional balance becomes affected and emotion plays a big part
> in the management of children. Then many mothers who have
> accepted employment haven't time to supervise their children ...
> the absence of a father reveals inadequacies in maternal control.[9]

This sensationalist reporting heightened the inadequacies felt by
mothers, and women became very concerned about the absent father.
Norma Jones remembered the absence of her husband as 'tragic' and
stressed the effect on her children. Her husband, Arthur, was called up
in 1942. They had met in 1936, as teenagers across the dance-floor in
Fitzroy. Two years later, when she was 19 and he was 22, they married.
During the war, he was absent for three years:

> if you've got a husband home all the time, your children would be
> different. See my children went without a father for three years. He
> was in the army for three years he'd just get a bit of leave every
> now and again. So I had to bring the children up on [my] own. It
> would have to be different I suppose, if your husband was there.[10]

It was difficult for her to assess the impact of this on her children:

> I don't know, really. I think it takes children a bit longer to adjust
> to things. They weren't used to having a man around telling [them]
> what to do and what not to do ... he was a stranger to them.

So you've got this stranger coming to your house. I mean to say you've got a husband there all the time and the children grow and they know their dad … but then all of a sudden a strange man comes into the house and the kids I suppose they just don't know how to take him … especially when they're babies and they don't remember much about him. I suppose they just got used to it [when he returned] … But it'd have to be different for children for a man to come back from the war and see their father all of a sudden …

As one investigation into prolonged absence in wartime subsequently found, the 'increased responsibilities of father absence [for mothers] had virtually become a new way of life'.[11] The wives of servicemen were forced to develop strategies to deal with the new responsibilities associated with caring for a family without a father or a husband. Their fathers' absence created dislocation for some children.[12]

The absence of a husband or fiancé was another motif in how widows remembered the war. The Second World War was a protracted, extended conflict. The number of marriages rose dramatically; the numbers of divorces after the war increased just as suddenly. For some widows, the absence of their fiancés or husbands became synonymous with a time of romance, as a period of dating and flirtation.[13] Mary Cooper recalls this during the Second World War when her husband, who, though he never served overseas, did so locally, and was absent for most of the war. She met Ashley at the age of 15. A persistent romantic, he pursued her relentlessly. He 'was boarding and he lived nearby' and eventually her mother suggested he move in, 'so he did and became part of the family'. He joined up when the war had begun. They married in 1944, while he was in the army. She expressed a desire to participate in the war effort more fully, but her ambitions for a term in the army were frustrated as:

I wanted to go into the army and become an AWAS [Australian Women's Army Service] and he said if you're going to be an AWAS we are going to have to break up our relationship because he didn't want me to be in the services … He didn't like the idea of me being an AWAS but I wanted to be but however I wasn't. I granted him that wish. He went his way and I went mine. I never became a member of any of the services. But I did my bit in other directions.[14]

Having been denied the opportunity to serve in the forces, she worked for Darrell Lea chocolates, and was very committed to her husband-to-be: 'I think we were meant for each other'. But, 'there was a period in

the time when I [felt] very lonely, I must confess. And he was away
in Western Australia'. She tells of how she met a sailor whom she
dated, although she 'couldn't get very close to him'. She broke up
their friendship when Ashley, whom she eventually married, returned;
her friend was 'devastated, brokenhearted', and she was 'lonely as
blazes'.[15] 'We've all had flirtation in our life', she explained, 'other
than that, Ashley and I were just true to each other'. The day he
returned she recalled with a sense of euphoria:

> It was a very exciting day that day he came out of the army and we
> could really start our life together. It wasn't very long after that that
> we opened a business ... I opened a baby wear shop in Sydney
> Road ... he went back to work at Prestige ... mill and life sort of
> went from there ...[16]

Her marriage lasted fifty years, until her husband died in 1989.
Since that time she has sought out her former romantic interest. Photographs capture a time she wishes to retain.

> I've tried to contact him since my Ashley died because I have
> photographs I'd like to give them back ... I don't want him as a
> person, but I want to give him these photos. I can't burn them. I
> can't burn those photos.

Cooper remembers her wartime experience through a romantic hue.
Because her husband returned from his war service, and she subsequently had fifty years of marriage, she can recall that time as one of
romantic innocence.

Absence also engendered anxiety about trust and suspicion
between couples, as marriages were placed under strain with the
absence of a partner over a number of years.[17] The Second World War,
Andrea Walsh has argued, 'provided fertile ground for a "culture of
distrust"'. With so many young men absent, and the future of relationships unclear, 'distrust and cynicism flourished'.[18] Margery Wittig's
narrative illustrates the ways in which absence negatively affected
romance. She met her husband-to-be, John, walking along the promen-
ade on a beach in Newcastle in 1939, when she was 20. One year later
they were married and in 1943 he was conscripted. He became
paranoid about her sexual behaviour in his absence, accusing her of:

> carrying on with Yanks ... it wasn't his fault actually because he
> was over there and he was lonely. I suppose and they say all kinds
> of things ... he got 5 pages back from me and it wasn't very nice ...
> I think he was lonely and upset about going over there.[19]

Many older women greeted the end of the war with great relief and do not recall it as a time of sexual experimentation nor of romance. Truda Naylor, whose husband Allan served in both world wars, recalled the burden and strain that had been lifted:

> We were too sick at heart to celebrate. We were only too glad to think it was all over. We were past celebrating. It was the younger people who celebrated. It was just terrific relief for us … It was like coming out of an illness or something you don't celebrate do you?[20]

Truda Naylor had, by this stage, been a veteran serviceman's wife. Allan Naylor had served in the First World War, at Gallipoli and in France. He remained in the army reserve and he and her brothers 'couldn't wait' to join again. 'Normally they were gentle men', she reflected, 'but they couldn't resist the comradeship, or something'. Truda was opposed to his going to war again, and it puzzled her why he did so. She didn't try to stop him as it would be futile: 'I wouldn't have had a chance.'[21] Naylor presents a stoic picture of her experience. At 94, she chose not to be nostalgic for another time and place. Unlike some of the widows who were younger and single during the war, she attached little romance to her narrative of absence or war.

KOREA: 'THE FORGOTTEN WAR'

Of all the wars Australia has participated in, the Korean War has been assumed to have had least impact on the men and on their wives and families. This is a symptom of the way in which it has been forgotten. It, as one historian has written, 'passed out of the public mind almost as soon as the ceasefire was signed in 1953 and the Australian troops were withdrawn'.[22] Korea foreshadowed Australian and American involvement in Vietnam, drawing on the same Cold War rhetoric, ideological perspectives and beliefs that later shaped the Australian commitment in Vietnam.[23]

While there is now an emerging Australian literature on the Korean conflict, it continues to be a largely undocumented war in terms of its impact on families. Histories of the war have been concerned with accounts of battles, and the context of the Cold War, rather than the experiences of soldiers or the impact the war had on their lives and their families.[24] Letters, diaries or memoirs written during this conflict, have not attracted as much attention as those of soldiers who served in the Second World War or in Vietnam.[25] The issues surrounding the silence on the Korean War have recently begun to be analysed. Why are some wars considered appropriate for commemoration and others not? These questions are now being raised and examined in relation to the Korean War.[26]

The Korean War began in June 1950 when fighting broke out between North Korea and South Korea amid the heightened tensions of the Cold War. The United Nations (UN) Security Council declared the war an act of North Korean aggression and UN members were invited to send troops. Australia was one of the first nations to send units to Korea.[27] There were, by the end of the conflict, 1584 Australian casualties with 339 killed and 29 taken prisoner.[28]

Olwyn Green lost her husband, Charlie, in the Korean War. Married in January 1943, he returned from the Second World War in 1945. After attempting a series of 'very ordinary jobs', he decided to go back into the army. Green claims this was all he had been trained to do. The army had 'sent him in a direction [which] was inconceivable … and leaving him stranded as it were … with nowhere really to go … All he'd been trained for [was] war and he was exceptionally good at it.' When it was suggested to him that he go back into the Army, he joined up for Korea. Green is unusual among war widows because she published a personal account of her grief, in her autobiography, *The Name's Still Charlie*. She was inspired to do so when his battalion decided to establish a memorial to him. In her book she documents the way in which she came to terms with Charles Green's death and how she dealt with the memorial built in his name. She reflects on how she idealised him and how she moved through this experience. It is a telling comment on the lack of public expression of such emotions within Australia that it took Green thirty years to allow herself to express this grief openly. Green recalled that because her husband Charlie was killed in the Korean War, there was little community sympathy for her. When he died in 1950, she lived in Grafton, which was an advantage as it turned out, because:

> if I hadn't been in Grafton where I knew people I think it would have been a thousand times worse because there wasn't much sympathy for the Korean War. Very few people knew anything about it – why they were there … a lot of people would have thought anybody who went to the Korean War was a fool and that doesn't help. That wouldn't help anybody who lost someone in Korea or Vietnam.[29]

The humiliation that came with the public erasure of the war was carried by its widows. Green conflates the present forgetting of the

Korean War with the past, as she remembers that the war did not attract support, although other sources show that in 1950 support for the war was strong. Later forgetting of the Korean War, she believed, reduced her and others to the status of ordinary widows, and this took away their sense of national service. A lack of recognition, it was believed, undermined their own sacrifices, and thus they remembered the war as unpopular.

The wives of soldiers internalised the lack of recognition given to their husbands. This is often articulated through a sense that their husbands' and their own efforts were not adequately acknowledged. Jean Rayner's husband, Louis, was a driver in the Korean War. They met in early 1957 when she was 17 years old, and she was living in Sorrento near the officers' cadet school. They were married in March 1958. Although not a combat soldier, Lou nevertheless resented the dismissive attitude of many people that the Korean War was not a 'real' war. 'One thing that did annoy Lou about the Korean War', Jean recalled, with indignation:

> was that people called [it] a point[less] action, not a war. Even when I became a war widow, I was asked point blank, 'how come you're a war widow?' … And they said, 'you're not old enough for [the] Second World War and you are too old for Vietnam. Now I was asked that point blank. And I said there was such a thing as Korea. And anyway [they said] 'was that a war?' … if they hadn't kicked up a stink about Vietnam, would have been the same thing. Put it out of your mind and forget it, it didn't happen …[30]

Rayner believed that:

> Korea [is] still not finished … it's a waste of time sending these chaps in … you'll never sort these wars out and so what's the point of wasting lives. Doesn't get anyone anywhere [during the Vietnam War] … Lou turned around … and said it's another Korea all over again … When they brought 'em home, Lou said … 'There you go', he said, 'they're not getting recognition', he said, 'we didn't get it either … we never got it'.

Recognition is a recurring motif in Rayner's story. She emphasised that the recognition her husband did receive, from his soldier friends as they played the Last Post at his funeral, would have been very important to him. Lack of recognition is a theme which is repeated in testimonies by war widows, as they too, carry the burden and legacy of 'forgetting'. Rayner links the belated recognition of her husband's

Lawrie and Jean McNeill, 1959

and her own contribution to the view that the war does not have the significance it did in 1950.

Jean McNeill's husband served in both the Second World War and Korea. She recalled that Korea and Vietnam were certainly forgotten wars, and for her generation, they are overshadowed by the Second World War. 'When you talk about the War,' she recalls,

> I suppose to my generation you ... think of World War I and World War II and you're inclined to overlook Korea and Vietnam ... The thing that always amazes me ... [is] they called Vietnam and Korea a police action. Surely they were war whatever they chose to call them ... There was some horrible things happen in every war and yet the Vietnam veterans seem to be more affected by it, more psychologically affected by it, which amazes me I mean there were [atrocities] ... in the Second World War that must have been horrific, flame throwers etc. Surely Agent Orange couldn't have been worse. I don't know if it's because we hear more about them ... whether the people who were affected in the Second World War didn't like to talk about it. But that always puzzles me.[31]

She claims that the treatment the soldiers returning from Vietnam received, 'was disgraceful, I think ... Nobody wanted to go. Nobody asked to go and to be treated so shabbily on their return. I think that was really disgraceful.' The view that the Korean War becomes forgotten is conflated with a sense of criticism of her husband's involvement in the war: 'or overlooked, almost. It just happened. Nobody seems to talk about it much ... They say we shouldn't have interfered ... [But] Somebody had to do something.'

Jean Nelson's husband Ron served in the Korean War, and like others, she felt his contribution has been neglected:

> those boys never got any credit or anything for what they did. They went away ... and a terrific amount of them gave their lives. But that wasn't recognised ... And they didn't get what they was promised when they got home.[32]

A lack of recognition and acknowledgement form a part of Jessie Moreland's testimony. Moreland, whose husband Robert had joined the navy in 1948 at the age of 18, had already served in Korea when they met in 1953. She was 19. They met on his leave and then he returned for another twelve months to serve in Korea. Both Korea and Vietnam are overlooked, she believes.

> I don't think people ... want to know about it ... People even now ... returned servicemen are fighting for things they are entitled to and people laugh at them. They think, oh, you know you were only in Vietnam but you know those boys went through a lot. Korea is another one you never hear much of it. If you go to a memorial or somewhere like that and it's always the First World War and Second World War ...

To Moreland, both wars seem absent from public memorials, and to her this suggests an erasing of her husband's efforts from public memory:

> when my husband and I went to Darwin ... and we went up to this big memorial place they just then put on Korea and Vietnam ... You never ever see, no matter where you went, very rarely you found that Korea and Vietnam was ever mentioned. So it was like they tried to wipe it off the earth but no one ever wants to talk about it. But even the governments don't want to talk about it. I think it's a thing that we got involved in with Americans and they had to do it. And I honestly think that was the whole problem ... Men are sort of fighting for their rights that it's really come out. Before then you never hear of it. You never read anything, say five years ago, about Korea and Vietnam. Never, no. It's only the last two years that really it's been in the open.[33]

Moreland reads her past experience through the forgetting which she believes has characterised the subsequent lack of public acknowledgement of the Korean and Vietnam wars.

Moreland lamented that her husband's contribution was not recognised and by association, she too felt hurt. She recalled the absences that the war created and the impact on her marriage. Her husband John had already served in Korea when they met and from the beginning, the marriage was marked by many absences.

> These were shocking. You [were] left on your own ... you sort of didn't know where they were going or anything because in those days everything was top secret ... he'd be on leave and then there'd be a knock at the door ... many times he never ever finished his leave ... they often never used to know themselves ... You didn't know when they'd come back. Like he might be away three months, four months.'

During his second visit to Korea, she didn't see him for twelve months, but, as his wife, there was little she could do about it, as women were expected to follow their husbands:

> In those days you accepted [it] because the wife had nothing to do with the services ... The wife didn't know. It was like he used to go to work and never used to come home for weeks and weeks ... You just had to cope with it if you married a serviceman. That was just life.

Her husband spent six years in the navy and then joined the air force. The wives of servicemen were not expected to be consulted and they were expected to live their domestic lives according to the dictates of the army: 'Wives in those days did ... follow their husbands like sheep. Whatever the husbands used to do, women used to go along with it'. Reflecting on this period when he served, she commented that 'we never saw that much of him'.[34]

Others tell a similar story of absence, and of women's stoicism in dealing with this gap in their lives. In 1950, Joyce Richards was engaged to her husband, Mervyn, after knowing him only seven weeks. They were married five months before he went to Korea, and spent a month together in Sydney before his ship sailed. He had been in the navy since 1946, and when the Korean War broke out, he was put on 24-hour notice and there was a mad rush to get married. The men in the navy had to spend twelve months abroad during their time of service, and this was a testing time on the marriage:

You only had to rely on letters, you couldn't ring up … and I can
look at it now … how you could be influenced by other men in the
office … I'd had a bit of married life and I'd got into this vacuum
of not having companionship or anything like that … One of the
men got a little bit keen on me but he could see what was going to
happen … You could see how that could happen because you're
just drifting away. It's this big vacuum there.[35]

War widows remember the Korean War as a forgotten war and in
their memories, they draw together the lack of recognition of their
husbands with what they perceive to be the broader neglect of the war.

VIETNAM: 'THE DIRTY WAR'

If recognition, or lack of it, was a motif for remembering the Korean
War, then the Vietnam War is heavily weighted with a mixture of
outrage, resentment as well as silence.

The wives of Vietnam veterans are unanimous about the impact
the war had on their husbands and on their marriages. This war, more
than any other, has brought attention to the impact on soldiers' relatives
and marriages. Perhaps the controversy surrounding the war allowed
Vietnam veterans' wives to articulate its impact. As with other wars, its
effect was not uniform nor necessarily evident at the time. Wives of
Vietnam soldiers dwell in their stories, on the controversial aspects
of the war. While they accept the representation of the war in this way,
at the same time they resist this as the only characterisation.

The story of Australia's entry into the Vietnam War has been told
comprehensively elsewhere.[36] Australia's involvement in Vietnam from
1962 to 1972, was the largest military commitment of Australian armed
forces since the Second World War.[37] What began as a small advisory
presence in 1962 of about 30 officers, advisers, and training instructors,
escalated into a major military commitment which by 1967, involved
8,300 Australian troops. As the American government escalated its
involvement, so too did the Australian. During the ten years Australia
was involved in Vietnam, 50,000 soldiers served, 17,000 of whom
were conscripts.[38] It was the conscription issue that ignited mass
protests and inspired a generation of young men to resist the draft. The
National Service Act was introduced into the Australian parliament
in November 1964. It stipulated that all 20-year-old men had to register
for national service. Birth dates were selected at random and those
whose dates were announced were called up for service. In 1966 the
first conscript left for Vietnam.[39] The anti-conscription and anti-war

campaign involved peace groups, women's organisations and the left in protest against Australia's involvement in the war. In total, the war claimed 519 dead and 2348 wounded.[40]

In writing on the Vietnam War, historians have concentrated on activities on the home-front almost exclusively in terms of the growing force of anti-war protesters, and the social movements they spawned. This is a history of public events, and of how these events have been mythologised, remembered and packaged.[41] Military historians, on the other hand, have written their histories from the viewpoint of the returned soldiers, especially in relation to the impact of the use of the defoliant Agent Orange and claims for compensation.[42]

In these histories, the experiences of soldiers' wives, and war widows have remained absent. They are portrayed with their husbands as either victims of hostile attack by demonstrators and others, or as uncaring and heartless supporters of an untenable war.[43] My research shows that wives of returned men cannot be characterised so easily and their stories suggest another layer of trauma, one often not identified in the historiography of the Vietnam War.[44]

The embarrassment with which the war is now remembered has significantly affected memories of it. As Ann Curthoys has argued, contrary to images in the popular imagination, there is no evidence that protestors hated the soldiers, or attended welcome home marches to abuse them. Indeed, very few veterans mention 'themselves experiencing or witnessing hostile actions by protestors'.[45] The mainstream press reported welcoming parades rather than acts of confrontation. In April 1968, the *Sydney Morning Herald* reported the return of veterans with the headline, 'Young Vietnam Veterans Get Warm Welcome'. It was reported that:

> Sydney ... gave Australia's newest Anzacs a warm welcome ... It was a magnificent military parade. The crowd, estimated at about 6000 outside the Town Hall alone, treated the young Vietnam veterans ... The men marched on – past the people, past the prime minister, past the policemen, watchful for demonstrations that did not occur ...[46]

This is not the way some soldiers and their wives now remember it. The anger, Curthoys argues, at participating in a war that failed 'is deflected onto the protestors, who are understood as attacking them personally rather than the governments that sent them there'.[47] The anti-war movement, she concludes, continues to be a 'source of historical disagreement and debate'.[48]

Soldier's wives internalised their husbands' angst, and interpreted protesters' hostility to the war as a slight on them. By the late 1990s, this too could be identified as a way of dealing with grief and anger. The wives, imbued with military culture, could not imagine criticising either the government or the men for going to war. For some soldiers' wives, the controversy over the war has meant that their memories are determined by the need to defend their husbands, while the passing of time has altered the views of others.

Olwyn Green recalled how she got 'very, very upset about the way people behaved. This blind response to the negative aspects of the Vietnam War and dumping all their negative thoughts on the men themselves. That really, really upset me.' 'Even the RSL', she stressed, 'didn't admit veterans because they weren't volunteers'.[49]

Noela Hatfield disagreed with the attitude of the protesters who agitated against the war, and with what she remembers as their treatment of the soldiers. She married her husband, Robert, in 1955. Five years later, he joined the army. He was sent to Vietnam in April 1968 and returned in May 1969. She claimed the behaviour of the protesters was

> very very rude. It was all wrong the way [the soldiers] were treated it was terrible … Like they were spat on … hit with things … it was terrible … Bob always said they should never have been in Vietnam to start off with. It's a waste of part of your married life to go somewhere where you shouldn't have to be … they all said Vietnam had nothing to do with us … We lost a lot of those boys which was very unfair … They should never have been sent into a war zone …[50]

Hatfield now views the time he spent in Vietnam as wasted, both in terms of her marriage and her children. In retrospect,

> I was younger then. I've really gone more against Vietnam more now than what I did then, I suppose because I think, well, that part of your married life was wasted and it's not fair on your kids but we shouldn't have been there.[51]

Ann Templar is also ambivalent about the war, given her husband's death from cancer in 1993 which was related to war service.

> But I still think he did what he had to do. And I wouldn't have changed it … If I had the time over again I wouldn't change it now … I don't know whether we should have even been there. And that's probably something I choose not to sit and think about.

Her attitude towards the protestors has been affected by the images of the anti-Vietnam War movement which has emerged in the popular media. It remains the lingering image for many Vietnam War widows:

> I think it's dreadful, but then I suppose people couldn't see any other way. They did what they felt they had to do, too, and whether it be right and whether it be wrong … The violence that occurred, the things that I've seen on television, I think was uncalled for and dreadful. But it's mob rule. It's what happens. I can't abide the thought of anybody burning a flag. That's just a symbol and has been to us always. I just think that's reprehensible. That again is something that I don't think probably ever set out to be done on the spur, in the heat of the moment … and what I've seen on television in recent years of what happened on those moratoriums and the protests I understand that people feel they have to have their say, but it's not the way that I feel things should be done …[52]

Glenis Hargen, whose husband George served in Vietnam in 1969 through the regular army, shared this view of how the soldiers were treated:

> It wasn't right the way they were treated. They were only doing what the government told them … The people in Australia didn't understand what they had come through and I think if they would know what they had gone through they would have been more sympathetic to them.[53]

Josephine Betts, whose husband Francis was in the air force when they met, was angry that he left five children behind in 1969, to serve in Vietnam. 'I thought he was a mongrel', she recalled, a 'complete rat. I was quite cross … It's a man's world and … they trot off and leave us behind'. But this did not soften her view of the protestors, nor of conscription. While compulsory military service did not attract widespread hostility, the selective system of conscription became increasingly unpopular.[54] Betts recalls that she would get:

> so upset. I could have taken my tommy gun to all of them. I was so angry … What right did they have to say that we shouldn't be there. The government said to our fellows, 'you go'. I felt for the conscripts … it was very unfair. It should have been one in all in. None of this business of the little balls … One in all in.[55]

The image of the protestors as attacking the soldiers on their return has lingered and is perpetuated in these accounts as her anger about her husband's lack of recognition is merged with an attack on the demonstrators.

Loris Pini recalled similar experiences of her husband, Desmond. 'He joined the army in about 1953, 1954'. Initially, she was:

> very anti-services … in fact … I wouldn't go out with him if he had come down in uniform to visit me … What I really felt was I couldn't see the point in an Army when we weren't at war … I have now … that Australia must have their defence forces … but at that age I just couldn't really see the point and I suppose in a way it was shutting out the fact that he could have been sent to war like my brothers had been so it was probably a reaction to them being away.[56]

But soon she defended him and objected to the treatment the soldiers had received:

> That is the main thing that knocked these boys around was the fact that when they came back it was as if it was their fault that they'd gone … [In other circumstances] They would have been welcomed home. Even their own RSL didn't really accept them for a while … as real war heroes which they were; they were sent there the same as others were sent to war. And it was a dirty war because really they never knew who was their enemy … in other wars they did know.

The unknown enemy was crucial in defining the Vietnam experience: 'They never knew who was the enemy and who wasn't … that's why it was such a terrible war they didn't know who they were against and who they weren't'. The Americans were also to blame, and 'of course when the Americans … brought in all that chemical warfare and sprayed the jungle and some of them [were affected] by that, that didn't help matters'. Loris considered she and her husband were fortunate not to have had any children, 'because a lot of the children that were born … deformed … and a lot of the men couldn't have children after that'. Pini was not entirely supportive of the war effort:

> at the time I was angry he was going. I really was. I don't know why I was angry, probably personally rather than the actual fact that it was a war. It was probably from my own feelings … I always maintained that we would not have had as much trouble if they'd allow the Korean War to finish … I don't know we had the right to be there … [but] there was a great fear of Communism in Australia … I have no animosity [towards the Vietnamese].

Pini felt veterans were forgotten because nobody would take responsibility for an unsuccessful war. People would say, '"what would you know, it was no war" … because it was political. No-one would accept the responsibility'. The negative talk and the abuse 'added to their stress', which was internalised by wives as well.[57]

Others did not agree with their husband's participation in the Vietnam War. Rosie James' husband, Robert, joined the air force in 1952, when he was 16. He had been posted to Malaya and they had lived there for three years. She objected to him going to Vietnam and distanced herself from his decision: 'I didn't want him to go to Vietnam. Who would want them to go? I never wanted him to be in the forces anyway ... I didn't want to lose him ... that was his choice, not mine.'

James concealed the fact that her husband was in Vietnam, because she did not want to bear the brunt of humiliation she believed was associated with the war: 'To tell you the truth I didn't tell anybody ... It [was] almost a shame thing. You've got attached with it that stigma and that shame ... it's something that had to be hidden and something that was shameful'. But externally,

> the controversy that arose over it was so heated in places and it was so controversial that those who were opposed to it ... were very angry about it so you copped the brunt of some of that anger and I preferred not to do that and therefore ... I hid it and didn't want to have anything to do with it.

On a more personal level, in terms of:

> my own personal, ethical and moral ... standards ... the treatment of the local people over there, I felt ashamed to be a human being, ashamed to have any connection with what happened there ... I felt ashamed to have some sort of part in being married to somebody in it ... Ashamed to be human ... I still don't say to people ... I didn't talk about Vietnam ...

James was unusual to be so outspoken and vocal about her resistance and hostility to the war. She also chose to see it as a coincidence of circumstances:

> My husband wasn't the air force. My husband wasn't Vietnam. Because he happened to be in the air force ... he happened to go to Vietnam ... I was proud of him, but not *because* of what he did or didn't do in Vietnam ... Yes, I was proud of him ... but it's not closely linked and connected here ... it's not that I was ashamed of *him* for having been in Vietnam ... they were two separate things. So I'm not in conflict about being proud of him and ashamed of him: that's no conflict whatsoever. The conflict would be in terms of Vietnam per se, whether I acknowledge or I don't acknowledge and that would be the only conflict, irrespective of him.

Rather than condemn the protestors, her resentment was directed towards 'the non-acknowledgement of the governments ... that there were quite profound residual ... psychological damage to those who were in Vietnam where there was no compensation for these people'.[58]

Beverley Schmidt drew distinctions between those men in the regular army, and the conscripts who were forced to go and serve in Vietnam. Her husband Terry joined the army in 1959 and he was a soldier when they married in 1961. Personally, she felt that 'they should have never gone ... Did not agree on the conscripts, poor little devils'. Terry made a choice to go. The hostility towards them was misplaced, because they 'were soldiers [and] they did what they were told to do'. The energy of the demonstrators was misplaced, as 'these demonstrations get on my nerves. They make me more angry. I can

Pat Medaris in the navy

understand where they're coming from. I know what they mean … but don't pick on the boys … Go to Government House, demonstrate there'.[59] By association, she felt slighted as well, and the demonstrators became the focus of her resentment about the lack of appreciation of the difficulties the soldiers experienced.

Pat Medaris' husband, Jack, was in the navy for nearly 23 years, joining at 17 and being discharged at 40. They met each other in the navy in 1952 when he was 23 and she was 25. Medaris spent three and a half 'wonderful years' in the navy herself. She had to resign after marriage: 'I suppose it was just taken as a matter of course because all women had to resign from everything'. She recalls the impact the Vietnam War had on her children at school:

> It was … very controversial … that was when the children were growing up. The eldest girl was into high school … it affected her [because] she was with girls whose brothers were in the draw … it was upsetting for them.

Jack Medaris, husband of Pat, 1949

She described the ways in which it was difficult for her children:

> You'd go past and you'd see written 'murderers' and all that sort of
> thing. It was quite taunting at times but I think they were so used to
> their father having been in the navy it didn't affect them in the way
> it might [have] ...[60]

The hostility remained when he returned. Medaris felt she too carried
the responsibilities of the war. In 1966 or 1967,

> I can remember going to Flinders Street Station meeting him one
> time. And they'd all just arrived back and I was waiting there and
> Jack came up and he was in uniform. We'd planned to have some
> lunch somewhere ... and a lady passed the most terrible remark to
> both Jack and I [to the effect of] it's a pity you didn't stay home and
> look after her ... instead of firing ammunition at innocent people
> and all this sort of thing. And it upset our day ... I can understand
> how they [veterans] went off on their own and did their own thing
> because people absolutely shunned them. It wasn't their fault. They
> were sent there ... They were very angry. They didn't understand it.

Her feelings were mixed about the Moratorium and the protests
against the war, and her own position was ambiguous. 'You knew you
were implicated and you knew you were in it because your husband
was in it. And then I wondered just what effect it was going to have
on the children.' She recalled her daughter, who was 16 at the time,
brought some friends home from school, and this girl said, '"where's
your father?" and she said, "oh he's away in the navy" and she said,
"he's not one of those is he?"'. Medaris justified her husband's actions
as 'doing his job', feeling in hindsight that she needed to do so: 'if you
get sent here, sent there, that's the job ... And that's the way he saw it.
And I thought that was a good attitude to have. And he divorced
himself of any blame on him.'[61] The memory of the ill-treatment of
their husbands suggests the ways in which these women too have
internalised their sense of betrayal and abandonment. In focusing on
the ill-treatment of their husbands at the hand of the government the
women too have internalised the sense of betrayal and abandonment.

Phyllis Muller agreed with her husband that it was 'better to fight
the enemy in their backyard than let them come into your backyard'.
She met her husband Keith in 1953, when she was working for the
Australian airline TAA. He had been a pilot in the Royal Australian Air
Force (RAAF), and then served in Korea for ten months. He was
awarded the Air Force Cross for his work in Korea and served in
Vietnam. She believed:

it was very sad, I think, the way they chose the boys to go to Vietnam. I think that just wasn't right … Yes [I agree] I used to see things the way he saw them … His statement to me about Korea was he couldn't understand why anyone would want to fight for such a godforsaken country.[62]

Maureen Matthews was more outspoken about the problems she faced when her husband was abroad. She married Robert Matthews in 1957. Robert was a 'Legacy boy', his father having died on the Burma railway. He was trained as an electrician, but wanted an army life. As an army wife, Maureen found the television coverage of the Vietnam War disconcerting and unsettling, which was reflected in how society represented and remembered the war. The negative representations for her reflected a sense of betrayal:

> Vietnam was in my living room every night … You couldn't really get away from it. It put a cold shiver in you … And they never ever said anything good. It was all bad. And then you'd see people marching in the streets and all that sort of thing and what people don't realise, and it upsets me … but you know yourself, [when] there's a bully, and if you don't stick up for yourself, that bully will overrun you and overpower you, well I think a country is only as good as its defence …

When it's a job, she reiterated, 'it doesn't matter what you think'. She felt humiliation at some of the tactics of the demonstrators:

Robert Matthews, husband of Maureen, in Vietnam

Maureen and Robert Matthews, 12 January 1957

> They were adamant that we shouldn't have been in Vietnam, well, perhaps we shouldn't have been. But I thought very very poorly of the people that burned the Australian flag and burnt their cards and wouldn't face up to the fact that their number was called and I think a lot of people underneath … are frightened and I think it takes guts when your number is called to do the right thing. Because if we didn't all do the right thing we'd all be in one helluva mess.

More directly, reflecting on her feelings at the time:

> I didn't like Vietnam. I didn't feel underneath myself in a way that we should be there but when I thought about it, I thought the way I looked at it we were really there to give America support … She came to our aid in our time of need and I think people tend to forget that they're too quick to bag … America.

Then the Matthews:

> bought a home [in Brisbane] … and a lot of people in that particular area were university people that were sort of mouthing off about Vietnam but I couldn't see that they were doing anything constructive. And I sort of felt … hurt actually but I just went about my business … I must admit my sons' school … [was] very good. [63]

Matthews was ambivalent. While she disliked the Vietnam War, she also despised the treatment she believed soldiers were given by the demonstrators. The protestors became a focus for her antagonism against the war.

The dilemma facing national servicemen was best put by Paula Voltz, whose husband Rex was a conscript who served in Vietnam between 1969 and 1970:

> It affected the servicemen and women because I mean they were over there defending Australia and here were people marching against their involvement. And I mean some of them didn't have a choice. Like my Rex went and he was a national serviceman. They say, 'oh, yeah, you could have done jail' and everything else. But well, he didn't want to do jail …

Her husband confronted the protestors, and she too is critical of them in her retelling of the incident:

> He certainly wasn't taking it very well. Well, he virtually just told them, you know, in no uncertain terms what they were and they didn't know what they were talking about … I used to defend the servicemen and women over there.

Protestors become the focus of much of the angst associated with the war. Rex Voltz committed suicide in December 1985, an event which inspired Paula to begin work for the Vietnam Veterans' Association.[64]

Wives of Vietnam men spoke openly of absences that strained their relationships. Because these events are more recent, and Vietnam was a tainted war, there is little romantic association with this absence. This was not however, an empty time, for the difficulty of carrying the strain and burdens of an unpopular war, and trying to keep domestic life harmonious made a significant impact on them. The absence for more than a year of Noela Hatfield's husband 'puts a very big strain on your marriage', she recalled. The unpredictability of his absence made it difficult for her:

> it is a lot of strain … I was left home with three children to rear … it was very difficult … they brought it in that the men were entitled to five days home if they wanted to go home, but I think that was the worst thing they could have done … You try to settle down to being apart from each other and then they come for five days and … we didn't sort of settle much after that … I was glad when the 13 months were up. We even got to the stage when we used to argue in letters, which was wrong …

The absence of a husband and father engendered anxieties, frustrations and required a significant adjustment for some families.[65]

Domestic demands were difficult to cope with, because 'you're the one left at home with the kids and they fight and I don't think there is anything worse than three fighting children'. Noela's mother had had the same problem left at home for three and a half years with four children during the Second World War.[66]

For others such as Ann Templar, absence became a very significant part of her marriage. Her husband, Wayne, was in the regular army and served in Vietnam between 1969 and 1970. Throughout their marriage, he was absent three or four months at a time, more than once a year, and this became a way of life. While he served, she looked after the children and took responsibility for them alone:

> It was tough because I had three young children. But we always lived in the army area … so there were a lot of people in the same situation and people just bonded together … but it was tough. The youngest one fretted. The youngest one didn't sleep for the whole year his dad was away. He'd scream himself to sleep …

When he returned, both of them had to adapt to a new routine: 'he didn't know how to be a heavy handed father because I always did all the disciplining and that part of it was hard'. The family underwent a significant adjustment:

> I was used to being on my own. It was hard on the kids. And it was hard on all of us when he was home every night … because he was just like the fifth child … I often wondered why he stayed sometimes. Because really I had all those years of having to do everything, of having to make all the decisions myself and it was hard for both of us. For me to include him and to not do things automatically and for him to actually have to be a part of decision-making because in the army he just did what he was told and basically that's what it was like at home.[67]

Others also recalled that their children were not immune to the effects of their fathers' absence. Loris Pini claimed that the 13 months her husband served in Vietnam affected her son: it was 'very hard … my youngest was 16/17 months … didn't know his father for over twelve months … the little fellow didn't know him at all'. The vagaries of waiting and waiting for news were very difficult to deal with:

> I did get word to say he was on his way home … then I was notified that his replacement hadn't arrived … and he would not be home … You can imagine what trauma that did to nerves … twice that happened.[68]

Ann Templar also recalls the terror of waiting for news of her husband:

> We were told that if someone was bringing us bad news there
> would be three people in the car ... a driver ... a commanding
> officer ... a padre ... Every time we saw an army vehicle [we
> would] count heads. And if there were three heads we were sure
> they were going somewhere in the area.[69]

Beverley Schmidt's husband Terry served two tours of duty,
including three separations from his family of more than twelve
months. Letters were very important in sustaining contact. He wrote
each day from Vietnam, but insisted that she destroy the letters when he
returned. But in his absence, 'every time you saw a car come up, your
heart's in your mouth ... the priest used to come ... when you saw it go
past you say, "Oh, thank God", but oh God that poor whoever it is'.[70]
Being alone also had its downsides as people would be suspicious of
her activities: 'having no men around ... the other personnel who
stayed behind got a bit carried away'. Prowlers knew women who were
on their own, and would 'come peep at you through the windows and
bang on your windows and doors'. On one occasion, her father came
to stay with her, creating rumours, that she had a man staying in her
house. He moved out, 'because [he] thought I was getting a bad name'.

The absences Pat Medaris endured were difficult at first:

> It was very hard at first ... the eldest girl was born 12 months after
> we were married which was the normal thing in those days ... Jack
> was sent away when she was eight months old ...and he was absent
> for 12 months.

This absence set the pattern for the next few years. He was sent away
again when the second child was six months old; and was absent from
the birth of their third child. He was posted to Vietnam in 1963–64: 'the
children hadn't seen a great deal of their father ... [not] much at all
really. It was just come and go sort of thing ... '. She recalled the
difficulty of coping with the children and the absences:

> I remember he'd said he'd be back at a certain time. And I got a
> telegram to say they had arrived and I said to the children 'now
> look, your father will be arriving home tonight ... making sure that
> you're good girls'.

But another telegram arrived which said he wasn't coming after all, and
they wouldn't see him for two or three months. One of the children
said, 'are you sure or are you just making it up ... he has said that
before'.[71] Medaris was convinced that, looking 'back on it and I don't

think they had the same childhood that a lot of children around them did. Simply because there were places I couldn't take one I had to take three'.

As an army wife, Maureen Matthews believed she had no choice in the way in which she would lead her life while her husband was away at war:

> well, that was my husband's job … of course I was brought up in the days when the man was the head of the house and I still believe in a man being the head of the house. You can't have two heads in a house. Somebody has to be the top … As far as the children went their father was the boss and what their father said, went and I never ever went against him in front of the children … And I always made sure that he was praised up and I used to tell them how lucky they were that they had such a great dad … In every relationship you do have the downside you think, 'Oh, I'd like to kill them', but I sort of kept that to myself and I think it was a good thing.

She described the way she ran the household while he was away:

> When you are on your own and your husband's away, things filter back … and you're the woman at home, balancing the budget, doing all the hard yakka with the children and … you feel as if you're missing out. But when a letter arrives that tells you how much they miss you and they realise that you're doing a good job and they're looking forward to coming home, it puts a different light on the subject … keeping in contact is very important, plus my husband had arranged before he went to have flowers sent on certain [occasions] like an anniversary or on my birthday …

Others did not identify it as such a problem. Roma Pressley said that in marrying her husband William, who was passionate about the navy, 'I knew what I was getting into. It didn't really worry me'.[72]

Women's memories of the wars were shaped in a myriad of ways. The Second World War inspired narratives of tragedy and romance. In the Korean and Vietnam conflicts, wives internalised the burdens of war, and the stresses that came with it, including lack of recognition of their husbands. They felt they had made their own contribution, and resented that their sacrifices were not acknowledged. While they discussed the wars in terms which have common currency, they challenged the representation of these wars. The embarrassment with which the Vietnam

War is now remembered has affected memory, and this both perpetu-ates and sustains the mythology surrounding the war. The protestors become the target for much of the antagonism about the war and its impact.

These are the stories of those whose husbands returned from the wars. The remembrances of those widows whose husbands died during war, which is the subject of the next chapter, are shaped by other considerations – nostalgia, and a life-time reluctance to relinquish memories of their loss.

CHAPTER FOUR

MEMORIES OF DEATH: LOSS, NOSTALGIA AND REGRET

the passing of time is intrinsically traumatic.[1]

Death in wartime shapes a distinctive response of bereavement. The tragic and sudden death of young men propels mourners into specific expressions of loss. For many of the wives of the men who died in battle, death was never entirely mourned. This chapter looks at the memories of women who lost their husbands in war. It considers the ways in which they grieved for their lost ones and how they have come to understand their lives in light of this tragedy.

A common theme emerges in the testimonies of women who lost their husbands in war: their partners remain idealised. Usually, with death comes a review of marriage. In bereavement literature it is observed that initially the marriage will be romanticised as perfect love and a complete relationship, but this view gradually subsides as other memories are recalled and considered, and the less ideal aspects of the relationship are remembered.Some scholars have argued that it is only when 'the bereaved remembers the dead person as the "real" person he was to her, then mourning is progressing successfully'.[2] Idealised memories make resolution difficult.[3] The fantasy of perfection remains like a persistent shadow in the narratives of those women who lost their husbands during wartime. In some cases, it emerges as the defining characteristic of the interplay between memory, mourning and identity and becomes a way of displacing grief in their lives.

NOSTALGIA

Mary Ellen Reid was born in Ararat, Victoria in 1919. At the age of 19, she married William Simpson. She had met her husband at the Stawell

64

Gift, the prestigious race which is run annually in Stawell, near Ararat, Victoria. Within the first twelve months of their marriage, they had a son, Alan William. Like so many of her generation, her family had direct experience of the war. Her father and his brothers had served in the First World War, and two of her sisters joined the army during the Second World War. When her husband enlisted in the air force in Sydney, she may not have anticipated the tragedy that was to change the course of her life forever. In 1945, her husband was declared missing in action. She recalled how, with the arrival of the telegram which was always a foreboding sign of the impending news of death,

> I was getting Alan his tea and my father come down with the telegram … they opened it and read it 'cause they knew it was bad news – it always is when you see the telegram boy coming in … so father brought it down I was very upset and I vowed that night that I would never remarry until my son grew up. We both prayed for him that night …[4]

Mary and William Simpson, late 1943

For many years, Simpson lived in hope that her husband would return and she believed that no man was capable of measuring up to his high standard as a husband. 'And I never ever did marry again', she reflected, 'I had many an opportunity but nobody ever … come up to him'. When the soldiers began to return from the war she was distressed watching them come back to their sweethearts. The return of soldiers would not bring joy and happiness for her as it did for others. She could not separate herself from the tragic event, and the shadow of his death was cast over her for the rest of her life as a permanent presence: 'it was hard, terrible … the flag was flying half mast … You know it's with you all the time, it never leaves you, never ever will'.[5]

She felt the loss acutely when the other soldiers returned and she fantasised about her husband returning:

> I used to dream you know of meeting him at Spencer Street station, what I would wear and what I would put on Alan. I could see him running to meet his father but it just wasn't meant to be. I think life's planned out for everybody. We all have a tick beside it but you're going quicker during wartime.

The fatalism she came to believe – that it was 'meant to be' – helped her to come to terms with the meaning of her husband's death over a period of time. Neither his presence nor his memory remains foremost with her now, but she recalled how for years afterwards she harboured a hope that he would return to her. Her identity became intimately tied to his memory.

> You remember, you just never forget … I always thought he'd come back and I went on for years and years because it was only 'missing' beside his name and I made sure even when it went to twenty years I thought he'd still come back that he could … have loss of memory.

The memory had frozen over a number of years and was being lived out as a fantasy. Accepting his death remains difficult for her to come to terms with: 'I've never accepted it, never, I don't think I ever will accept it. It's happened, I know that … he has a sister too and she's never accepted it.'

The brief married life they shared has become romanticised in her recollections. They were:

> very, very happy, very happy. We used to go everywhere together, he was very attached to his son [I was] … the only woman in the world that he ever wanted to be with, this is over fifty years, I suppose it's silly …

The permanence of their love endures for Simpson: 'a thing you never get over, never and I always say in life you'll fall in love and your first love is your only love'. Remarriage was never a possibility. 'I wasn't meant to remarry', she states emphatically. The ways Simpson understood her fate as a widow – as 'meant to be', and the romance of a 'first love' – show how she came to understand the tragedy of losing her husband, deal with the death retrospectively, and understand her current situation.

Simpson spent much time thinking about a grave site, because her husband's body was never found. He was on his:

> last flight … in France and we never found out what happened. The whole crew they all went missing and we have an idea, the Red Cross, that two of our planes collided and a lot of the bodies went into the sea. Some were found, some were not. He was one that wasn't found …

The absence of a grave-site made grieving very difficult. Simpson never experienced the sense of closure that can be achieved by witnessing the body. Widows were expected to accept this without complaint, and, coupled with a lack of emotional support, certainly it made any sense of closure extremely difficult: 'there wasn't any of that about like you'd get now … actually I can't ever remember getting any emotional support at all. You just fought through it yourself. You were just told it had happened and that was it'.

Simpson was not alone in sustaining a hope of her husband's return. Other war widows who had lost their husbands during the war were equally determined to preserve a romantic memory of their husbands. Eve Harris, whose husband Albert was shot down in Germany in 1943, recalls how her love intensified for him over time. 'We were only married for six years … ', she remembers, 'I suppose time dims everything. I love him more now than I ever did … I realise his worth … he was [an] honourable, decent human being'.[6]

What these women share in their testimonies is a desire to continue a connection with their deceased husbands in shaping their identities, and to frame these stories through nostalgia – that is, through a vision of a world without loss.[7] Nostalgia is melancholic because it involves 'losses that alter the self's history: the loss of one's youth, the loss of loved ones, the loss of "futures."' It consists of 'pining about one's past'.[8] Women who lost their husband in war are informed by such considerations: their memories and their senses of themselves are sustained by 'nostalgia's desire that things might be different'.[9] While it has often been assumed that nostalgia can be a form of disavowal, it can also be a way of looking forward. As others have observed, it can be a means of moving between mourning – where the self is affected by loss, but where there is a rebuilding of the inner world – and melancholia – where the mourning is never compete.[10]

Nostalgia is most commonly associated with fantasy, and certainly the women whose memories are discussed in this chapter are imbued with a desire for memory as a way of re-writing the present. Indeed, memory is a means of 'creating a self-esteem that helps us rise above the anxieties of the present'.[11] Nostalgic myth, imbued with fantasy, serves to mediate between 'the past and individual consciousness. It can function by erasing a memory or an object from the past and displacing the anxiety induced by it into a more pleasurable and less threatening object or scene.'[12] Nostalgia can also replace the 'imperfect present with a perfect past where values and meaning are condensed'.[13] It is a yearning for the 'other' to be present in a 'perfect' way.[14] More fundamentally, nostalgia is an attempt to 're-enact reunion with the lost object'.[15] This is often expressed through photographs, which become a repository of desire for another time and place. Visual reminders became very important in the attempts by war widows to sustain themselves and to resist loss. The photograph, and the narration within it, for instance, 'will itself become an object of nostalgia'.[16] Souvenirs such as these help to 'authenticate a past'.[17] Yearning for this past indicates the search for a 'simple and stable past as a refuge from a turbulent and chaotic present'.[18] Often a nostalgic yearning represents a time when 'choices were simple and responsibilities clear'.[19] A collective nostalgia reinforces these impulses and desires, in sharing the meaning of events.[20] Nostalgia indicates resistance to 'the ultimate decay of finite lived experience', and the loss that is associated with this process.[21]

To some extent, all the women in this book speak in nostalgic terms, for grief is always concerned with forms of nostalgia, with a longing for a world where loss is absent. Those whose husbands did not return indulged in a particular form of nostalgia, not only yearning for a world without loss, but for a world of perfection. In attempting to negate death, they also denied grief.

A part of Simpson's narrative is a glorified image of her brief marriage, which became internalised. It took on the status of an idealised relationship, and assumed perfection.[22] Inevitably, once perfect love has become the way in which a relationship is remembered, it can never be matched by anybody else. In framing her memory in these terms, Simpson justified her resistance to forming romantic attachments and eschewing a new relationship.

RECOGNITION

Jean Fry was another widow who lost her husband during the Second World War. Brought up in Lindfield, the youngest of seven children, she grew up with, and married, the boy next door, James Rollo Fry. His two older brothers had been killed in the First World War, and he 'grew up in the shadow of that awful loss'. They were married in 1941, and within three months he enlisted in the air force. Rollo Fry was a navigator serving with the RAAF in Britain and lost his life on 13 June 1944, while returning from a raid over the Ruhr. Their daughter was born two months after he left Australia in August 1942.[23] In recent years some, mostly young people have asked her why a man would leave his pregnant wife to go to fight for Britain. Fry experienced such questions 'like a blow between the eyes; to me [it was] criticism of my husband', and a 'total lack of understanding of the wartime relationship Australia had with Britain'.

Jean and James Fry

Fry draws a sharp distinction between what she perceives as two groups of widows. What hurt her most significantly after the death of her husband was that the two groups – those who lost husbands during the war, and those who lost husbands after the war – are not recognised as having distinct experiences. She holds strong views about this and resents the claim of 'war widow' by women who may not even have been married until after the war, or perhaps not been widowed for fifty years after the war. Fry claims the identity of 'war widow' for women who lost their husbands on active service during the war. She claims:

> I call that a real war widow … These others I call post-war widows … Well, you [can] just imagine the difference between what we real war widows went through. The trauma of your husband never coming home. Never seeing their child and you being left with this less than a living allowance and the other ones who had joy of their husband … there would be some relationship between you left, and also they had the joy of seeing their children.

She conceded that returned men suffering from war-related injuries could be difficult. As we will see, some of the wives of the men who returned claimed that their husbands were not the men they knew and that they returned altered or even transformed in some way. Women whose men never returned considered it would be a privilege, for at least those women could share their future with their husbands. 'I know they probably had a difficult time', conceded Fry, 'with the men when they first came home, but they *came* home and that was the man of their choice that they had married and here he was home'. The ways in which this distinction was not, and has not been taken seriously by some people has remained a point of contention and a source of pain for widows like Fry. The sacrifices she made after her husband's death have not always been recognised. Erasure of the distinction between war widows and post-war widows has undermined her own identity as 'war widow'. 'That is very hurtful to us', she claimed,

> It belittles us. It makes nonsense of all the effort we've put for the last fifty years which doesn't compare with them having their husbands for twenty, thirty, forty or fifty years. Having their husband to help pay the house off. I've paid this [house] off myself. Having to rear the children, educate the children, buy cars.

The anger of losing her husband is a tragedy that has never left her. But as a 'battler', she has no sympathy for those who use loss to cling to the past:

you get over it, of course, in the end. I have no patience with these women who every anniversary of their husband's death they go into grief ... That's nonsense, you've got to get on with life and I always try to do something positive ...

In refusing to dwell on grief and on mourning, Fry reflected an attitude prevalent among her generation. But in talking about her grief, she reveals an expressiveness more common in recent times:

There is an awful hollowness there, but it's not grief. The grief was something that you had to fight with at the time ... It was something that lived with you the whole time ... it's something that gnaws away at you and you're conscious of it all the time. I can only say it really was like recovering from a major operation. Some part of me had been cut away and I had to learn to live without it ...

The pride Fry attached to being a war widow and losing her husband in a sacrificial context was a part of her identity as a war widow, which gave her a sense of purpose:

because they had died for their country ... it means something ... there is little sort of core pride ... OK, you've lost something but you've lost it in a cause ... you feel you've just earned a little better place in Australia because you have done something for Australia ... I think I've had that feeling all along. That you are something a little bit special.

The sense of being 'special' and earning a place in Australia's history mitigated her loss and grief, which was why she so resented the lack of distinction between the two groups. 'That's why', she explained,

I dislike these girls coming in calling themselves war widows, who don't know the meaning of it ... they really don't know what it means. Even if they had the last two or three years of illness with their husbands ... when you've married you expect to have that at some stage. But not this in the prime of their life giving their life overnight just like that. Yes, it makes you feel just a bit special.

For Fry, those whose husbands had returned should not be entitled to use the term 'war widow' because they robbed the real war widows of *their* special status, of their identity as war widows, which she believed was sacred and precious. She feels returned men have treated her with more dignity and pride, treating her 'as something a bit special'. Conflating the two sets of war widows 'belittles what we went through which cannot be compared. Theirs could have been ghastly if they had a lingering illness ... ', she contended, 'And if they died within the first ten years, OK, I'd say that would be a war widow. But not fifty years later.'[24]

MOURNING

Shirley Tilley's experience defies this categorisation between what Fry would call a 'true' war widow and one who is not deserving of that status. Tilley also speaks in terms of nostalgia and regret, but her story is also one of anguish at the denial of her loss.

Shirley Joyce Tilley (known as Joyce) was born in Albert Park in Melbourne in 1920. She first met her future husband, Arthur Thornton, in 1936 when they were both working in an exclusive department store. They soon became the 'store sweethearts'. When he turned 21, in 1941,

Shirley Joyce Tilley (photo carried by husband)

Shirley Joyce Tilley and husband

Shirley Joyce Tilley's husband, Arthur Thornton (original inscribed 'To my wife and sweetheart with all the love in the world from Arthur 18/8/42')

he joined the air force, and one year later they were married. After their marriage, they had spent about six weeks together when he returned from leave. Initially, she was 'devastated' but 'proud' that he was going off to fight in the war. She recalled the moment when he sailed with as much emotion as she had felt that far-off day:

> my parents took me down the beach. And we saw his ship going out in the distance … I think it was called P23 … we stood on the shore and just watched her disappear and I never saw him again. This is where the tears want to come. You'd think I'd be adult enough to be over it by now.

The news that he was missing devastated her. The details of his death remain vague, as was often the case when airmen were declared missing. The hope and anticipation that he would return remained with her for the rest of her life, and she always wanted to know more:

> One of the crew was found a prisoner of war and of course you'd think he'll be a prisoner of war and this is going on for months. 15 months later he was presumed dead. I have to recover a bit now. He died … April 10, 1944. Once again you hoped against hope even after he was presumed dead and when the end of the war came you hoped again that he'd be found.

The hope of his return nourished her for many years, until:

> I received communication … to say that they had found the debris of the plane and they presumed that the plane had exploded in the air. So I didn't know whether he was killed on the plane, whether he parachuted out and was killed, whether he landed and was killed. I don't know how he was killed.

These indeterminate details of his death haunted Tilley for the rest of her life. Not only did she attempt to retrieve the details of her husband's death, but the memory of her first husband remained an obsession with her even when she remarried.

Joyce recalls that, ironically, her second husband's birthday was the same date of her first husband's death and it was very hard to celebrate and mourn at the same time. On her wedding day, almost like an omen, she received a letter, and a photograph, from the air force to say that her first husband's grave was in Denmark. This was contrary to what she had been led to believe. On retelling her story, Tilley reflected that she never properly mourned for her first husband. The details of his death and the absence of a body firmly became implanted in her mind:

> I tried to contact one of the members of the crew that lived in Melbourne and he wouldn't see me ... Which is against everything I'd heard they came back and saw the widows. And I was young and naive ... if I had more get up and go I would have gone to see him ...

She expressed a profound, almost desperate, sense of a missed opportunity, as well as an inability to mourn her first husband properly. She recalled dreams that reflected her intense longing and preoccupation with Thornton. In her unconscious he is a distant figure who remains unattainable and elusive, but one whom she desperately longs to be with:

> All my life I have not been able to grieve properly because I never saw him dead and I don't know how he died ... I dream that I can never catch up with him; that he's catching the train and I miss it. I go to his mother's house and he's upstairs and she won't leave me in the house. All sorts of dreams. And I still have them to this day. But that what it's like to be a war widow, even though I married again and [have] two beautiful children.[25]

Recurrent dreams were prevalent among the war widows, especially those whose husbands had died during the war. Dreams, it is claimed, are drawn from our experiences and represent things that we cannot accept. Our dreams are 'evidence of something so dismaying, so shameful, so terrifying, that it must not be shared'.[26] The importance of dreams is reflected in the testimonies of numerous war widows and suggests a subliminal, internalised loss. Marjory Miller's husband Rex enlisted in 1940, three years after they married, and served in Palestine and Tobruk. He was a second field ambulance transport driver, who was killed in a bombing raid. After he died, she remembered how she would 'dream that he'd come back ... we were apart, sort of engaged. "O, fancy him being away all the time and he's not even showing any interest in me" ... always the distance.'[27] Eve Harris claimed she had a premonition about her husband Albert's death. 'I knew already', she stated,

> because I had a nightmare ... I had this nightmare and I said to my aunt ... 'I had an awful nightmare last night' and she said tell me about it. ... I was telling [Albert] 'I'm sorry I can no longer be a wife to you' ... he was terribly upset ... Now why would I say a thing like that to him? ... Then it was only a few days later that we got the word [of his death].[28]

Ironically, Joyce Tilley is now a war widow for the second time, the Department of Veterans' Affairs having deemed Larry, her second husband, to have died from war-related illnesses, polio and cancer of the oesophagus. During the post-war period, those around her believed it was appropriate to attempt to annihilate the memory of her husband, rather than to allow the grieving process to take its course. Her mother destroyed the letters between her and her first husband, and the photographs which she had cherished of her first husband, as a way of trying to assist her daughter to relinquish the past. But this attempt to silence and repress the grief in order to 'move on' had the opposite effect. Because Tilley never had an opportunity to express her longing and yearning, which is part of the mourning process, her life-long grief never moved towards resolution:[29]

> When I married again … my mother took everything … she felt that it wasn't right that I still had everything around because I was married again, I was trying to make a new life. So she took all the photographs, all the letters, all the telegrams, and I think she destroyed them so I had no letters.

This attempt to repress the memory of her first husband, and contain the public expression of grief, did not help Tilley to overcome her trauma and grief. Keeping his memory alive was considered to be shameful, but negating grief only exacerbated and prolonged its presence. Tilley was unable to mourn because of various attempts by herself and others to deny the past. The story of not being allowed to grieve serves to legitimate her desire to cling to his memory.[30]

In her retelling, Tilley makes the inevitable comparisons between the two husbands which are mediated through feelings of nostalgia and regret. Moreover, her story is one of denial of death, as she finds it difficult to imagine Thornton dead. With no body or evidence of death, she found comfort in sustaining that denial.[31] By keeping the fantasy alive, she clings to the hope that he might return, and is fixed in a state of yearning for him. The acceptance of Thornton's death:

> took years. I can remember I went to a film … called *Random Harvest*.[32] … And in it [Ronald Colman] had amnesia, so [my] fertile mind [says] O, yes, he's got amnesia, he's somewhere in Europe and he doesn't know who he is. See you hope … even when I remarried, at the back of my mind I hoped … because the second marriage wasn't particularly happy, and I then reverted in my private times to remembering Arthur which was the worst. If only my second husband had turned out happier. I couldn't have regressed so much. Larry however was popular with other people.

It was inevitable that she would deem her second marriage inferior to the first. Tilley stated she felt sorry for her second husband. He was in the air force, but did not serve overseas, though he had wanted to, because he had contracted polio while in an air force hospital. She married him because the pressure to marry was so great after the war and the 'sheer loneliness' humiliated her, despite the warmth and support she received from her friends. 'If I went out with them [and] their husbands', she recalled, '[they] had to dance with me because Shirley was on her own … You must look after Shirley'. In retrospect, she wasn't in love with Larry, 'he turned out different. Some of it might have been my fault. After all, I don't think I'd ever fallen out of love with my first husband …'.

Memories of her first husband filled her inner life and during her 'private times' she remained faithful to this memory. Even though the second marriage was difficult because of her husband's bouts of drinking, she takes some responsibility for contributing to the tension because of her inability to forget her first husband:

> We made a … pact that we wouldn't not talk about Arthur … and we openly spoke and I rather appreciated that attitude from him … Later on in life he began to resent it … I think I helped in the deterioration of the marriage. I tried not to, but I think I must have …[33]

Although her friends and her relatives attempted to be supportive through her loss, they did so in the way that was typical of the day, by denying death, and encouraging her to attempt to suppress rather than express grief. Inadvertently, they were complicit in ignoring her loss, making it difficult for Tilley to 'move to the stage of accepting that the loved one will never again return'.[34]

The death of her second husband precipitated real mourning for her first husband.

> How can I say this with out making myself a monster? A certain amount of relief and yet sadness for a wasted 50 odd years. Regret that he hadn't turned out better. Regret that it could've been my fault. A lot of regret. And then I started to think more of Arthur that had been more or less put into the back of [my] mind through the years …

This is an expression of regret for the possibilities which never materialised and feelings of guilt for her complicity in the demise of the marriage. The details of her first husband's death continued to obsess her:

If the plane exploded in the air would there be anything buried, or did he get out? Did he get out with the two that were prisoners. I don't know how he died. I'd love to know how he died.

She asks herself:

if I knew he was killed instantly [or] even if I knew that he'd suffered at least I'd know and that's haunted me and ... until I know for sure always will because I loved him very much ... I feel I've lived ... but not really deep down had true happiness ... That's self-pity and I hate myself for feeling like that but I can't help it ...

Recollections of life with her former husband, albeit brief and temporary, are entrenched in her memory:

I tried to push it into the back of my mind to make a go of the second marriage because deep down [I felt] this is partly my fault that this marriage is breaking down but it's too difficult ... Songs particularly and now the film that I'm watching and of course that's maudlin again. I like to watch all the films of the pre-war ... I'm picturing myself at the Regent Theatre sitting watching them. It was hard to get on with your life ... the dreadful part about it is I think far more of Arthur than I do of Larry in my thoughts in the last five years. It was like I suppressed it and they just flooded out when he died. So I'm mourning my first husband again.

After Tilley's death she allowed herself to mourn and to grieve her first husband. Her testimony was filled with guilt and with angst, guilt about not allowing her second marriage to succeed. She continued to idealise the first marriage and fantasise about possibilities of life with Arthur, and invests the very meaning of her identity in these possibilities: 'You'd like to think it would have been rosy ... he would have continued his study and he would've been an accountant ...' But she is resigned to the possibility that the haunting memories of her husband:

won't end until I die ... I have the feeling that one day I'll catch up with him. But I only remember him as young, and not old. How do you get over that? At least when I die, it will be the end of the memories ...

When comparing her husbands, Tilley contrasted the experience of the two men in terms of absolutes. She remembers Arthur with 'wonderful memories':

you remember all the good points and you're inclined to forget the other. Arthur didn't have many bad points ... he was a good man and he would have been a good man ... I wonder if he would have been bald now!

Larry was 'selfish. Wouldn't do anything that he wouldn't want to do; wouldn't meet you half way ... '. If it had been a socially respectable thing to do, she would have left him. She reasoned:

> I'll be perfectly honest – I would have left him years ago if I'd had the money to do so but our generation didn't. And I didn't have the confidence to go out into the workforce then that I had a bit later on. So you'd stay with them.

Tilley was extremely disappointed with the second marriage, regretting it, internalising her grief and suggesting that she was to blame as well:

> I had two different lives. But life goes on ... but you grieved inside. That's the maudlin part ... I've painted Larry very black and I'm a bit sorry about that ... no marriage break[s] down by one person ... Both contribute to it. I'm as much at fault as he is. That's trying to make me a martyr but I'm not ... but I wished I hadn't married again ... I wished I had pursued a career ... But then I wouldn't have had my children, grown up and happily married.

Another lament was the fact that her children were 'not very interested in Arthur, which disappoints me a bit, but they're not'. They appreciate that she cannot mourn Tilley very much , 'because he disappointed me in so much in my marriage'.[35] Tilley's narrative is one of a woman who suppressed her mourning after the war and could never separate herself from the memory nor identity of her first husband. Her life story is reduced to two narratives: one of lost possibilities, the other of a socially appropriate marriage, which was flawed and full of limitations and shortcomings.

Tilley is an exception in this particular study, in having married again after the death of her husband. But in experiencing lingering grief and pain she was not alone. Virginia Gerrett lost her husband during the Second World War in a sea battle for which she believes her husband never received the recognition he deserved. Born in Mildura, in 1913, Gerrett grew up in Melbourne. She studied art at Brighton Technical School, and by the time she had met her husband, Gerrett was working in public relations for a fashion agency. In 1934, she met her future husband, Gerry, who was 22, and they were married in 1936. He had joined the navy at a young age and by the outbreak of the Second World War had risen to the rank of lieutenant-commander. She had two children with him. Her first daughter was born in 1937, her second in 1942.

Her husband died in an accident while on duty in October 1944. He was declared missing for some time before any details were known.

Gerrett's anger at the lack of recognition of his sacrifice as well as of her suffering as a consequence was conveyed dramatically as she retold the story of her husband's death on a burning ship:

> I want to say here … the captain was killed and the commander of the ship was also killed … no-one said anything to anybody except the newspapers published what Gerry did to help save that ship in his dying hours that he … made the effort to have got people going

H. B. Gerrett, husband of Virginia, 1939

Virginia Gerrett and daughter Caroline, 1940

and saved the ship ... Nothing ever did I hear from anybody. There was no medal or anything. Nothing ... I utterly resent that there was nothing done about it. And since then I have never received his medals which I was entitled to. Never have I received them, I think that whoever is responsible ought to be ashamed ...[36]

Fifty years after the event, the pain of loss was lasting and persistent. Her injury was never acknowledged:

> In some way it should have been made up to me. Somewhere they should have decorated and given him something … he did deserve something but he got nothing and I'm resentful and I don't care who knows it … I've never talked about it …

Gerry continues to be a hallowed figure in her memory. She remembers her wedding day when: 'we were standing at the altar … but I can remember a shaft of light sort of came down through the windows and … shone on Gerry and I thought … he looks almost spiritual'. She preserved this idealised memory of Gerry:

> I could have married several times … I never found a man as fine as Gerry. I had so many chances … I don't think I've known anyone more utterly sensible … really caring for one the way you really want to be cared for. People don't know that any more; men don't feel that they are responsible for women to the nth degree right through to the bounds of thought … If you've had it good [once] don't think you can repeat it …

Idealisation becomes a way of resisting trauma and loss, and the possibility for further intimacy becomes unlikely. Satisfaction with another partner is difficult in the face of this image of perfection.

As with Tilley and Simpson, Gerrett found the lack of knowledge about her husband's death hard to accept. The thought of being '"buried at sea, buried at sea" … It's uncopeable …' She had solid support from the commander's widow: 'She was a great friend … and she stayed a few nights with me [because] she was also going through it'. Gerrett found an emotional anchor and a meaningful structure through her career, which allowed her to deal with her grief. By keeping active through a busy professional life as a journalist on the Sydney *Sun*, and then on the *Women's Weekly*, she could move forward. But in her private moments, the hope that her husband would be found taunted and tormented her through her dreams:

> When you go to bed that's your business and you howl yourself to sleep and you have evil dreams. I can't tell you the dreams … Always I was scrambling over rocks because I knew that I'd find him somewhere where nobody knew [he was] being washed up. And those dreams they went on for two or three years … the dreams are just terrible. I think back on them and they are nightmares … Somehow they would find him … You think for a long time that it's not true …[37]

These themes are reflected in Mary Baldrin's story. Baldrin's first husband, Arthur Hopper, also died at sea. She was born in 1907 and married Arthur Hopper in 1936. After he joined the navy in 1940, she never saw him again. She eventually learnt that he had died as a prisoner of war. She recalls how she sustained an enduring hope, and how difficult it was for her when the other men returned:

> It was hard. One thing you must never do is … never give up hope. Never give up hope … But then the time comes when you realise … I kept thinking even … perhaps a couple of years after the war [he would return] because you see there were men who'd been like Arthur who had got away somewhere and they didn't come back until later. Because they got away somewhere … oh, you never give up hope …[38]

The fear of life without the bereaved sustains this hope, as does the lack of detail about death. Hopper persisted, and she kept going to the military hospital, even after the war. She did remarry, but not for twenty years: 'I never thought I ever would … I didn't expect to because we were a very happy couple. It never entered my head that I would but strange things happen in life …'. The telegram which stated that he was 'missing believed lost at sea' gave her a little hope: 'well, you always keep on hoping. I often thought, "oh well, he might have got away" … but you have to accept it in the end. You just have to accept it …'.[39]

The lingering hope of return also informed Sylvia Brown's testimony. Brown is another war widow who experienced the loss of her husband at an early age through a naval disaster. She, too, was a navy wife, marrying the sea as well as her husband: 'I was a typical navy wife … I had no choice … he loved the sea more than any woman, including me and I accepted that …'. She was born Sylvia Mathews in the Melbourne suburb of Brunswick in 1913. She married the boy next door and they shared an interest in music. Her husband Arthur joined the navy in 1925, and was a passionate seaman. They were married in 1932; their only child, Betty, was born a year later.

In Brown's case, the timing of the telegrams heightened the trauma in a tragic situation. She recalled the moment she received news of her husband's death:

> I was in Sydney sharing a flat with one other … navy wife … I got home from David Jones … and there was a telegram on the mantelpiece and Mona burst into tears when she opened the door … So I looked at the telegram and … she put her arms around me

Arthur John Brown, husband of Sylvia, Cairo, October 1940

and said, 'there's bad news lovey' … I opened the telegram and it said that John had – I should have imprinted [the words] on my mind in fire, I guess, but [it was] 'your husband missing at sea, presumed killed. Sympathy from the navy' – words to that effect.

Sylvia Brown, 1966

Her worst fears were allayed when she then received another telegram
from her husband, reassuring her that he had survived:

> about an hour later, another telegram came from my husband to
> say 'everything OK, received your parcel, thanks darling, letter
> following'. That came two hours after the telegram. I thought,
> thank God, he's all right! But of course that telegram had been

sent before the navy one came through. And that night his
mother rang me from Melbourne ... and she said, no it's true
Sylvia, he has died.[40]

It was easier to believe that he might have survived and this hope
reassured her momentarily:

> I kept hope, hope against hope that the first telegram was wrong
> and the second one from my husband was the correct one, because
> it was later ... however it was true enough and when Grandma
> Brown ... rang up ... I said, 'No, no, no mum, it's all right, he's all
> right. I've just had a telegram'. And I read that out to her over the
> phone and she burst into tears of course. It was her eldest son. She
> didn't know it then but she was to lose her youngest son ... early in
> December in New Guinea and he was not eighteen ... She had
> those two tragedies to deal with within a couple of months.

Brown used a range of strategies to dealt with this grief. The immediate
response was shock:

> Lots of tears and still come occasionally ... because it was a real
> loss to me because we were really in love. We were really in love
> and not only that we loved each other in a brother and sister sort of
> way ... he brought a breath of fresh air into my life every time
> he came home from sea because he was fun. He had a sailor's
> way of looking at life and he was so different from anybody that
> I ever knew ...

Unlike other wives, for whom the absence was tiresome and tedious,
Brown does not remember this as a negative aspect in their marriage.

The first moment that she realised she was actually experiencing
mourning was a confronting one. Ironically, it was in a public rather
than a private place, where emotions were, after the war, meant to be
contained:

> My first sense of deep loss was [when] I went into Collins Street
> ... to buy a good pair of shoes to go to [the] award [which
> decorated her husband posthumously] and I burst into tears ...
> I wanted these new pair of shoes to go with a black dress I had
> ... when I was trying on the shoes, I realised I was in there
> in mourning and I started to sob ... I just didn't have any
> control ...

Even so, she hoped for his return, because he had been 'missing,
presumed killed'. A few months after his death, she wrote to the three
sailors from the ship who survived. One sailor responded:

he said there was no hope for my husband because he was on watch with him on the very night it happened that the three torpedoes that had struck the ship ... he wouldn't have survived because he went straight down to his cabin and I thought bitterly, '[he was] probably going to write to me' because we wrote frequently ... I wanted to know if I still had any hope ... up until then I'd hoped he'd been alive because he was presumed killed ...

Hope remained her companion for many years. Brown had the opportunity to remarry, but declined any offers. Her daughter resisted having a stepfather, and this resonated for her, because of her own family history. Does connecting the two stories become a rationale for avoiding further intimacy? In the retelling, she conflated her own experience with her stepfather and her daughter's insistence that she not remarry:

I had a stepfather. There was never nothing wrong with him; he never laid a hand on us ... I was in the dog house because I wouldn't call him father because I remember my own father who also came back and died one year after World War I... he came back with shell shock and gas poisoning ... I adored my father ...

She clearly did not want to relive her experience through her daughter:

I don't think she had anything against this particular man, I think it was just the fear of having a stepfather and of course I used to be sent to my room time after time because I wouldn't call him 'father' ... I said he's not my father and never will be. ... I settled for 'pop' and he didn't mind me calling him 'pop' ...

Brown believed that coping with this sort of grief tested one's strength of character: 'I think you have to be a fairly strong character to cope with grief in the long-term basis and you have to have a certain amount of humility in your make-up'. Her sense of lost opportunities was balanced by her need to move forward rather than dwell on what could have been: 'I probably would have had more children if he'd lived and come back. But, well, that didn't happen. But it's no good grieving over that when you're got the rent to pay and things to do. You've got to be a realist.' There was never any question that she would marry any man who had not been in the armed services. She certainly would have married 'if my little girl hadn't felt so strongly against having a stepfather'. But even when Brown met suitable men, 'I said I couldn't marry anybody who hadn't served in the war, naturally ... I feel they'd done their bit ... my father and my husband fought and died under that flag ...'.

Another war widow, Pearl Sutton, also lost her husband during the war, but unlike the other women whom I have discussed, he died in an accident in Australia when a bomb exploded while he was training other soldiers. He did not serve abroad and so the accident was not associated with the heroism attached to the deaths of other soldiers. But this was no less tragic for Sutton as she became a single mother and found she experienced as much distress and anguish as that of any other war widow.

Pearl Sutton met her future husband Lewit Stanley John Sutton (Stan) on the train going to work. She was born in 1919 and lived in New South Wales most of her life. They caught the same carriage to work each morning. One day when she had hurt her finger and 'it was all bandaged up', he 'asked her what happened and it all started from there'. They married in 1940. She was a dressmaker, and opened her own business at her home in 1939. He joined the army in that year, at the age of 21. His death and the birth of her only child – a daughter – almost coincided. Her daughter was born on Saturday, 13 March 1943, and Stan died on Monday, 15 March 1943. She was 23 years old at the time and 'very alone' during the pregnancy. The expectation at the time, she recalls, was that grief was something war widows simply had to overcome:

> Oh, I don't need to be reminded. It's there all the time sort of thing. I never ever want to remarry or anything like that … No counselling at all. You just had to get over it the best way you could. It was terribly hard to accept. I think more so when you haven't had a funeral to go to.

He was the first man she had dated and he is still emotionally an important part of her life.

Her husband died in a bomb explosion along with thirteen other soldiers when stationed in Western Australia. He never knew of his daughter, as 'the telegram which you relied on for news in those days never got there in time'.[41] Sutton visited his grave in Western Australia:

> It was what I always wanted to do … It was a big thing for me. When you can see a grave, you can learn to accept things. You know. If you've never had a grave to go to or a body to see you just don't realise it. It's hard to accept.

There was a sense of lost opportunities: 'Well, yes, you had your dreams … the sadness part was that he didn't know he had a daughter … We were both so thrilled I fell pregnant before he left.' Future plans remained unfulfilled: 'We had great plans as to what we were going to do after the war. We were going to get a home. Have more children, [that] sort of thing'. She was relieved when he was sent to Western Australia, reassured that he would be safe. 'When he was sent over there, I was just so happy because I thought he's not in the war … You think … there's no war … where he is …' Like Brown, she could not dwell on the past because of her daughter: 'for her sake, I couldn't live in the past. She didn't understand because she just never ever knew … her father.' At that time, the dreams, emotional investments and aspirations of women were built around a future with their husbands:

> You built your whole life around them. There was no other interest sort of thing … we were gonna get a home. And the strange part about it [was] we were always going to live in this area. Then when I was looking for a block of ground I didn't look anywhere else, just around the corner … [Dreams] all folded.

Sutton felt the death of her husband acutely, and resented others who believed that the brief duration of their marriage did not warrant an extensive grieving period. In retrospect, she believed she was not given an opportunity to grieve. In what was believed to be supportive and sympathetic behaviour at the time, the news of death was kept from her because of her poor health. She writes that the telegram which notified her of her husband's death, 'was delivered to my previous address … [and] you will find this hard to believe they just pushed the telegram under the door'. It was eventually taken to the post office, 'and my mother on hearing about it collected it from there because I was so ill at the time they kept the news from me for several years'.[42] When the news broke, there was a reluctance to acknowledge her grief or adversity:

> Some people say, 'well, you were only together two and a half years'. But that's got nothing to do with it. Your feelings are just as strong. If you've had forty years with somebody that's a bonus. It was really hard when the war ended … It was devastating, especially [when returned soldiers would] come to see you and they'd have their wives with them and you'd think, 'well, that could have been me'.

The grief was debilitating and little support was offered to her after the war. 'I suffered badly with nerves for many years couldn't venture out. My daughter had to depend on my mother and good friends for any outings'.[43] She reflected that '[I] guess I just had to manage the best way I could there was no counselling or compensation in those days'.[44] Others had difficulties, to be sure, but their men did return: 'they go away young men but they come back with an old head on their shoulders, gone through so much and to come back sick, some of them were never the same again', and so it 'must have been difficult for their wives to handle, too, because they go away and come back difficult, older men'. However, ambivalent feelings were aroused for her when men returned. When the war ended,

> you just wished with all your heart that you could be there to welcome somebody … of course, if you visited your friends, they had their husbands. It was a difficult time. They had the things that you really wanted. Not that you'd begrudge it to them. Not at all. It was hard to take.

At the end of the war, she reflected that she was 'happy for them, I was happy for them, but as I say, I had the heartache too. They were coming home and Stan wasn't.' She didn't get involved in the welcome home celebrations and found it particularly difficult when the men returned to discuss her husband with her: 'The hard time was when the men came to see me … They spoke so highly of him. So well liked.' She didn't attend Anzac Day, as such an event would still arouse a sense of loss. 'It's not that I'm not interested', she argued, 'I'm just not strong enough'.

As we have seen, Olwyn Green also lost her husband while serving. As he was killed in Korea, she experienced the loss in a different way to those who lost their husbands during the Second World War. Green reflected on the pre-war generation, and how war meant something in particular for them, which her generation did not share:

> There was no real questioning of the rights of the war … it was a cause and they had done the right thing … That's their pride in what they've done … I don't think it would have done them any good to have had … what their sons had done questioned and dishonoured. I don't think that would have helped them one bit … It would then have been [considered] a total and absolute waste. How do you adjust to that …?[45]

She married her husband Charlie in January 1943 while he was serving in the Second World War. He returned around Christmas in 1945, and she was shocked at his condition 'because he was so yellow and so thin … The image I first had of him was this dashing man … and here was this [man] so hollow and so yellow and so thin, I felt I didn't know him.' As with many soldiers, he had not been trained for anything else, and went into very 'ordinary' jobs. He returned to a vacuum, so he decided to join up and go to Korea. She was living in a small country

Olwyn and Charlie Green, 30 January 1943

town when she heard of his death in 1950 and described her reaction on learning of his death:

> There were no words to describe that … that will never ever leave me. It's brutal beyond belief … It's physical. I can only describe it as so physical. So physical that … the body does [go] through the same feeling every time it's triggered … you have the same shock. It lessens but there's the same shock … the whole mind and body and soul.

Nonetheless, she understood that women became social outcasts in widowhood, because culturally, you 'are immediately suspect … I sense[d] [that] very quickly'. The letters she had collected were burnt, an act which she believed was necessary as a way of moving on from the death of her husband. Her view encapsulates the attitude towards mourning and grief in the immediate post-war period:

> I've got to get rid of all this past; I've got to get rid of all this and I burnt all except a few. I'd say a mixture of 'I'm going … to get on with my life. I'm going to wipe out the past and I'm going to get on with it. I can't cope with all this' … Too devastating for me to understand.

Green was fortunate to have her personal story memorialised where her husband's deeds were given explicit and public recognition. In 1980, a memorial was built in his honour at Lismore by his 41st Battalion. A number of officers had been especially interested in Charles Green's range of service across three branches of the army, and they believed Charles was '… a man who had achieved a significant, if not unique, range of service'. For those who memorialised him, Green bridged 'those worrisome distinctions … between enlisted, part-time and regular soldiers. We wanted to generate the idea of unity in the army'.[46]

When she was approached about the memorial the memories were rekindled after years of retreating from his memory. Being consulted jolted her. She did not remarry: 'it's hard to explain because it wasn't that I didn't want to … I suffered from terminal guilt … and my assessment of my want of understanding … of not endeavouring to understand more'.

Nonetheless, despite an attempt to deny death in the early stages, her identity remains tied to her husband's: 'We all in our own way – foster that – and I wouldn't want it otherwise – foster the heroic warrior image and the woman who loses the heroic warrior takes on some of that heroism herself … '. Part of this, and the status associated with being a war widow, was related to the sacrificial death. Others also defined their identities through their husbands:

> I would say that's very real in my life ... I suppose if anything its increased, the way men come up to me and assume that because I'm the widow of this man that I'm just like him. They are wonderful to me, there is no question about that. Furthermore, I have to say that what was interesting is the Korean community [in Korea] have done it even more than our community ...

It was important for her to keep the memory of her husband alive, in large part because there has been such little recognition.

> Well, it's making amends for the lack of recognition that the public is not prepared to give, that the government was not ready to give because what he did should have been acknowledged and there are a whole lot of people who have written why it wasn't and I just don't want that life to have been lost without people knowing what he did and what kind of person he was. If I got the ability to correct [this] I will.

Green has documented her journey through grief in her powerful and evocative memoir, *The Name's Still Charlie*, written in 1992. She encapsulates the dilemma she experienced after Green's death. Green was unusual of the women in this study as she eventually sought counselling for her grief. Being told by her counsellor that she had idealised her husband rather than remembered the real man with all his faults, she asks:

> *The real Charlie?*
> Jolted, I recognised something was at odds. There's the unchanging, handsome hero Charlie in my memory. But in my nightmares there's the rejecting, unreachable Charlie.
>
> *Why?*
> Did I really know him after all? I didn't know Charlie of the farm, or Charlie of the battlefields. When he came home ... at the end of 1945 ... He kept silent about his out-of-life-years, grappled with the future, as a civilian, till hope gave out ...[47]

In a final letter written to her dead husband, Green attempts to come to some closure and reconciliation with memory, and the place of the past in the present is replayed through dreams:

> There's no point in questioning or regretting the past. It's gone ... Our marriage was a lifetime ... Lately, I've stopped having the bad dream that you were so far away and couldn't get in touch with me.

I hated that dream I had over and over again. I could never
understand it ... [I had another] very different dream. You came
close to me.[48]

In this reconciliation, he remains an anchor and a part of her emotional
life. Therefore, she has not looked elsewhere for fulfilment:

I worked and saved to fill in the years ... I feel content, and ... rich,
even though I've never filled the gap you left. It wasn't an empty
gap. I've always had your love to sustain me ... You are the finest
human being I have ever known.[49]

She laments the hopes that did not come to fruition, that were not
realised:

It's what happened to his dreams that I have to live with. That's
why, whenever I drive through the country, I can't forget, and I
can't heal. I see Charlie's dream, a continuous frieze ...[50]

Green dwells on missed opportunities, another life and chances unrealised, of the 'big dreams in all those letters written during the war,
when we were apart'.[51]

It is significant that it took Green until 1980 to feel she could
express her grief. The repression of it immediately after the event was
characteristic among war widows after the war. Faye Longmore, whose
father Joseph Longmore (known as Paddy), departed for Korea in
September 1950, died 29 October in the same year just before his forty-
eighth birthday. He left his widow, and seven daughters, the youngest
of whom was two years of age. When reflecting on this deep loss, Faye
Longmore recalls how the repression of grief was debilitating for her
family, especially for her widowed mother:

Our mother was devastated, her health broke and never fully
recovered. The family members were separated for some time and
poverty descended. A memorial service was thought inadvisable
due to Mum's distress. The repression of grief had a destructive
effect on the family – remaining to this day.

Referring to the Next-of-Kin programme, which aims to acknowledge
the bereavement families of men who died in war, Longmore expresses
hope that the commemorations organised by this programme, 'will
hopefully help us with the healing process the absence of a funeral
service did not'.[52]

In a similar way, Lois Murphy found herself resisting an overt
expression of grief when her husband, James, died in December 1969
while serving in Vietnam. She recalls how, despite having great support

from other members of the air force, she felt restrained, although others
were perhaps more demonstrative. Murphy recalled that:

> When you get that sort of support you feel a wimp if you've cried
> over everybody. You don't slobber all over everyone. You try to be
> a little bit strong. The day that Brian was buried we had the greatest
> wake ... they needed to get their sorrow out. They were in a bad
> way ... It was a huge funeral.[53]

In retrospect, she recalls, 'I honestly and truly don't think I grieved.
The way I grieved I suppose was to relive those days'. She left her
three youngest children aged nine, six and three behind on the day of
the funeral, thus perpetuating a silence, but has since regretted that
decision:

> Looking back on it, I should have taken them all to the funeral.
> They should have all gone to the funeral ... They would have
> realised that that was it ... And we were going to bury him and that
> would be where he would be ... We would know that he was there.
> As it was they just didn't cope ... It wasn't a topic of conversation
> ... you do what you think is best at the time.

There was little support available for her in terms of grief counselling:

> You sunk or swum ... you either stayed on top or you went under.
> There was nothing. No follow up. The only follow up was from his
> mates ... And I hear people say this ... 'you're only a war widow
> for so long'. Then people say, 'you should be over it by now' ...
> Some people grieve for the rest of their lives. Well, I suppose I do
> to a degree. You know, a little bit, but nobody knows. I got on with
> my life and I did the things I needed to do ... I've lived a solitary
> life. I've had a heck of a lot of fun tho'. I've had a ball.[54]

The individual quest of grief, however, is something she believes,
others cannot share. 'You don't understand until you've been there.
You've got no idea. None. You can try to imagine but you've got no
idea. Such a shock ... because death is so final.'[55]

Women who lost their husbands during the wars encountered
specific difficulties as single mothers. All of them joined the workforce and, while it was not uncommon for women to be active in
the paid workforce at this time, they were unusual in that they were the
main breadwinner at a time when it was still considered appropriate for
men to be the major wage-earners. Nevertheless, increasing numbers
of women were joining the workforce, often in a part-time capacity.[56]

The economic stringency that she was forced to endure was a
great blow to Fry, who found life as a single mother a strain. The

question of fatherless children became a much talked about issue after the war, affecting the emotional and financial lives of war widows. The role of fathers in the post-war family became a source of anxiety and concern. In those families that had lost a breadwinner, the state became a surrogate father, taking the role of provider and financial supporter.[57] Fry and others claim that their experience cannot be compared to that of women who did not have to endure this burden of single motherhood. In her case, she 'kept a positive outlook' for her daughter's sake. She had a difficult time financially. When her husband went into the air force in April 1942, she was three months pregnant. The allotment for those entering the air force was 25d per week for the spouse with no children. With all of her commitments, it 'took a lot of ingenuity to survive and keep the home together'.[58]

Sylvia Brown's daughter's resistance to having a stepfather echoed her own experience and she decided not to remarry because of it. She was conscious of her daughter not having a father: 'I wanted my little girl to have everything her father would have given her and as far as I was concerned she has got it'. She made the decision to go out to work early, in order to provide her child with these benefits.

Virginia Gerrett had two daughters whom she cared for while she continued her professional life. Olwyn Green and Pearl Sutton both worked and each tried to raise her child with the best effort she could muster. Jean Fry expressed dismay and distress at having to be a single mother, and worked as a librarian for the accountancy firm, Price Waterhouse, where her husband had worked before the war. She 'battled' hard to ensure her daughter was raised with all the opportunities she would have had had her father lived. Olwyn Green discusses the impact on her daughter of her father's death. Even now,

> she won't talk about it. I have great difficulty to get her to talk about it and I've tried to take her off to functions where people are honouring her father because they've been doing that ever since he died … She cannot cope with it. She cannot go to functions to do with it. She just says, 'I can't cope with it … I didn't explain to her, I didn't know how to … she thought he died because he cut his finger … he went away and … abandoned me [in his daughter's eyes] and can't explain duty.[59]

Pearl Sutton 'took in sewing to keep with expenses', eventually took up a job in a record and book store where she worked for twenty-five years. 'Life is so much better now. A few years ago, I had a friend come to live with me so loneliness is a thing of the past.'[60]

The memories of those women whose husbands never returned from war would haunt them forever. The disadvantage of war widowhood is more pronounced for women who lost their husbands during the war; indeed, some are bitter about the ways in which they were treated. Even for widows themselves, what is a 'real' war widow is highly debatable. Their memories document a time when stoicism was the appropriate response to grief; indeed, it was seen as inappropriate for them to continue their mourning. These are narratives about romance, lost opportunities and perfect love. Underlying these memories is a pronounced nostalgia which becomes a way in which grief and death are denied. There are issues about missed opportunities, and rebuilding a life without a husband, which was socially and culturally very difficult to do. These women upheld the identity of the 'war widow' to varying degrees. They cherish memories of their husbands, and carry an internalised grief. The paradox that lies at the heart of these stories is that while war widows remembered their lives as lost opportunities, they also eliminated any hope of future options because of perceived obligation to their lost partners.

CHAPTER FIVE

THE QUESTION OF SILENCE

I could never understand the secret.[1]

Histories of war have often been discussed in relation to questions of silence. The interminable struggle to talk about the grotesque, bleak experience of war is a theme that has overshadowed many survivor narratives. Paul Fussell has discussed how impossible it was for many soldiers to write and to speak about the conditions they endured in the trenches during the First World War. A language could not be found, let alone spoken, that could adequately convey the ghastliness of what they had witnessed. A recurring theme in many of these accounts is the 'presumed inadequacy of language itself to convey the facts about trench warfare'.[2] As many writers have shown, the symptoms associated with shell-shock, which has been characterised as 'male hysteria' by Elaine Showalter, became the only language through which returned soldiers could speak of their experiences. 'Soldiers lost their voices and spoke through their bodies', she observes.[3] It is ironic that a two-minute period of silence was introduced for Anzac Day as a collective form of remembrance, given that First World War participants found it so difficult to convey their experiences and those of the dead.[4]

What is spoken about and what remains unspoken, forms a pervasive pattern in narratives of those who survived atrocities inflicted during the Second World War. In the wake of different aspects of brutality and trauma came yet a further paralysis in the attempt to make some sense of unprecedented human tragedy. 'There was a new silence in 1945', writes Adrian Gregory, 'the silence after Auschwitz and the silence after Hiroshima, the silence in which nothing meaningful could be said.'[5] The gulf between language and experience, observes Inga Clendinnen, can be so disabling for survivors of atrocities, such as those experienced during the Holocaust, that they remain silent.[6] While many have written their stories of such events, others 'found no recourse save silence'.[7] For them, their release was one into 'chaotic solitude'.[8] The same could be said of prisoner-of-war survivors, not all of whom were willing to open themselves to the scrutiny and voyeurism of a waiting public.[9]

What has been the impact of this silence on those around the soldiers and civilians who survived these and other indescribable atrocities? The reticence of returned men, their reluctance to speak freely and fluently is now almost a cliché in discussions of ex-soldiers.[10] Related to this vocabulary of silence is the fact that it has not been socially acceptable or appropriate for men to grieve openly and in public. The testimonies in this study support such a view. Soldierly silence shrouded men in a protective shield. The silence became a pact between them that could be broken only in the company of an elite few. But the question of the impact of this behaviour on those around them has yet to be considered.

Their immediate families respected this silence. In many family stories, a father's tendency to relate war stories only to his soldier friends was accepted as another aspect of male camaraderie born out of extraordinary circumstances. Like many war widows, men of the generation before the Second World War sought solace in their community, rather than in the professional advice of the social workers, psychiatrists and counsellors who became increasingly influential after the war. Often, these men remembered through silence. But many widows believed that if men had been more forthcoming in discussing their experiences, they might have been able to deal better with problems that arose in their marriages. Military life was endured by disciplining the emotions, and this mechanism for survival was carried into civilian life when soldiers returned from war. Emotional anguish lay dormant beneath the surface of everyday routines. When it was unleashed, it often found its fullest expression in violence, with some men demanding that their wives and their children bear witness to, experience, and in some cases, internalise the force of their own guilt and trauma. Recently, Joanna Bourke has argued that men's silence suggests not the anguish of war and an inability of language to articulate its horror, but rather that silence masked the pleasure of killing, and of men's enjoyment of it.[11] The testimonies examined in this study offer a challenge to this argument, and suggest it was not the pleasure of killing that haunted these men and explained their silence, but rather the opposite. Silence masked an anguish that was often left unarticulated, but when it did find an expression, it left an enduring legacy on the families of returned men.

Truda Naylor recalls that her husband Allan, a First World War veteran, would talk about only those wartime experiences that were humorous and entertaining. It was a performance, a way of defusing the memory of death and grief. 'Occasionally little bits came out but they were the amusing things', she claimed; 'they were the trivia'. He also had not 'meant to inflict the memories' on her and 'he protected me a bit'. The silence was, however, punctured by nightmares:

> It wasn't obvious but at times during our married life he had dreadful nightmares … One night he nearly threw me out of bed because he thought I was the enemy … he used to fight … several times he fought me … as soon as he woke up he was all right … And actually when he was dying, when he was comatose, he was rambling about the war.

Naylor believed 'they kept it under covers. They didn't express themselves … Men talked amongst themselves … but they wouldn't talk to the women about it all.' She had tried to get him to write it down for the record, but he would not do so.[12] Other women remembered that their fathers had become as reticent about their wartime experiences as their husbands would later be about their experiences. Pat Medaris noted that her father, who served for four years during the First World War, including at Ypres and Pozières, returned injured after being shot in the back; 'you could put your fist in his back when we were children'. He didn't 'speak about it until the grandchildren came along'. The announcement of another war merely aroused a resistance:

> I'll always remember the night that war was declared, the Second World War, and he turned to my mother and he said, 'Thank God we've got girls. I haven't got a boy. I wouldn't want them to go' … He said 'I wouldn't have wanted them to go through what I've been through'. He said 'I know what it's like' …[13]

Jean McNeill discerned different approaches to experiences from her father and her husband. Her father served in the First World War, and he:

> talked about the war more than my husband. My husband didn't talk about the war much at all. I think in the First World War the comradeship was deeper … they kept talking about the fun times they had and slipped over the horror bits.[14]

Jean lamented that her husband 'didn't say very much at all … which was a pity … looking back now I'm sorry he didn't talk about it more. Life just gets busy … you don't talk about those things. It was a pity, though.'

Jean Davis recalled how her husband's silence was a source of regret and concern for her:

> even though … they don't say anything to you … they never get rid of what's inside of them. And … really a very sad thing that they wouldn't talk about it. Maybe if they could talk about it it wouldn't [have] got so sort [of] deeply imprinted … A lot of little things that would happen … like watching a film and you could see

Jean Davis

Leonard Davis, husband of Jean

... especially if there was a film like in the jungle which is where they *were* you could see he really didn't really like to watch that sort of thing. And yet he loved to read books about it. About the war ... I really think it affected him very deeply, emotionally.[15]

She could not know what it had been like for him: 'he'd come home ... you don't know how they feel but you can imagine that you'd been through this traumatic war and then full stop everything stops'.

Davis knew little about which regiment her husband served in, or what his wartime activities were. All she knew was that he served in New Guinea, and 'because they don't speak about it ... It was the Legacy fellow who came to see me after I became a widow who had everything about him written down ...'. She too regretted that 'he didn't speak about it. Even my children would like to know more history about him but he didn't speak to us about the war ... I don't think they do'.[16]

Doris White, who herself had joined the armed forces at the age of 18 in 1943, remembered how her father served in France in the First World War, but 'didn't talk about it much', and joined up again for the Second World War.[17] The Second World War seemed to usher in a different form of silence. White's husband, Leslie, served in the war for four years, and she remembered how he 'clammed up' afterwards:

> He was a man that kept things inwardly ... he wasn't as out-going and he lost a lot of friends in the war ... like real friends. He never come out with any friends ... he liked to joke ... but he couldn't communicate with me. I think if he talked more to me it would have helped him ... All he thought about was going to work ... he was a good provider ... I don't think he communicated with other people much, he just kept it in. I think that was a lot of his troubles ...

This behaviour was compounded by the fact that their youngest daughter died:

> he just closed up all together and he just sort of kept it all to himself which he had done all along ... he didn't talk about personal things ... That was a lot of his trouble. I couldn't talk to him ... he used to shut off ... He blocked it out ... that was his way he coped with it, I suppose.[18]

Nancy Murrell's husband Kenneth was reticent to speak with her about the war but he spoke freely to other men: 'They would never talk war with their families. Apparently they did up the club, that's why I think they drank and [loosened] their tongues. It wasn't a women's thing ... you never hear what they actually did ...'.[19] Her husband went to the war at 18 and returned at 26. The impact of this was that he 'was very secretive at times ... He always wanted to be with the boys where he could say what he wanted without being guarded or that sort of thing.'[20] Lorna Higgenbotham rationalised that '[t]hey didn't want to talk about death. I think they saw so much of death it was unbelievable ... Bill wouldn't talk on war.'[21] Jessie Morland claimed that:

> unless the men sort of told you a lot of things – like Bobby never
> spoke of it, so you don't know really what went through their
> minds or things like that. And you find a lot of men that went to war
> [and] never spoke of it, a lot of them used to take it – like my father
> – probably took it out on their children …[22]

'They used to keep it to themselves', she remembered 'unless they got
really drunk, unless he got really drunk'.[23] Nell Durnford summed up
her husband's response to war: men did not talk about war, because
it 'brings back too many memories'.[24]

Verna Phillips recalled a similar experience after the return of her
husband, Desmond. He didn't discuss his wartime experience with her,

> but once the boys got together … [they did] talk. He wouldn't tell
> you [about] anybody that was killed or anything like that. He
> wouldn't go through all those. I think he sort of tried to wipe
> that out of his mind. I don't know whether they spoke about it with
> the boys when they got together, because they all went through
> the same [experience] … I think the Second World War boys just
> closed things out of their mind … they wanted to come back and
> just start again … I can honestly say that I never heard Des talking
> about anything that he went through in the war.[25]

Silence also become a part of the experience of returned Korea
and Vietnam veterans. Public memories of war were framed by forgetting. Without the fanfare and ceremony of the Second World War, it
was easier to remain silent. In light of prevailing political and cultural
attitudes at the time, the widows of the ex-soldiers might have felt it
was probably more appropriate to do so. Olwyn Green described this
silence as a 'code'. She recalls how soldiers told 'good' stories, and that
you had to read the literature to discover how bad any of the wars were
and the experiences men had in them:

> It's a code, it's a code … they don't want to upset their family with
> what it was really like. The other thing they'll consistently say is,
> 'well, nobody will believe us if we told them', that the gap of
> understanding was too great. The other constant thing is that it's
> inexplicable they couldn't explain anyhow …

She observed that they had learnt to live by that code, and relive 'the
spirit of camaraderie' among themselves.[26] She didn't try to find out
more, to her 'everlasting regret'; she 'didn't ask and [she] wasn't
told'. Of Vietnam veterans, she observed that 'You can almost identify
a Vietnam Vet. They look different … they've got their own code.
They're beginning to merge now …' Green reflected that there was no

mention of the war in her husband's letters. This silence was in part because of the censorship, but it also pre-empted the silence that men brought home. Soldiers 'primarily didn't want to upset people', she claimed, and they idealised the future rather than dwelling on the present.[27]

Jean Rayner's husband, Louis, was a driver in the Korean War and his war stories were funny, frivolous and theatrical. He always talked about comical episodes: 'I didn't know whether he just didn't want to share that side of it or whether there was none. But he never used to say anything about those sort of things'.[28] Beverley Schmidt recalled how her soldier husband, 'Terry never spoke very much about the [Vietnam] war. When asked by relations if he killed anybody, Terry piped up and said "no ... you fire into the blackness". It's nothing to be proud of ... he drank a lot more.'[29]

Phyllis Muller also recalled how her husband Keith, who served in the air force in Vietnam, would:

> not [talk] in front of the family but when air force friends ... came home there was an expression I used to say to the children, 'well the hangar doors are open' ... we used to hear a lot then, but no he didn't talk very much with the family ... He wasn't a terribly outgoing sort of person at any time and he wasn't one who could sit and make small talk.[30]

Glenis Hargen observed that the silence for her partner, George Dick, a Vietnam veteran, manifested itself in a number of ways:

> Most Vietnam veterans don't talk about the war. They will to a man but they won't to a woman ... some of the things they had to do was pretty devastating to them ... one part of their life was secret, one part was for people who they wanted to know and the other part was, you know, 'mind your own business'.[31]

The way in which he kept his 'secrets' to himself was detrimental to their relationship: 'I don't know whether all Vietnam veterans are like this, but they seem to get something in their brain and it festered and all of a sudden it would explode.'[32]

Other soldiers could be a source of information when words failed men themselves. Loris Pini noted that her husband Desmond never 'talked much of it but other men who had served with him told me a lot of things in that respect ... his nerves were so bad'.[33] It created a particular difficulty of communication. Lorna Higgenbotham spoke of her husband William dealing with being surrounded by death. For him, death was an existential experience:

They didn't want to talk about death. I think they saw so much of death it was unbelievable ... Bill wouldn't talk on war ... He was a very gentle sort of quiet man but when he came back he realised life was different. He never believed in religion any more, saw too much death and he never talked about it very much at all.[34]

Noela Hatfield reiterated this theme:

I heard more about the Second World War than I ever heard about my husband ever being in Vietnam. When the men came back from Vietnam you heard ... . very very little about it. People ... make a lot of comments about the Vietnam war now and they say they hear more about the Vietnam war but if you ask my sons anything connected with the Vietnam war they couldn't tell you ... when Bob came back it was hardly ever discussed in the house.[35]

The silence of survivors has been a powerful motif in the public and private memory of all wars. The common experience that when men returned they retreated into silence points not only to a psychological response to wartime experience: as well, it was not appropriate for returned men to grieve openly when they returned from war. In the following two chapters, the impact of maintaining this silence is explored in the experience of a number of women whose husbands returned from war. The women who lost their husbands during the war experienced silence in a different way. The mystery of unknown circumstances surrounding sacrificial death would hang over them in an omnipresent, yet elusive silence for the rest of their lives. Another silence which is pervasive throughout these memories is the silence of the women themselves regarding their own experiences of the often volatile marriages to those men who returned. Women had few opportunities or avenues to articulate their disaffection and they kept silent about these often traumatic experiences which shattered and unsettled their expectations about marriage and intimate life.

This pervasive private silence, however, sits oddly with the plethora of memoirs and reminiscences of returned soldiers that have been published in recent times.[36] Silence is not the only way in which men responded, for the continuing fascination with war has meant there is an insatiable market for war memoirs. Many of these are accounts of wartime experience in various parts of the world, and during certain battles. One type of such writing seeks to capture the camaraderie and mateship of wartime experience, and endeavours to tell a story of adventure. Although these accounts can include stories of witnessing death, in many of these recollections the tone is one of adventure and humour in dealing with death. Peter Medcalf writes of how:

> We had to face the unpleasant task of burying the swollen, rotting remains. The job was made bearable by the varied jokes and comments from several humorists as the burial party sweated with shovels alongside the offending corpse ... We had pitched our shelters on top of the shallow graves the Japanese had dug for their own dead during the battle the week before, As Sad Sack observed, 'You got to admit, the place has atmosphere'.[37]

Some writers have chosen to represent their participation in war as a strict factual account of 'what happened', relating the various activities, movements and personalities of their battalion.[38] Other memoirs attempt to convey a personalised, more reflective account.[39] Yet others remember war in more sombre and subdued tones. John Kingsmill writes of how:

> Old men and old women make long and arduous journeys to visit these sacred sites ... and they would be entitled to ask why our fine young men died in places so far from home. The answer was perfectly clear and logical then. It is not so now, all these years on ... It was impossible to say how much our lives had been changed by the experience, any more than a prisoner can say as he emerges from jail. But changed he is, and he has to live with that.[40]

Roland Griffiths-Marsh was emotionally explicit recalling his Second World War experience in 1990:

> I closed my eyes. For five years and seven months I had been a frontline soldier. I had fought in four campaigns ... I had been wounded, injured many times, and had malaria, dengue ... amoebic dysentery ... for the first time in five years and seven months, [I] knew for sure that I would see tomorrow's rising sun; and for the second time in that period, I wept silently.[41]

Many of these memoirs were published during the 1980s and 1990s, suggesting that sufficient time had elapsed for the initial silence, which so many of these women described, to be finally broken. In the immediate post-war period, when death had been culturally 'banished',[42] the social climate was not conducive to recounting acts of death, killing and mourning.[43] This would have been especially the case for returned men, for whom war was proof of their manhood, understood in terms of the restraint of emotion, rather than its expression. Social mores deemed it inappropriate for husbands to confide in their partners and they did so rather in the camaraderie of men. An urge to record their stories for their families as they aged has also motivated ex-servicemen to record their thoughts and experiences.

By the late twentieth century, with a wider acceptance of the *need* for men and women to grieve or examine emotions through open, public discussion, and through testimony, the silence has been fractured.[44] In the past ten years, the number of self-help grief books has created a boom in the publishing industry. A space has opened for the discussion of grief both in Australia and overseas. Books such as *Living Well With Grief*, by Betty Riordan; *How We Grieve: Relearning the World*, by Thomas Attig; and *Growing Through Grief: From Anguish to Healing: Coping with Death, Suicide and Trauma*, by Gerard Dowling, point to recent trends in how grief has become publicly articulated.[45] Another such example is Stillbirth and Neonatal Death Support, which has organised grieving mothers who experienced stillbirths. It offered support and recognition to all those who experienced death following the death of a baby. In years past, this type of death was greeted with silence. One woman who used the service to find her son's burial place, forty-seven years after his death, spoke of the silence which prevailed in 1947, when he was born a stillborn child.

> It was the first time I had spoken to anyone. Even my husband never spoke about it, he just covered it up. You were not allowed to have your feelings. If only they [the doctors] had had enough sense in those days to give the dead baby to the mother. I'd have got over it.[46]

Organisations like the Centre for Grief Education, which was established in 1996 in Victoria, also illustrate a worldwide trend. It provides programmes and services, consultation and advice for those experiencing bereavement and publishes two newsletters. It holds seminars and workshops which cover a broad definition of bereavement and grief, providing a forum for discussion of a range of experiences. In July 1999, these included questions of grief and ageing, the child, men and grief, disability, grief among Aboriginal people, mothers, adolescents and suicide, and those bereaved by murder.[47]

Women knew, from the silence, that their men had been changed by the war. Memoirs, emerging forty or fifty years later, confirm this. In the next chapter, we consider how wives often internalised the trauma and guilt of their husbands, at a time when their own and their husband's grief and loss found little public acknowledgement.

CHAPTER SIX

MARRIAGE WARS

Warfare is not an event but a process.[1]

During the Christmas holidays of 1945, Gwen Davis, aged 23, was holidaying with a girlfriend and her mother at Queenscliff, a seaside resort on the coast of Victoria. At the guesthouse where she was staying she met a 'very good looking' young man, who was also holidaying 'with his mate'. The attraction was immediate, and he asked her to marry him almost straight away. She replied, as did many other women during this period, with an instantaneous yes. 'Hasty' marriages were common at the time.[2] William Robertson was still in the army when he met his wife-to-be. He had served in the jungles of New Guinea in 1942–43, having joined the militia in March 1939, six months before the beginning of the Second World War. When they met, he was 'doing administration work at Victoria Barracks in St Kilda Road', and in 1946 was discharged from the army.

Reflecting on that time, and the domestic drama that soon unfolded, Robertson stressed how, despite her initial attraction, there was considerable doubt in her mind about the suitability of her choice. 'I had my doubts', she confessed over fifty years later,

> whether I wanted to marry him or not because I began to feel that there were differences between us. I did discover that he had a bad temper and I didn't realise the seriousness of it. I was also too afraid of my parents to go to them and admit that I thought I could be making a mistake.[3]

Gwen's instinctive doubts and her husband's temper were crucial issues to which she would return while reflecting on the history of her

110

Gwen and Bill Robertson, 1946

married life. Years after the event she stressed the doubt in her mind as a way of emphasising the unease she felt about her future husband and as a means of explaining why she stayed in the marriage. In hindsight there were other reasons too. In her retelling, she explains why she remained in a marriage that later become psychologically untenable:

> I remember one weekend in particular he wrote to say that he'd be down the following weekend. And I began to feel that I was toey that he was coming down to Melbourne. I then realised that I had doubts as to whether I wanted to marry him or not ... I began to realise that what I felt was not love, that, I think, I was only attracted to him because somebody needed me, not that I realised that at the time ... I realised that was why I married him. Because somebody wanted me. And as my brother-in-law said to me some years later, 'he wanted you to replace his sergeant because he needed somebody to tell him what to do ...'[4]

Robertson's marriage became abusive, and yet she stayed in it. In offering explanations as to why she remained in a marriage which became so difficult, Robertson attempted to retrieve her self-respect and dignity. In doing so, she found an affirmative voice in her narrative, in ways which suggest that memory shapes certain 'concepts of person-hood and accountability'.[5] Once engaged, which she considered at the time a 'serious commitment ... almost like a marriage', it was difficult for her to reverse her decision. Despite her early doubts, she married Robertson in 1948, had a daughter by him in 1949 and a son in 1953.

Robertson lamented lost opportunities, expressed guilt about her husband and attempted to explain both of these emotions in an auto-biographical account. Reflecting on her marriage thirteen years after the death of her husband, her testimony reveals how 'all the meanings of the marriage, all its memories, will be thrown into relief'.[6] In this process, the bereaved 'reviews, piece by piece, memories, thoughts and feelings associated with the image of the dead partner'.[7] But her narrative is one where she not only laments the loss and death of her husband: she also endured a painful and traumatic relationship with him, and hers is a story of stoic survival and of painful humiliation. Robertson's journey suggests what others have pointed to, that identi-ties are shaped through memories and experience.[8] Her story reveals, too, the ways in which the 'self' is historically shaped.[9] After having grieved the death of her husband, the loss she comes to mourn is that of missed possibilities:

> I'm quite happy to be now who I am and to live the life that I'm living. The one thing I must say that I have missed which upsets me still because I've never felt that I've been loved by a lover or loved by a husband as so many women are loved by husbands.[10]

Robertson's oral testimony provides a prism through which to consider how women made sense of their volatile marriages to returned men. In Robertson's narrative and in the stories of other war widows who endured the dramatic mood swings of their husbands, 'the war' gave women a framework within which to make some sense of a domestic situation that was at times volatile and explosive. The 'war' becomes an ahistorical, intangible entity through which much of this behaviour is understood and explained. It gives a coherence, unity and clarity to memory. It becomes a metonym for women's trauma in ways that other events have come to represent complex processes. As Kali Tal has argued, for instance,

> the Holocaust has become a metonym, not for the actual series of events that occurred in Germany and the occupied territories before and during World War 2, but for the set of symbols that reflect the formal codification of that experience.[11]

In dealing with painful memories of anguish, 'the war' served to legitimise some men's erratic and unstable behaviour and provide a coherent narrative through which to explain why women remained in marriages that were themselves traumatic.

In this chapter, I explore in detail the memories of two women in particular. Both women witnessed their husband's traumas and experienced the impact of these traumas on themselves during the course of their marriages. In remembering, they offer representations of domestic life which dramatically challenge the image of the suburban family of the 1950s offering 'quiet security'.[12] Several scholars have mentioned the condition of returned soldiers,[13] while others have provided details of violence by men,[14] but the number of historical studies which examine the impact of returned men's physical and psychic injuries on the wives who had to endure the volatility and difficulty of caring for a returned soldier remains small.[15] In clinical studies, this experience has been termed 'secondary traumatization'.[16] In this formulation, those who come into contact with a trauma victim may experience considerable emotional anguish themselves.[17] In studies that have considered the experiences of wives, it has been found that a woman whose husband has suffered some psychic pain is distressed, and feels helpless, depressed, guilty and anxious. It becomes increasingly difficult to live under the pressure of the relationship, where he is unable to maintain the intimacy of married life.[18] Recent studies have noted that the 'troubled veteran is the focus of concern for most treatment agencies, his wife, who suffers considerable emotional and social distress, is often ignored'.[19] These experiences are not of course confined to Australia and had resonances throughout the world.[20]

I also explore the ways in which women have *remembered* the experience of marital conflict. These stories suggest that the sharp division between the war and post-war period is an artificial one when we consider questions of grief and of loss. Such tribulation does not fit easily into discrete chronologies. This is important because so much of the history of war in Australia has been written with little understanding of the lasting psychological legacy of war on future generations.[21] The impact of a world war was played out over the decades that followed it, both outside and within the domestic realm. But most of the existing literature has dwelt on the trauma of returned men, their symptoms and available treatments, rather than on the impact of that trauma on their wives and their children. To move towards analysis of this kind, the definitions of trauma need to be broadened so that it encompasses trauma within the 'private' as well as 'public' arena. As Laura S. Brown suggests, we need to 'look beyond the public and male experiences of trauma to the private, secret experiences that women encounter in the interpersonal realm and at the hands of those we love and depend upon'.[22]

TRAUMA

Gwen Robertson witnessed and lived her husband's trauma. She recalled, after his death in 1985, that her marriage had been a time of anguish, difficulty and pain.

She related the story of her husband's trauma in the following ways. Her husband returned from the war wounded across the bottom of his spine, after a number of bullets were lodged there. He survived an ambush in New Guinea, and was rescued by another soldier, who died while trying to save him. Robertson recalled the incident, which 'tormented [Bill's] mind':

> Evans was a short distance ahead of Bill and he saw that Bill had been wounded so he turned and came back to help Bill … one bullet or perhaps two hit the hand grenade around [Evans'] waist … as they exploded he was so close to Bill that the shrapnel from the hand grenades caught Bill along the left-hand-side of his body. He had a big hole in his left arm and he had all scars right down his left leg … .The bullet wounds in his back were horrific.

Evans died in the skirmish and the trauma of this event stayed with Bill Robertson. In his battalion book he gave an account of the battle, and his last words on the page were, as Robertson recalled them, '"I will never forget his last words before he died." And I think that actually

tortured his mind, particularly in the last couple of years when he was
… very ill and in a lot of pain.' Robertson emphasised that this note had
a profound significance. He did not mention what these words were,
just that: '"I will never forget his last words *to me*. *To me*, just before
he died" and that actually tortured his mind'. He carried these words
for the rest of his life. The impact for Robertson and her children was
painful and their story becomes, in the words of one observer of
trauma, the 'story of the way in which one's own trauma is tied up
with the trauma of another'.[23] Robertson's experience supports the
contention that traumatic events are traumatic because they are re-
experienced (not just remembered) repeatedly and well after the actual
time of the event.

The guilt of surviving death, and being saved by other soldiers who
subsequently die, is a burden which many soldiers have carried. The
repercussions of such an experience has been documented extensively
in psychological studies of returned soldiers.[24] Suffice to say here, that
William Robertson carried the burden of survival throughout the rest of
his life. His story illustrates the symptoms of survivor guilt. Soldiers
who witness the death of a fellow soldier often feel profound guilt for
surviving such an experience. The soldier becomes riddled with self-
blame and self-condemnation. He feels responsible for what he did not
do to alter the situation, and for his apparent inaction.[25] After the event,
the 'surviving self must endure the surviving' and the individual must
come to realise that 'it is not rational or appropriate to feel total responsibility for that person's death'. If a war veteran has not understood
that, he will 'blame himself for the death of a friend, whereas it was the
enemy who actually killed him'.[26] Where this 'burden of self-blame'[27]
remains, those who experience it have difficulty with intimacy, and
anger, rage and violence become more 'comfortable than guilt or other
forms of anxiety'.[28] The problem of readjustment by veterans into
civilian society has been examined in detail by social workers, psychologists and sociologists. The war self – which is structured around
the death principle – and the civilian self – which values and affirms
life – need to be brought into some harmony and balance, which also
includes integrating any trauma which is experienced within these two
separate selves.[29] Some trauma and survivor literature suggests that the
'trauma becomes embedded in personality and that there is an interactive
relationship between memory of the trauma and subsequent stages of
adult development'.[30] This condition can lead to limiting vitality in other
areas of one's life, such as in marriage and parenthood, when 'self-
punishment … permeate[s] all aspects of living'.[31]

One theorist has characterised the initial psychological symptoms of widowhood in terms of post-traumatic stress disorder (PTSD) and survivor guilt – both conditions associated with returned soldiers. Robert C. Di Giulio argues that

> typically, to characterise the psychological problems that affect combat veterans, PTSD includes numerous symptoms that also affect widowed men and women, especially within the first year of widowhood: re-experiencing of the traumatic event through flashbacks, dreams ... and other disturbances including loss of sleep, loss of appetite ... or numbness ...[32]

Widowed men and women experience 'survivor guilt' in which a person:

> feels guilty that he or she is still alive while another has died. Survivor guilt implies that the survivor was spared because of the death of another person. For widowed people, the guilt may be strongly felt because the survivor and the deceased were typically closer than survivors of mass disasters.[33]

The material in this chapter supports the argument that war widows internalised these dynamics when their husbands experienced both PTSD and survivor guilt.

William Robertson's injuries were such that he endured enormous physical pain and punished others because of this physical and psychological anguish. Gwen Robertson noted that his 'nerves were always bad and that's why he was bad-tempered'. His health deteriorated, and she recalled,

> it became more difficult for us all ... because of the pain he was in ... the part for us – myself and my two children – was the fact that he couldn't cope with his pain. He couldn't cope so we had to help him cope and he made us suffer too.

What was the nature of this suffering? In what could be considered a return to the initial trauma of events, and also an expression of his own self-destruction, Robertson recalls how in September 1960, her husband

> couldn't sleep very much at all and he'd be up out of bed wandering around the house ... and I just couldn't get any sleep. I just had to move him into the back bedroom ... he couldn't sleep and he suffered such terrible pain with his back that he would get up out of bed, he would crawl around the house on his hands and knees, he would bang on my bedroom door and kept us awake half

the night and he would yell and scream because he just couldn't stand the pain. He would bang on my bedroom door … [he] … just banged and banged and banged on the bedroom door so as we couldn't sleep.

The burden became far too much to carry. She and the two children could not deal with his persistent noise which upset her daughter, 11, and son, 7. He resented that he could not sustain 'the burden' of his injury and was tormented by his own trauma. He became dependent on her, like an infant:

> He wanted us to carry the burden. He couldn't carry it himself. So we had to carry the burden. He had to make us suffer. He was suffering why shouldn't we. He couldn't forgive society. The world owed him a living … I think it was because he was immature. I always felt that he was my eldest child. He's never [been] a husband. He was my eldest child, that's the way he was just like a child. He needed help. I hated him.

Robertson was also vulnerable to the mood swings and volatility Bill displayed in public. She recalled an incident towards the end of 1957 when 'his outbursts of temper were so great that we'd go away on holidays to … friends of ours … and there'd be rows …'. The catalyst was one incident where she had returned from shopping with a friend and:

> by the time we got back we were a bit late … and of course he started abusing me for being late back and … there was one great bust up in the car. And I got back from that holiday and I thought 'I've done all I can to make this a marriage', and that was the end of 1957 … so I gave up. Decided that I would go my own way. I'd make my own life in some way. That was the end of my marriage and that was only nine years after I was married.

Bill's anger and rage, which were part of carrying and struggling with his trauma, forced her to consider leaving him.[34] In 1962 Robertson approached a solicitor about her finances and the possibility of ending her marriage. Her solicitor advised against it, warning her that she could not support her children on her wages and that if she left him, 'he would fold up like a paper bag'. She felt she could not leave him at that time. Robertson internalised his guilt and felt guilty herself for considering letting him perish:

> I couldn't have deserted him because he was not a man who was able to cope on his own. He could have never looked after himself.

He could never have fed himself. He could never have been able
to cope with the outside world ... It would have been as if he'd
lost a mother.[35]

The sense of responsibility for his survival, and feelings of guilt for
his condition emerged in a dream – where undesirable aspects of
one's experience often find expression – which was prompted by the
interview:

It was in the house on the ... farm where we lived for 29 years ...
and in the dream I dreamt that I had left him and I walked into the
house and the house was in such a muck. There seemed to be
furniture all over the place and clothes all over the place and
everything very disorganised and he was just about to walk out of
the house to go and get a meal ... and in the dream I remember
feeling, 'Oh, he's got to get a meal for himself. I'm not here to cook
for him'. And I felt regret that he was having to go and find his own
meal. And then I woke up. And then I felt quite upset by the dream
and yet I've never dreamt about anything like that before ...

Robertson's sense of guilt and overwhelming burden of responsibility for her husband were not the only reasons why she had reser-
vations about leaving Bill. Married women who were contemplating
ending their marriages during the 1950s encountered several obstacles.
In 1957, the Anglican minister W.G. Coughlan concluded in his study of
'marriage breakdown' that, 'in spite of the advance of women towards
economic independence and legal equality, a number of practical
realities makes it extremely difficult for a wife to desert once she has
begun to have children'.[36] One of the problems Coughlan identified was
the 'difficulty [of] proving adultery, desertion, drunkenness or cruelty',
so much so that 'many wives who were dissatisfied with their lot and
are fearful for the children's future feel compelled, nevertheless, to stay
with their husbands'.[37] Divorces filed on the grounds of cruelty and
drunkenness, he reported in 1957, had 'increased in number by about
74 per cent in the last five years'.[38] Coughlan claimed this was not
because there were more men behaving in this way, but rather that
women are 'less and less inclined to suffer patiently at the hands of
habitually drunken and/or cruel husbands'.[39] Coughlan observed that
'physical assault ... is a much more common feature than is generally
realised or believed'.[40] As John Murphy has observed of this period,
grounds for divorce were difficult to establish and invariably involved
one of the couple providing evidence against the other, 'on grounds of
adultery, desertion, insanity or habitual violence'.[41]

Financially, it was difficult for women to survive on their own when women earned less than men. The outbreak of the Second World War created new positions for women in the traditionally male occupations, although they did not uniformly attain the same pay as the men who had formerly occupied these jobs. The newly established Women's Employment Board awarded women wages between 60 and 100 per cent of the male rates. Following the war, there was an increase in women's basic wage from 54 to 75 per cent of the male rate, but women's earning capacity remained considerably lower than that of men's.[42]

Robertson had worked in various jobs, none of which attracted lucrative pay. In September 1939, when the war broke out, she was employed in a pharmacy in Kew. She was 'not trained for anything, which was not unusual in those days'. During the war she worked in a factory producing micra – a conductor of electricity – which was used by the army. After being released from war work in late 1944, she was offered a job working in a dry cleaners in Collingwood and worked there until she became pregnant with her daughter in 1949. Single mother status attracted shame and stigma in the late 1950s and early 1960s.[43] As Judith Allen notes, women 'recorded the impact of changed war and post-war circumstances on their personal lives – but many more women experienced these same difficulties and did not seek divorce'.[44] Social ostracism, coupled with financial difficulties, were compelling reasons which deterred most women who entertained the possibility of leaving their marriages.

Robertson was not alone in expressing unease about her marriage, although other women did attempt to change their circumstances. In Australia, the divorce rate rose to an unprecedented level following the war, with the number of divorces increasing by 55 per cent from 1944 to 1947.[45] This was a corrective to the artificially high marriage rate during the war.[46] In March 1940, it was recorded that in Australia, 2,482 more marriages had taken place in the last three months of 1939 than in the same period of 1938.[47] In December 1942, the Registrar's Office of the Army and Air Force recorded high numbers in Victoria. The number of marriages for the month was 178; the total for 1941 of 1,363 was a record.[48] During the 1940s, the number of divorces also jumped, from about 3,200 annually at the beginning of the decade, to some 7,200 in 1945 and a peak of 8,000 in 1947.[49]

Nonetheless, the imperative to marry and have children was a culturally compelling one, and it was one that most women obeyed. By 1947, 49 per cent of women had been married by the age of 25, and this figure continued to rise in subsequent censuses, until, in 1961, it was over 60 per cent. The rise is dramatic when we chart it over a period of time. In the 1920s, three-quarters of all women had been married by the age of 35; in 1947 it was 87 per cent, and in 1961, 92 per cent.[50] By 1961, 91 per cent of women under the age of 35 were married.[51] Increasingly, women were addressed by politicians, social workers and advertisers as housewives and mothers.[52] Prime Minister Robert Menzies, for instance, shrewdly appealed to women in their 'private and domestic rather than economic roles'.[53] In 1957, the *Sydney Morning Herald* announced the 'Vanishing Spinster', when it reported that there were 31,000 fewer spinsters than 10 years ago. This was heralded by the Family Welfare Bureau director, May Pilinger, who declared that most 'women are better off married. It gives them security, social position and a good deal of happiness'. The president of the Business and Professional Women's Clubs in Australia, Jean Arnot, was quoted as claiming that: 'Two world wars deprived women of the chance to have a home, husband and babies. It's wonderful to see a return to the natural and a happy state.'[54] For this reason, the purpose of women attending university was questioned. 'Are these women who take professional courses at the University, involving at least three years of hard study and £150 worth of tuition, wasting the University's time, space and money by not following their careers after marriage?'[55] It was expected that a woman would devote her time and energy to making her husband's life comfortable and in doing so, offer support in his professional career.[56]

Coupled with a concern for these increased divorce statistics came an anxiety about the nature of the family. It remained the case that, as one historian has observed, the 'divorcee joined the spinster as a social outcast'.[57] Together with juvenile delinquency, divorce was seen as one of the areas of 'breakdown' during the 1950s.[58] Women's increasing entry into the paid workforce was similarly identified as disrupting the traditional family. According to Murphy, married women's participation in the workforce increased from 8.6 per cent in 1947, to 13.6 per cent in 1954 and 18.7 per cent in 1961.[59] For many women like Robertson, work provided a valuable source of self-confidence. Between 1960 and 1976, Robertson worked in two pharmacies, in Werribee and Yarraville. After rearing her children, and because of her husband's 'lack of conversational skill', she could 'barely hold a conversation'. She eventually became 'head' in the pharmacy. Within the terms of their marriage, Robertson had to seek permission from her husband to take such a position; otherwise, her daughter would have had to have left school at 14. She recalls how women often had to ask their husbands whether they could let them go back to work: 'how humiliating to have to say "let"', she recalled.

Marriage guidance councils emerged to counter the trend, and emphasised restructuring one's personality to accommodate the changes married life would bring.[60] The marriage guidance movement was begun and sponsored by churches, especially by Anglicans like Coughlan who believed that such guidance should be provided by the clergy who promoted Christian ideals.[61] He formed the Marriage and Family Council in Sydney in 1948.[62] Coughlan believed that marriage counselling was best practised by the clergy rather than 'experts'.[63] The institution of marriage was constantly being assessed and reassessed by the state and the clergy in terms of the suitability of those whom they married and why.[64]

The emergence of marriage counsellors reflected anxieties and concerns about marriage, suggesting the possibility that it was an institution in need of renovation. The churches were behind these developments and at the forefront of reform.[65] Coughlan put forward a forceful case for the introduction of marriage guidance in 1948. He argued that if the incidence of marriage breakdown increased, 'western civilisation and society are doomed to extinction'. Marriage played a crucial role in future personality development:

> It is now clear that in all relationships of men and women, and especially in the intimate relationships of marriage and family life, the pattern and tone of the whole personality will determine the reaction to the varied circumstances and strains of corporate living.[66]

As marriage guidance counsellors became professionalised during the immediate post-war period, and with the rise of the social worker during the 1950s and 1960s, marital problems were believed to be better solved by professionals.[67] In May 1960, Attorney-General Sir Garfield Barwick announced that the government would offer assistance to marriage guidance agencies. In order to qualify, counsellors would 'have to undergo a course of instruction and pass through a regimen of selection of particularly searching nature'.[68] Married women were apparently the preferred group to be employed as counsellors, because of the perception that they 'have greater understanding than single people'.[69] Advertisements stipulated that applicants be 'married men and women in the 30 to 50 years age group ... preference would be given to those applicants who had studied psychology and/or sociology at university level'.[70] Others identified the problem in terms of equity between men and women. Constance Cooke argued that two factors militated against successful marriages. First, the inferior economic and social status accorded to women and second, the lack of 'sex adjustment' between the average woman and man. Mutual respect and unselfishness would solve these problems.[71] This view that modern marriages should be based on an ideal of partnership and egalitarianism had gained some currency among the middle-classes during the 1950s. But this continued to be understood within a framework of the sexual division of labour, with men's identities being shaped by their role as breadwinners and women's as homemakers.[72]

Marriage counselling during the 1950s and 1960s stressed the importance of maintaining marriage and adhering to Christian ideals. Coughlan optimistically noted that women had become more assertive and bold in their expectations of marriage and in their response to cruelty. 'It is undeniable', he asserted,

> that the advance of women towards equal status ... has been a major causative factor in the spread of marriage breakdown. The wife of today is not nearly so willing as her mother was to tolerate any behaviour of her husband which seriously offends her ... she will not endure physical or mental cruelty, or financial deprivation ... or indeed any of the indignities that may be a part and parcel of a discordant marriage ... women today, even more than men, tend to go into marriage with definite expectations both of a material and non material kind.[73]

The testimonies of the women in this chapter offer a more complicated picture than what Coughlan presented in 1957. His optimism was misplaced during the 1950s and 1960s, because while many women may have been more vocal in their opposition, they tended to remain in marriages that were emotionally volatile and at times, cruel and violent, because of their sense of obligation.

Some women believed that they were ill-prepared in their knowledge of what marriage entailed. Joyce Richards, whose husband had served in the Korean War, described marriage in the 1950s,

> like going through a brick wall and the gate was shut – there was no going back because there was no easy way out in those days. You had to just make a go of it because there was no way ... Women ... have got more support today ... Everybody just had to learn to put up with all the bad things as well as the good things.[74]

The transition from the single life to the married one often involved a sense of loss. There was a 'huge wrench' going to the in-laws:

we went through this grieving process because you left your job
and you left your family and you went to an entirely different area
… You just had to wear it. I wouldn't tell my mother that I was
feeling so unhappy …[75]

The chronic housing shortage which beset young couples following the
war created widespread difficulties for couples attempting to establish
an intimate space.[76] This exacerbated the situation for Richards:

And in 1950 there was no accommodation available – we were
lucky (in some ways) to have a room or a house to share with
Mervyn's father (whom I hardly knew!). Other people were living
in garages, sheds, anything you could find.[77]

Men were equally ill-prepared. Olwyn Green describes how her
husband Charlie had been trained in warfare, but little else:

For six years he had been honing skills that were … as necessary
for peace as for war: anticipating, resolving, organising, managing
men. But who, except a few in the New Guinea jungle, knew of his
vision and his potential?[78]

After several unsuccessful attempts on the land, her husband became
restless: 'I can best explain Charlie's unrest in his own words. He was
always saying "racehorses will gallop". How could he passively continue in an unachieving role?'[79] This restlessness drew him back into
the army, which he rejoined in January 1949. In retrospect, she recalls
that time: 'Shock leaves what feels like shell holes in my mind'.[80]

Given the turmoil of her marriage, Robertson fell in love with
another man, but neither she nor he were prepared to leave their
marriages. Roberston framed this as another loss of possibilities:

In 1958 I met a chap … and we fell in love. But we were both
married. And that's now just over 40 years. And we still love
each other. And they call it unconditional love. Because under all
conditions that I've had to go through, I still love him … The one
thing missed in life: haven't been loved.

Robertson become a carer, and a nurturer of her husband, despite
his illness and patiently endured his temperamental nature. The circumstances of her marriage meant that she was a father and a mother in
rearing the children, although the impact on the children was difficult
to measure at the time. In retrospect, she concluded that they certainly
suffered from his behaviour. She recalled of her son, 'I think he still
has to come to terms with his experience as a child because I am
sure that they both look back and realise that they unfortunately had

a very turbulent childhood'. Her daughter speaks more openly of her
memories of Bill Robertson and recalls the time that he attempted to
choke Robertson, and her daughter tried to drag him off her. Her
daughter told Robertson,

> 'O mum, one of the dreadful things I can remember is the night he
> tried to choke you', she said, 'and I'm screaming at him, "leave her
> alone, leave her alone", and here I am … as a child of 12 or 13,
> trying to drag him off your neck, and he was 6ft 3, and screaming
> to Gary come and help me come and help me get him off her'.
> Poor Aileen's … hidden that away until she's admitted it to me two
> years ago.

Her son has:

> never spoken about those things so [Bill] was never a father …
> he never talked to his father about anything. I mean he wasn't
> a husband and he wasn't a father … I'm sure now they have come
> to terms with that but they realise that there was something in their
> lives as children that they just didn't have, that was a father that
> a lot of their friends had.

Part of the effect of Bill Robertson's wartime experience was the loss
of a happy childhood for his children.

To what extent Robertson's husband's behaviour was a result of
the wartime injuries is very hard to judge. Robertson tends to assess the
situation which arose as a combination of factors, not least of which
was the pain suffered from the war injuries. 'I often asked myself that
over the years', she reflected,

> I wasn't always sure whether he put on his spasms of pain or …
> tried to make it appear worse because he just wanted my attention
> like a child or whether he was in actual pain. I think because he was
> mothered by two older sisters so I would say that his behaviour
> wasn't totally to blame on the war … I don't think he was able to
> cope with life regardless … perhaps 80% the war.

The ambivalence of the role of the war expressed here reflects the
ambiguous meaning of war widow itself, for if injuries were not the
cause of his condition, then it throws into question this status.

Robertson identified her husband's background as another factor that might have determined his behaviour, and his response. Her
husband was a child during the depression and the youngest of seven
children. His was a deprived childhood and he was drawn towards the
army for that reason:

that's why he joined the army at 19 ... [to] ... have some sort of a life away from this poor country family because they were just poor people who worked as labourers ... So I would say he had a very deprived childhood and that has helped me understand in the last three years ... that his life was unfortunate as a child and a teenager and perhaps he was bitter about that even but never said ...

Robertson was atypical in this study as a widow who sought counselling after her husband's death and remained in it for three months.[81] This gave Robertson the space and the freedom in which to express a new sense of self. During this time, she began to 'remember who I was before I was married'. She also found a religious explanation for her experience: she began to accept that her life was 'what I'd been meant to go through because of what I could learn from it'. She learnt compassion in what she had gone through, but others found her strength and change difficult:

> they began to see that I was changing and they couldn't accept the change; they preferred to think of me as being sick ... somebody that they had to help. They couldn't accept the fact that I had got on top of it all. People are like that. Especially women. So this year I have been myself ... I am quite happy to be me because I know who I am.[82]

She spoke about a process of renewal, strength and affirmed identity after Bill's death. On one occasion, she returned to:

> the house and it was dark and cold and it was just like walking into a coffin and I walked through all the rooms into the house ... but as I stood in the kitchen ... suddenly that room wasn't dark and cold and damp and suddenly it was a bright Saturday afternoon the sun shining brightly as it was the day we first bought the house in 1950 ...

This journey back was a part of her renewal and relinquishment of the guilt and the burdens she had adopted and absorbed from her husband: 'it was just like walking through somebody's coffin and then within a short period of time the house was ready to fall down. That's all part of going back and then coming back to a new home'.[83] As a firm believer in apparitions, Robertson was sustained by the apparitions she claimed to have of her husband. She spoke of one apparition that finally affirmed her sense of self, and absolved her of her guilt. She spoke of seeing her husband's ghost, as a way of feeling comforted by his reassurances:[84]

wearing a dark striped suit. He's got his RSL badge on ... Now
he's gaining more confidence ... O what a handsome man ... he's
saying 'please forgive me. I'm sorry for what I did ... to you ...
all'. All the other ghosts are there, including her mother and father,
saying, 'Well done Gwen, well done'... And they have the biggest
bunch of flowers for you ... All these flowers ... they're saying,
'Well done'.

In the memories of her marriage, Robertson used the war experience of her husband to make his violence explicable and understand-
able. Her experience provides a representation of family life in the
1950s that is not tranquil and harmonious. It suggests domesticated
trauma – where the boundaries of periods of war and post-war are
blurred, as the trauma of war returns to shape the identity of those
around the traumatised soldiers. Robertson's narrative is told as a way
of understanding how she dealt with a difficult marriage and why she
stayed in it. She witnessed her husband's trauma and at the same time,
internalised his guilt of survival and assumed responsibility for him.

MOOD SWINGS

Another war widow whose marriage was affected and shaped by the
war service of her husband during the Second World War was Isobel
Russell. She met James Ford in 1942 on a blind date which had been
arranged by her mother while he was stationed with the Australian air
force in Britain. Both of them had joined the air force just before the
war, she in Britain, he in Australia. 'I had a very strong feeling about
what was happening', she confessed. But as a woman, it was more
difficult for her to join the services at that time. 'When war was
declared, of course I was called up and my father absolutely hit the
roof. He couldn't believe that his daughter would take herself off.'
Despite these differences with her father, she 'loved her time in the
armed forces'. Her rebelliousness carried her through it and she loved
'knowing that I was doing something that nobody had done before ...
having been brought up in an era where you were more or less told
... that boys were cleverer than girls'.

Her father also disapproved of her marriage. Ford recalls how,
'within an hour, James Ford told me he was going to marry me'. They
married in 1943, and in 1945 she left Britain as a war bride bound for
Melbourne. A rebellious, feisty woman, Ford was able to withstand the
demands of her father. The story she tells of her marriage repeats her
familial story of rebelliousness and assertiveness. Like Robertson, she

Isobel Ford, United Kingdom, 1942

recalled the emotional volatility of her husband and his dramatic mood swings. James Ford also carried a back injury after he returned from the war. He had been:

> shot down … and he had a very bad back problem … and he was very sick and so life wasn't very easy for me … he was very

Isobel and James Ford, December 1943

volatile. He would fly off the handle at the least little thing and
[it was] very difficult for my girls ... I think it was justified by the
pain ... He hit me in his temper and I went to the doctor and I
explained this to him. And he said, 'Look, you must remember that
the problem isn't there, it's ... in his back [it's] such a mess. So it
wasn't easy.[85]

Her husband was a complex man whose mood swings and violence
were founded in his wartime experiences and in the subsequent pain
he endured from them. Other aspects of his character, such as his
generosity, offers a counter-balance to this behaviour, and was especially important in sustaining her through the early years of her marriage.
In retelling this story, Ford used humour as a way of dealing with the
intensity of her relationship and the mood swings of her husband.
She noted how her husband would attempt to redeem himself by giving her presents after they had clashed. Humour allowed her to cope
with this memory, as well as heightening her ability to resist and confront him. Asked whether the war affected her marriage, she replied
unequivocally:

Oh yes, very much so! ... the thing is we did very well out of it.
I might add because every time he put on this terrible act he'd go
out and buy you a fur coat ... that's what he'd do ... [He] was
very generous.

But clearly this generosity was not enough to sustain her and there
were times when, in hindsight, she should have left him:

If I am to be honest, I think had I anywhere to go, which I didn't
have except for friends, or ... family ... I think I would have left
him ... I did leave him a couple of times and I always went back
and then he was the kindest person you would ever meet ...

In her autobiographical account, Ford was less concerned to justify
attempts to leave her husband and felt less guilt about his behaviour. In
her retelling, she presented herself as more active and interventionist.
In dealing with such a volatile partner, she developed a number of
strategies in order to temper his moods:

You had to learn strategies to live with him because he was a very
complex man, I suppose. I loved him but I wasn't in love with
him at that stage because that had gone ... What's the point of
saying sorry when you do the same thing again? I think you lose
respect ...

For Ford, there was a very direct link between his behaviour and the war injuries he sustained. But she was also keen to highlight that he had several sides to his character, that he was not simply a tyrant. In doing so, she stressed that he had a gentle side and was a complex personality:

> there is no doubt about it, he used to have nightmares ... he'd be crawling around the bed frightened that he'd fall off the edge of the bed ... He was sick. There's no doubt in my mind ... because he could be this gentle, very kind person ... So I had to look after him ... I had to be there ... It was difficult; very difficult.

Having to look after him made it difficult to leave, although Ford resisted him and certainly her ability to cope with the marriage stems from voicing her frustrations and expressing her unhappiness.

Although what Ford euphemistically called the 'blow-ups' left a lingering bitterness and anger in her memory, she preferred not to think of him in these terms during this period of their lives:

> Some time ago I suppose I was resentful and hurt. I was angry. I felt this sort of anger ... he was devastated every time he did this and yet it was very hurtful. When I think of him now, I think of him mainly in the early part of our marriage when our children were young. And it was very good. Excellent actually ... But I think honestly ... I was frightened of him. And also I couldn't come to grips with this sudden flying off the handle ... .

She found it very difficult to devise strategies in order to cope with his mood swings although she attempted to do this for her own survival.

> I'd been pretty placid and when you're not used to that it's difficult. It is very hard to know how to respond. It didn't matter how you responded; it didn't make any difference. I use to hate Christmas because he always used to blow up at Christmas. In fact I still hate Christmas.

She attempted to explain his moods and his volatility in terms of being a complex man, who had sustained a number of war injuries. She admitted that she too could be difficult, but stressed how she struggled to find a way of dealing with his volatility and preferred to hold onto his more positive attributes, as a way of countering memories of violence.

Ford's experience of volatility, violence and tensions challenges several prevailing assumptions about family life in the 1950s and 1960s as stable, harmonious and tranquil. It captures another narrative about domestic life and women's role within it: as a carer, provider and emotional supporter. Ford asserted that the wartime injuries which her husband sustained were responsible for his 'blow-ups'. Like Robertson, she too would have left had she found support networks available. In this context, she constantly challenged her husband's behaviour and resisted any passive acceptance of his actions: 'I used to sound like a gramophone record. I used to say, "One of these days you'll be sorry". This went on for twenty years.' Two episodes suffice to illustrate her resistance and show her trying to retrieve some strength and agency in a situation in which she felt alienated and isolated. In her narrative, she is the 'battler', the fighter who retaliates and challenges her husband's behaviour. In doing so, she controls the situation, as well as the memories of these events.

In 1958, after one of their confrontations, she waited until he left for work, she then called in the carriers, put all the furniture in store, and booked into the Southern Cross Hotel in inner-city Melbourne with her daughters. 'It was really quite pathetic in many ways', she later recalled. She and her two children stayed away for about ten days. He set about 'trying to woo and have dinner with us'.

Two years later, in 1960, another episode erupted.

> Something I said [made him get] up and [he] tipped [over] the card table ... That's it and I walked out [to the kitchen] ... I had all these different sorts of crockery and I remember ... opening the doors and taking out piles ... throwing them on the floor and smashing them to pieces and he came in and he said, 'you're hysterical'. What I didn't throw on the floor I threw at him ... And I was crying and tears were streaming down my face ... and as he came up to me, I said, 'Don't you slap me!' And I grabbed hold of his wrist and twisted his arm around and for about two months his hand was like I'd torn his ligaments ... And I'd smashed practically everything. I had to get it out of my system.

Ford internalised her husband's violence and aggression. In her recollections, she found it difficult to reconcile the two sides of his personality. She attempted to keep the peace, and to monitor his behaviour, in order to prevent his outbursts. As she described it:

> I was frightened ... but when he'd get into these moods I was frightened and conscious of everything I said to him. I had to be conscious all the time of everything I'd say in case he flew off the handle ... for no reasons and it's very difficult. And yet as I say, the other side of him was so different. He was thoughtful, kind, very affectionate.

Like Robertson, 'the war' was the way in which she gave her story coherence, 'to better manage or contain it, to present it convincingly to others and, finally, to have done with it'.[86]

Ford developed a psychosomatic response to his memory and her fear of him. When she discussed her husband after his death in 1973,

> much the same as I've talked to you, I then would suddenly ... start this trembling in my stomach and I would shake for about sometimes ten minutes. It didn't happen every time but it must have been something that was very deep rooted for me to feel that because it certainly affected me ... and I couldn't control it.

These shakes stopped after two or three years. She didn't know whether the response 'was going back and feeling frightened'. As Janet Sayers observes, when 'disillusion in men, or their loss, is denied any psychological or symbolic representation, their death can result in psychosomatic symptoms'.[87] One way in which Ford coped was to document and write down everything, to get it 'out of my system'. Keeping a diary in the late 1950s helped her to regain her equilibrium, and 'stay on a level keel with him', something she found very difficult to do. There was no doubt about his love for her and his loyalty to her, and no doubt this would have been an attractive part of him. None-theless, years later, she experienced a sense of guilt for not doing more for him:

> I started to think about all the things that I had done wrong. I don't know whether I did or not but this is all part of the grieving process that I really got out of my system ... I felt guilty that I probably hadn't been patient enough and I should have done this and I should have done that ... By nature I'm fairly philosophical. I accept things as they come ...

Volatility and mood swings were common when men returned from the war. A number of men exhibited volatility and mood swings when they returned from the war. The 'war', became an all-encom-passing explanation for their behaviour. Margaret Wittig, who married her husband John in 1940, was open about the state in which her husband returned. They had been apart for four and a half years during the Second World War, but on his return she discerned a restlessness in his manner:

> You never make up that time ... Don't think I'm nasty with this but [all] my husband wanted to do was drink ... And he give us hell ... you can't blame him because what the poor devils went through over there. I did at that time. I'd a cut his throat if I hadn't got in

trouble … he used to get up of a night and he'd go out but he couldn't stay in the house … you'd stand on the balcony and watch to see if he was coming. He'd be away all hours of the night.[88]

Jean Thomas' husband, Morris, served in New Guinea during the Second World War. They met on a tram, just after the war began. In retrospect, Thomas was forgiving of her husband's behaviour; 'you sort of forgive them for a lot but you never forget', she said. She recalled that her husband had been violent:

> he was a good father, he never abused the children or anything, but [returned men] abused their wives and we didn't have any support … punch-ups, a lot of punch-ups, and then you'd fight back but then men are pretty strong, aren't they, and they usually have the upper hand; however, we survived it and we stuck it out and stuck together. But as he got older he matured a little bit and got a bit mellowed and got … a lot better actually …[89]

The army, she concluded, 'taught him to be cruel; very cruel some-times; abusive, nasty, rotten mouth, rotten fist. But he never hit the children which was good I suppose, in one way.'[90] Her tolerance of him wore thin after a while, and she reported that: 'I nearly walked out a couple of times on him with his bad tempers and nerves and what have you … We stayed together all those years. I dunno how I done it but I done it.'[91]

When she pressed her husband, he responded as many married men would have during the immediate post-war period. Thomas would ask,

> 'Why do you go to the pub after work for?'
> 'Oh, just to sit and have a talk.'
> 'Well, come home and have a talk to me and the kids.'
> 'Well, no we talk men's talk.'
> 'But you're with 'em all day what the hell do you have to talk to 'em [about] from 5 to 6 in the big swill?'

For Thomas, the 'toughness' they shared in their upbringing was crucial, and this sense of a shared understanding bonded her with her husband: 'Perhaps if I'd a married better I wouldn't have had to have gone through the hardships as much as I did but however … I know he loved me. He really really did …'[92]

Lorna Higgenbotham concurred that when men returned from the Second World War, the condition of their 'nerves' had a detrimental effect on their ability to be intimate and to communicate. Her husband

William served in Egypt, Borneo and New Guinea, and was away for three years. On his return from the war,

> [h]e was never cruel or anything to me or my children ... but our life was totally different ... He wouldn't go back to church with me any more. No, he didn't believe in that ... When he came home from the war if he knew anybody ... he'd be that glad to see them, he'd only be talking to them for a minute or two and he'd have to get away because of nerves ... their nerves were shot to pieces and they just couldn't talk to you. They'd love to see you and they didn't know how to express themselves ... they were thrown in amongst the people and said get on with life. That was it. And I think they just sort of took life well, as it came and tried to enjoy [what] they had left ...[93]

ADJUSTMENT TO CIVILIAN LIFE

Following the war, there was little assistance or counselling for returned soldiers and their families. While there was acknowledgement in medical journals that repatriation needed to be dealt with urgently to avoid the mistakes of medical authorities in treating soldiers of the First World War, these insights were largely confined to discussions within the medical fraternity. The veterans of the Second World War returned with disabilities and problems that were certainly recognised at the time in psychiatric journals and repatriation studies.[94] But initially there was a lack of understanding of stress and trauma, and no insistence that the grief attached to it be publicly articulated.[95] In a book published in 1945, *Psychiatric Aspects of Modern Warfare*, the Melbourne psychiatrist R.S. Ellery predicted that the individual soldier is likely to become a 'mental shipwreck' unless there is support for him in adjusting to civilian life.[96] Adjustment to marriage once again would be difficult. 'Absence, by altering the marital perspective, may cause difficulty for the married man who returns from active service', he wrote. They would have to expect some change in their relationship, and the 'wife ... may find her returned husband a far different person from the man she imagined was hers'.[97] He accurately predicted that he may become:

> morose and irritable ... nagging and harsh ... Divergence of interests may implant the seeds of mistrust. Alcoholism or in-fidelity, in the emotionally unstable, may cause a breach which good intentions are unlikely to heal. Yet in many cases, the chief obstacle to successful marital reunion is simply the inability to

bridge the gulf caused by having grown apart, both intellectually and emotionally, in the years of enforced separation.[98]

Research published in the *Medical Journal of Australia* supported Ellery's findings. In January 1945, Andrew Dibden, of the Australian Army Medical Services in Glenside, South Australia, stated that more care and attention should be given to the psychiatric problems of returned soldiers. The experience of the First World War highlighted the shortsightedness of the 'folly of the policy then adopted, that of giving the man a pension and treating him at a repatriation centre'.[99] In a study undertaken of men who had been invalided from the Middle East, Dibden concluded that 'approximately one-third of discharged servicemen with psychiatric problems require further help, even though their claim for a pension may have been refused'.[100] As Garton notes, some 'couples existed peaceably enough, some even prospered, but others created their own private hell'.[101] The tensions which arose were also reflected in popular culture, in the form of fiction and film continued throughout the post-war period.[102]

After the war, there was an emphasis on the nature and the structure of the family, and the survival of marriage. Indeed, following the war, 'the psychology sections in the armed services were wound down or shut down'.[103] Paradoxically, it was usually not the psychological condition of the returned soldier that was under scrutiny by medical professionals, nor how their wives would cope with them, nor the impact their return would have on their marriage. Rather, the emphasis was on the ways in which the gender roles had been changed during the war, through women's participation in the paid workforce. Women's heightened independence and sexualised identity was seen as cause for considerable concern.[104] Ellery expressed this alarm of gender role reversal when he asked,

> What, then, of the women in uniform? Will they who have worked in the auxiliary services, who have savoured the dignity of a uniform and tasted the independence which money and position confer, go back willingly to the washing and cooking?[105]

He predicted that the adjustment problems of the 'ex-service' woman would be severe, and the 'unsettling influence of war may unfit her either for motherhood or a career, and the pursuance of either objective may end in a neurosis'.[106] While he agreed that women would not suffer to the extent of their husbands, he warned that should 'the loss of uniform, however, mean the loss of employment, women may suffer frustrations inimical to their mental health'.[107]

Discussions about the adjustment problems of returned servicemen dominated the medical press as well as the popular media.[108] Rehabilitation was not perceived to come through a public and open expression of grief, but through strategies which concealed this condition. It was argued by C.M. McCarthy that rehabilitation was a political and social problem and that the medical profession should begin to consider the problems associated with it. The most successful means of rehabilitation was a job placement. 'Work is treatment', it was argued, and a 'close liaison must be maintained between the medical advisers and the organisations of employers and employees'. The incidence of 'post-war' neurosis increased the scope of the problem, where returned servicemen feel 'embittered, disillusioned, insecure and hostile'. He predicted that if the serviceman felt unappreciated, post-war neuroses 'will be an even greater problem than the neuroses of war'.[109] Existing equipment and facilities were inadequate and the welfare of the community would be served best 'by salvaging ex-service personnel with neurotic symptoms and reduced efficiency'. The community needed to decide whether to prioritise the obligation to 'the demobilised service man and woman over and above the duty of the individual citizen'.[110]

In terms of war neuroses, wrote Douglas Galbraith, of the Australian Army Medical Corps, the responsibility of the medical profession:

> does not end when we get the patient over the acute stage of his or her illness ... It is also part of our responsibility to provide supervision, help and counsel until the man or woman is once more restored to the privilege of full employment.[111]

The definition of successful placement is that 'the man or woman will, in spite of the disability, be competent to hold the job down by sheer ability, and not because of the sympathy of the employer or because of any governmental decree'.[112] Another commentator, H. Hastings Willis, noted that while there were promises that these matters were going to be dealt with in a different fashion, 'old mistakes have been made, the same old failures of readjustment have recurred and we have with us as big or bigger problems than we had in 1920'. Rehabilitation was not enough; the 'neurotic ... requires to be dressed up again as a civilian ... our task is to make a civilian of him again'.[113] The ex-serviceman must rehabilitate himself and in order for this to happen, the public must change its attitude towards neurotics. At present, there is 'a tendency to cultivate neurosis and to exaggerate the problem of the neurotic. Furthermore, the attitude of the press is not helpful'. The journalists 'ensure for the disgruntled an excess of publicity which satisfies their vanity, but gives them very little real help'.[114] Recent clinical studies point to the continuing impact of post-traumatic stress disorder on Second World War veterans.[115]

Despite medical discussion of the problem, many men received no help and their changed circumstances induced by the war meant that men and women had to accommodate a different sort of marriage. With this came a sense of loss. Higgenbotham remembered that 'you come and meet a strange person. It's very hard to get together again'. The birth of their son drew them together, and they 'just accepted whatever was put in front of us'.[116] The different men who arrived from war strained some relationships.

Myra Davies believed her husband, Willie, had changed through his war service in the navy, during the Second World War. 'He was never the same', she insisted, 'Never the same. I never knew … him to be violent but a few times in later years he got a bit violent and did a few stupid things when he was drunk … It was pretty damn difficult'. The navy certainly 'changed his personality from what I'd first known'.[117] Children also had to cope with their changed fathers. Her daughter:

> hardly ever saw him … He was away, for a start. And when he did come home he was always at the pub … I think with her it's an automatic shut off, remembering him being drunk and perhaps [aggressive] if he got a bit cranky.[118]

In Myra's assessment, the navy gave her husband a purpose in life, which he found extremely difficult to replace in civilian life. The navy gave him a sense of identity:

> When he came out of the navy … he was just another person and he didn't get the same recognition as he got in uniform and that was pretty hard for him to adjust [to]… because … he spent his entire life trying to sort of find who he was himself. … [he] was always looking for some reason to try and feel important and never quite found it because I think he felt unloved by his own father … he really battled all his life to try and be recognised which was rather sad really.[119]

Even those women who barely knew their husbands claimed the war had a profound effect on them. 'I didn't know him very well before he went away', confessed Barbara Potter, whose husband William served in New Guinea.

> I only went out with him for three weeks. And when he came home
> I was only going out with him for about six weeks … We just knew
> we wanted to get married … I took a very big risk, I suppose, and
> we had a wonderful marriage.

They never fought or argued, although she later in the interview admitted that he had significantly withdrawn into his garage all night and on weekends: 'I wouldn't do that all over again. I'd change that, I'd change that certainly'.[120]

The incidence of marital conflict described by these women is at odds with one of the prevailing images of marriage at this time. These representations of domestic life in the 1950s and early 1960s project a picture of family life that is different from the more familiar one of tranquillity and harmony. These testimonies suggest that family life was directly threatened by the residue of the war. These women witnessed, and lived with, and at times, internalised their husbands' trauma. They carried within themselves a constant reminder of how the public and private intersect, and how trauma is not confined to the experiences of the men who returned, but becomes a part of the lives of the women (and children) who have to endure it. The 'war' becomes the all-encompassing explanation of why men behaved differently, and why they could not change their patterns of behaviour. It is an irony that while these men had fought for freedom and democracy, they often could not admit to democracy in their domestic lives, and did not allow women freedom to express themselves. The wives of many returned soldiers had numerous opportunity to see, experience and understand the impact of war. The society they lived in, however, did not provide war widows with the 'cultural forms and occasions for remembering' nor did it allow them to articulate these experiences.[121]

CHAPTER SEVEN

'OVERLOOKED':
KOREAN AND VIETNAM
WAR WIDOWS

And yes there's war widows who haven't had a chance to tell their story too, but usually it's them holding up the vets.[1]

THE KOREAN WAR

'No other democracy' asserted the *Sydney Morning Herald* in July 1950 as Australian troops reached Korea, 'has a more direct concern in blunting the thrust of Communist aggression in Asia'.[2] The importance of the war was in no doubt. 'Another world war might break out almost any day'[3] predicted the press, but this importance of the Korean War perceived at the time was lost over the following fifty years. In 1950, so close to the Second World War, war was fresh in people's minds, and the threat to the 'free world' seemed to be real once more. American military intervention, it was reported, was necessary in order to hold 'back Russia from an eventual attempt to seize world control' as the United States faced 'the greatest risk in its history, the risk that the Communists might strike elsewhere while the nation's strength is at its lowest point as a result of the Korean war'.[4] It was Australia's responsibility to 'prepare with utmost speed to make whatever contribution the latest decision may entail' and to assume 'the degree of responsibility held by a country so situated as Australia … forced by geography to keep a watchful eye on happenings in Asia'.[5] The burden was a heavy one and time was at a premium, for every 'month lost in putting those defences in order is a month of peril. We are faced with a grave national emergency, and it can only be met by a united national effort'.[6] The Korean War was the last war in which a wholly volunteer Australian military force saw active service.[7]

As the Cold War receded, the Korean War diminished in official memory. Overshadowed by the impact of the Vietnam War and its effects, and the broader weight of significance of total war, the Korean War has not attracted the same attention as other wars.

As we have seen, the death of Charlie Green was a profound loss for his widow, Olwyn. Green's account, which was rare among war widows, conveys the anguish of a war widow's experience, and is especially unusual in its consideration of the Korean War. The lives of others were also affected by the war, but these stories have not yet been told. Jean Nelson's husband, Ron, served in the Korean War for about two years. He returned, and 'kept having blackouts'. It was 'nervous hysteria' that caused it and little could be done to assist him.[8]

Mary McLeod's life was certainly transformed by her husband's experience in the Korean War. Born in Port Pirie in 1923, she met her future husband Kenneth at an air force station at Port Pirie where he was stationed. He had joined the army in 1938, at the age of 18. They were married in 1944, twelve months after they met, and soon had two children – the first in 1944 and the second in 1945. Kenneth McLeod was a member of the permanent Royal Australian Air Force. In 1947 he served in Japan as part of the British occupation forces, and was stationed there for nearly three years.[9]

Soon afterwards, the Korean War broke out and he participated in it with great enthusiasm. In retrospect, McLeod was cynical about the troops' eagerness to be part of another war:

> They were like small schoolboys. They couldn't get there fast enough. They were really frightened that the Australian government wouldn't let them be in it. But of course what they didn't know was the horror they were going to see.

The impact of this 'minor war' on her husband, she claimed, was profound and long lasting. 'He was never the same again, though. Well, if you take a gentle man, and make him kill, he'll never be the same again.' McLeod never underestimated the impact the war had on her husband, and on their marriage. Grief for this experience could not be publicly articulated. Her husband contracted tuberculosis and this had a dramatic impact on their marriage, their children and on their lives together. Once he returned he was quarantined, 'as if he was an animal in a zoo'.

Both his mental state and physical state were affected by the war. In the way in which she retold the story, 'the war' gave his behaviour

Mary and Kenneth McLeod

and his experience coherence, and became a way of dealing with his disability. She believed that his condition, after losing part of one lung and then contracting rheumatoid arthritis, was caused by war. The psychological impact of his involvement was she believed also considerable:

> I always believed that it was caused by being forced to kill. When
> you can see the damage you've done with bombs or ... the river
> running of blood after you'd fire at people he never recovered from
> that. And so many of the men, no matter what they say, they don't
> ever recover. It's always been my opinion it's not Agent Orange
> that drives the Vietnam [veterans] off their heads, it's what they
> saw. And the gentler the person, the harder it is.[10]

Mentally, her husband had been transformed from:

> a very happy man ... into a man that was sad ... A man who was
> very easy to live with into a man that could be very difficult to live
> with or you might say he [under] went a personality change. From
> a man who was socially adept and wanted to mix with people he
> just didn't want to mix with anybody any more.

He expected much of his son, 'to act as though he was a little soldier
and salute and say yes, sir ... He changed my son's personality. From
a very happy child, he turned into a very morose man.'[11]

After he returned from the war, she found herself 'living with
somebody I hardly knew'. She had lost and began to mourn the man
she had married, as their relationship was transformed: 'I lost a happy
husband. A man with a good sense of humour.' The impact on her
family and her children was devastating. Over the subsequent years, he
had minimal contact with the children, as was the practice for those
who suffered from tuberculosis in the 1950s and 1960s. He was put
into Rankin Park hospital in Newcastle and the children were allowed
to see him intermittently:

> When he got tuberculosis he was away for three years so I had to
> cope with four children on my own ... in those days, if you got
> tuberculosis, they locked you up like you were in jail. He was not
> even allowed to touch his children.

He was in hospital for three years and she had to cope with four
children on her own:

> he lost his children as well ... His children didn't know him and he
> didn't know them and this is where the trouble came in particularly
> with the two older children ... It affected those two mentally ...
> [they] resented the fact that the two younger ones got all the
> attention because they gave him all the attention ... they never
> really gained contact with him ever again.

The private, domestic world is inescapably affected by the world of
wars and air forces and armies, irrespective of the magnitude of the

particular war. Although he attempted to find employment, 'he could never settle because his lifestyle had been taken from him when he lost his career … he loved his flying'.[12]

McLeod reared the children for many years as a single mother, and was forced to survive on her own. She encountered advances from other men which made her sexually vulnerable: 'And of course … in those days I was young attractive woman … you were a grass widow marked for … anything that thought they could get hold of you. I sent them packing very smartly, I wasn't interested.' Kenneth McLeod was forced to leave the air force but the impact of his illness continued for the rest of his life. McLeod recalled his dramatic anti-social behaviour, and she felt bound by the pressures of the day to care for and nurture her husband: 'I could not accept a social invitation ever from the time he left that hospital because if l did he wouldn't go with me. And there's a lot of people will tell you, you don't go on your own.'

Despite these difficulties, their marriage lasted forty-seven years. Like other women in this study, she pointed to the few opportunities women had available to them to enable them to leave their husbands during the post-war period. The overwhelming assumption was that marriage was for life, and leaving a marriage was shameful and un-tenable:

> it couldn't have been too bad. But then of course we grew up with the idea that you married someone you stayed married to them. We didn't throw away the baby out with the bath water, as the saying goes. Every marriage, in all relationships they always go through bad patches. And today I think it's just too easy to get away when the bad patch happens. If you keep going, you'll get through it.

The motif of the stoic survivor runs consistently through McLeod's narrative. An acceptance of the difficulties which she endured became a part of her survival strategy: 'One has got to accept what happens. You can go through life moaning and whingeing and grizzling … why should they have to put up with it'. McLeod encapsulated her gen-eration's prevailing view towards tragedy, loss and grief when she prided herself on her ability to restrain any expression of emotion:

> I was brought up by people who believed you laughed at tragedy, it was no good crying over it. I'm a woman that doesn't cry not even when [Kenneth] died … I didn't cry when my mother died. I didn't cry when my father died.

Many women use the motif of the stoic in their narratives. McLeod believed that the repression of the 'bad' memories should not be considered a problem: 'That's in the past and there's nothing that brings them back. You could learn to live with your memories. And strangely we ... do [and] suppress the nasty parts and remember only the good parts [and] why not?' Despite the length of her husband's illness,

> you remember the fun you had. You can remember some of the arguments you had. I remember if he overstepped the mark and I got very cross with him ... he used to go out and buy me a plant. So many plants out there [are] from when I got cross.

Her response to grief suggests she believed that the survival strategy of any tragic event was to endure and not to become fixated on the negative aspects of life. As a Christian, she believed misery and unhappiness were not the way to relieve one's grief. Her Christian belief allowed her to find a philosophical acceptance of her life and focus on:

> only the happy times and the funny things that happened. Don't try and dwell on tragedy. Don't alter anything. You don't alter anything by being miserable. Any dramas that happen. I believe in God. That these things are sent to try us. And I believe what Christ said ... You can't change anything by being miserable and unhappy about it. You've changed nothing. You've got to accept what's happened to you. And that's my philosophy. To accept what's happened and just put up with it and do your best ... what's the use of me whingeing about what's wrong with me? It doesn't do me a scrap of good and it's only boring to everybody else.

In McLeod's view, consistent with her generational upbringing, the need to grieve and the expression of grief are perceived as a weakness or a form of impolite behaviour.

McLeod believed she had learnt a form of self-sufficiency as an only child, so she was used to being alone and protecting herself. The theme of strength and endurance emerges in the way in which she tells her story of 'surviving' as a single mother. She went to Korea in the first few months of the war and stayed there for a period of time. 'I took it in my stride', she recalls, 'it was something you had to accept ... I was brought up to think that a man's job was important. You accepted his job and that was it'. Her growing up, too, had made her tough and resilient. Her mother, who contracted arthritis in the 1920s, was crippled from it. She admired her mother's stoic strength which allowed her to endure her physical handicap. McLeod believed she had inherited the 'tough', determined and pragmatic approach to life that her mother adopted in order to survive. She was, she believed, 'ahead of her time', a determined woman who did not allow her disability to inhibit her activities.

McLeod tells her autobiography as the story of a stoic survivor, and the 'war' offers a unified and coherent way of speaking about her husband's illness and affliction. In recalling her experience in this way, she reflects the tendency of women of her generation not to dwell on death and loss, but to endure without sentiment. Her loss is expressed in terms of what could have been, and lost opportunities, but she is also at pains to stress that she exploited the opportunities which were made available to her throughout her life. An irony in her story is that, as with other widows, while her husband attempted to survive in wartime for freedom in peace, she found herself trying to survive and find her own freedom in difficult domestic and marital circumstances. Losing the man she had once known brought grief and loss, but women like McLeod chose to deal with this by resisting despair and struggling through with what they had – an approach which was both productive and enabling.

VIETNAM VETERANS RETURN

The return of the Vietnam veteran has captured the popular imagination and, as we saw in chapter 3, it continues to be an area of contention and debate. The literature on the psychological damage to Australian returned Vietnam veterans remains surprisingly slight, especially when compared to the American material.[13] However, it is worth summarising here as some of the more recent findings will indicate the condition of many returned men when they came back into family life.

Some commentators argue that Australian soldiers were not traumatised in the same way as American personnel, although the psychological literature suggests Australian soldiers suffered from the effects of post-traumatic stress disorder like their American counterparts.[14] There is no doubt caution needs to be exercised when comparing the two experiences, because of the difference in combat exposure, and the better-integrated and more cohesive units in the Australian army.[15] While Australians were rotated as individual soldiers, which would have heightened the difficulties of their adjustment, most did return home with their own units.[16] This was in sharp contrast to the situation for the American returned soldiers, who were removed from the close and integrated community of the unit, and thus denied peer support that may have assisted with reintegration into society.[17] But there is ample evidence to suggest that Australian Vietnam veterans certainly suffered in similar ways to their American counterparts, if not to the same degree.

The Australian commitment was much smaller than the American and it was only in 1969, when Australia's military involvement was highest, that a psychiatrist was included on the staff of the Australian field hospital. In total, for only two of the ten years that Australia was involved was there a psychiatrist to assist troops.[18] In 1982, it was found that sleep disturbance, feelings of fear, and anxiety and depression, apathy and anorexia were among the most common effects reported. 'Personality disorders' were less in evidence among Australian soldiers than among their American counterparts, while diagnosis of 'anti-social personality' was registered as only 4 per cent of psychiatric casualties.[19] Those who are prone to violent behaviour, it has been argued, 'had a history of aggressive problems in childhood'.[20] In March 1990, a team of researchers, Christopher Tennant, Jeffrey H. Streimer and Helen Temperly, reported that many Australian Vietnam veterans were 'continuing to experience PTSD many years after their war experience'.[21] It was reported that regular soldiers had a higher psychiatric casualty rate than conscripts; two-thirds were regulars and one-third conscripts.[22]

In the period after the war, Vietnam veterans have continued to encounter problems and difficulties. In the Royal Commission into the Use and Effects of Chemical Agents on Australian Personnel in Vietnam (1985), the major psychological problems associated with the war were listed as PTSD, depression and alcoholism. The Commission listed other effects, such as risk-taking, suicide, violence, instability and underachievement. Other factors which were identified as severe problems among returned soldiers included lack of intimacy within families, generally feeling alienated and detached, and suffering from a lack of self-confidence. PTSD symptoms such as nightmares, guilt feelings and nervousness could not be treated in Vietnam because there were no facilities there, though in some cases the symptoms had occurred before soldiers returned. No debriefing or readjustment programmes were available for veterans on their return, which left them isolated. These symptoms were most common among soldiers who were exposed to combat, and in many cases the symptoms of PTSD were delayed. Those who suffered a delayed PTSD experienced the symptoms in a number of ways, including the occurrence of nightmares, or a feeling of detachment from the outside world. Following the war, there were few official facilities available to assist Australian soldiers.

In Australia, 'depression' was the most commonly reported psychiatric complaint among a group of 200 Victorian veterans who were surveyed in 1982. This was likely to cause marital problems, unemployment and drinking.[23] Alcohol dependence and abuse was identified as a problem for some veterans. The incidence of alcohol abuse seemed to be higher among those who served in base camps than among combat troops.[24]

Violence and other anti-social problems were evident among returned men, although it is important not to exaggerate this picture. A profile of 200 Victorian veterans was compiled by the Vietnam Veterans' Association (VAA), and it 'listed irritability as a problem in 10% and rage/violent temper in 17% of veterans'. All doctors who gave evidence to the inquiry cited 'rage' as a symptom. In hospitalised veterans, the majority had episodes of overt violent behaviour. Many of the widows reported these symptoms, even if their marital relationships were satisfactory.[25] Violent behaviour was directed towards wives and was a factor in contributing to marital problems. Veterans who were violent, however, were found to be predisposed to violence before their service in Vietnam.[26] Suicide rates among veterans were also not as high as has been assumed.[27]

Many soldiers returned to civilian life unscarred, but some had difficulty reorientating themselves to a domestic situation. The increasing resentment among Vietnam veterans that they had not been properly rewarded and recognised for their efforts, it has been argued, hindered the healing process. To deal with the increasing problem of readjustment to civilian life, the Vietnam Veterans Counselling Service was established in January 1982 and within six months had centres in every major capital city. Soon country centres were also established to provide families with support.[28] The Vietnam Veterans' Association of Australia also offers support to soldiers and their families, and became a voice for veterans. The association argued that soldiers and their families had been affected by the herbicide Agent Orange, usually in the form of abnormalities in children.[29]

A Vietnam widow's mourning

Paula Voltz's experience most powerfully challenges the view that Australian serviceman experienced traumas different from those of American soldiers. Her story illustrates how one woman coped with her widowhood and how she channelled her grief and loss into political agitation. Dealing with grief in this way was unusual in my sample of war widows, as Jessie Vasey was the only other prominent example of a war widow who become politically active.

Voltz met her future husband, Rex, in 1967, after he had been involved in a fight near the well-known Young and Jackson's Hotel in Flinders Street, Melbourne. She went to assist him and soon afterwards, they began dating. They were engaged in 1969, the same year Rex Voltz was conscripted to go to Vietnam. He was discharged in 1970 and they were married in August of the following year. This was her second marriage, as she had been first married in 1964, just as she turned 18.

Divorce was not the norm in the mid-1960s. In 1966, a year before Voltz met her second husband, the marriage figures had not abated since the 1950s. In 1966, 59.6 per cent of all females in the 20–24 age group were married; for the 30–34 group, the proportion was 93.15 per cent. Divorce remained unusual – 12 per cent of all marriages in Australia in 1970 could be expected to end in divorce.[30]

On her husband's return from Vietnam, she was not aware of any untoward behaviour, because 'I was glad to see him and he was glad to be home'. The one thing she did observe was how he missed being 'over there with his mates', which was not unusual as many soldiers also felt guilty about leaving without their friends.[31] He found the readjustment very difficult, and she made the point that many made then and have made since the war, that 'they don't get debriefed or anything for service men and women have to fit back into society ... even though Vietnam was an undeclared war, it was war zone, a combat zone'.[32] There was enormous strain in being taken from the battlefields of Vietnam, after twelve months and placed directly into civilian society which had no understanding or appreciation of the experiences. Such a dramatic transition 'left the veteran physically back home but still psychologically in Vietnam'.[33]

It has been argued that military psychiatrists attempted to minimise the psychiatric impact of warfare by limiting the tour of duty to each soldier to twelve months or so, and allowing for periods of rest and recuperation. Statistically, this was shown to be a successful strategy as the numbers of those with psychiatric problems needing medical discharge for the armed services was indeed reduced, 'to an all-time low of 1.5% [of all enlistments] compared to 23% during World War Two'.[34] In the American case, these psychiatric problems were instead concealed by narcotics, alcohol and marijuana.[35] Australian soldiers did not record the same level of drug addiction as Americans, although this cannot be said of alcohol abuse which was identified as a problem among veterans.[36] They shared with their American counterparts, however, the difficulty of adjusting to civilian life, without orientation.[37]

Rex Voltz found readjustment virtually impossible. Voltz may not have been representative of the average veteran. But even by the late 1960s, the climate was not supportive of open grieving. Voltz had become violent and aggressive in ways which were inexplicable to his wife, and to himself:

> He'd sort of have these uncontrolled rages. And he didn't know why and I didn't know why. And I didn't know there was anything wrong with him. I didn't know anything about Vietnam veterans or toxic chemicals or anything. Neither did he. I think we were just both unprepared for it … The Vietnam veterans basically looked very healthy … but it was inside the head that's where the problems were.

Voltz also saw changes in other aspects of her husband's behaviour:

> Before he went away [after he had a few drinks] … he was always very jovial very happy kind of guy. But now when he went to a pub he got really nasty if he was drinking spirits. It changed his whole personality.

He also became more violent towards her:

> The first time he hit me I turned around and said to him that had better be the first and last time but it wasn't … I think it was about nine times we broke up and went back together … I guess you keep on hoping.

Like other veterans, his nightmares, outbursts and violence became a part of wrestling with his wartime experience:[38]

> he'd have nightmares where he'd all of a sudden grab you around the neck and fighting for your life or else he would be reaching over for his rifle, which of course was not there. He had many suicide attempts …

Studies of the wives of Vietnam veterans like Voltz, show a 'pattern of secondary traumatisation, where those in contact with a trauma victim themselves experience the effects of the trauma as it is relived'.[39] Unable to witness this trauma any longer, Voltz took her son and moved 'into a unit on my own just to get a bit of space and try and see if it helped … but in his uncontrollable rage he had to find out where I was …'. Voltz was adamant that it was Vietnam that created these conditions, and he internalised a 'violence that made it very hard for him to live with and for myself to live with'.[40] He was then placed into psychiatric institutions, and a number of other hospitals, until in 1985, he committed suicide.

The legacy of this wartime experience also affected their children, both of whom suffered birth defects. These were related to the chemicals used in Vietnam, and Voltz blames her husband's violent behaviour on Vietnam. His violence 'made it very hard for him to live with and for myself to live with'. They both knew that the end would be devastating:

> He was a volcano ready to go off. At any moment, at any given time … These blokes have explosive outbursts of rage and they can't control them. Rex knew in the end and so did I what was going to happen and every time he felt like that he used to go down to the Anchorage [The Salvation Army hostel] so that the kids wouldn't see him … and that was how it was … He'd just come back the next day.

Following her husband's death, Voltz was driven by a sense of mission to improve the conditions of veterans. She channelled her grief into becoming active in the VVA and lobbying politicians. She wrote tirelessly to ministers and politicians, to the Department of Veterans' Affairs and hospital doctors, to protest about the lack of attention given to veterans and to pressure them into doing something about veterans' problems. She wrote to the Prime Minister Malcolm Fraser and others who claimed there were adequate services available for Vietnam veterans. Eventually crisis centres were established and she joined the VVA in 1978 in order to learn as much as she could about the effects of chemicals on the central nervous system. Her own anger and sense of loss were focused onto the activities of the Association:

> You could say I had a bee in my bonnet. But it was more than that. It was just that I was determined that no other veterans are going to go down like he did and no one else was going to be made to suffer like our family had and so I just decided to go in there and I worked night and day. Didn't matter what time it was. I went out crisis time. I went out. Go out to the veteran's home and their families naturally and just talk to them, trying to talk the vet down you know, just listen to them … And then you sort of make appointments and different things for him to go and see people. And also try and help his wife, girlfriend, mother whoever, understand … They always seem to have bad times late at night or early morning because that's the time overseas when … they're put on picket duty so they have trouble sleeping.[41]

She 'threw herself into it for six months' and took veterans home who had been 'told to leave by their families'. Her children suffered, as her attention was elsewhere: 'I know that working in there and going out on crisis calls meant that I was away from my kids for extended periods of time'.[42] Voltz's efforts were rewarded when she was presented with an Order of Australia for her indefatigable efforts to assist Vietnam veterans and their families. Voltz's story is a timely reminder not only of the lasting impact of the war on some veterans, but also of the dramatic impact of their behaviour on those around them. Voltz responded to this crisis through her political activism.

The outspoken and assertive way in which Vietnam veterans began to articulate their demands for recognition coincided not only with a mood of activism and change, but also with the greater acceptance of public expression and display of grief and loss.

This change in the 1970s and 1980s is apparent in the reportage of a public tragedy, like the Granville train disaster, which occurred in NSW in 1977, claiming 80 lives. The *Sydney Morning Herald* reported that psychiatrists were encouraging the relatives of those who perished to express their emotions and their grief. One psychiatrist was quoted as saying, '[t]hey must be encouraged if possible to talk out their grief, and cry about their loss – this is a crucial and natural way of overcoming their bereavement'. Another psychiatrist at the Prince of Wales Hospital asserted that 'relatives, friends and neighbours should not try to distract the mourners from their grief', and that they should 'try to get the bereaved people to talk out their grief, to weep and relive the memory of their loved ones'. Professor Beverley Raphael, a specialist in grief counselling argued that anti-depressants and drugs were not the way to cope with tragedy. 'Emotional release', she claimed, 'should be encouraged through crying and expulsion of anger and sadness'.[43] There was an open expression of grief. In a mass which was held to celebrate the dead, injured and bereaved, '[s]everal mourners wore black armbands or black ties, and many wept openly'.[44] In another church service, '"tough men", including some of the rescuers, had tears in their eyes throughout the service for those bereaved by the disaster'. Trevor King, from the Salvation Army, was quoted as saying, the 'men in the congregation seemed, on occasion, even more moved than the women. I have never seen so much feeling in my life. One really tough-looking former boxer had tears in his eyes'.[45]

Almost twenty years later, the shooting by a lone gunman at Port Arthur of thirty-five people provided the nation with another occasion to grieve openly with an unprecedented outpouring of emotion and loss. There was no reticence in the headlines which greeted the country the morning after what was described as 'the nation's worst mass killing'. The *Age* set the tone for the week of reportage that followed when it announced that 'communities across the nation were mourning their dead'.[46] There was no doubt of the need for the families of victims to release their emotions, but experts also advised the community as a whole to do so. It was reported that twenty counsellors were on hand at Port Arthur and Hobart, 'ready to deal with anyone who needs to talk about their experience'. Professor Phillip Morris, at the centre for War Related Post-Traumatic Stress Disorder, stated that it was 'important that people have access to counselling and that there is some form of debriefing for groups of people who have been traumatised'. The state government of Victoria set up a counselling service for Victorians 'caught up in the Port Arthur tragedy'.[47] In the first church service to mourn the dead, 'Tasmanians wept in the streets and Hobart's central business district grew quiet as mourners filed [into the church]'.[48] Grief bound a community together, as they shared a humanity 'with those who died and with those left alive, deeply wounded physically and psychologically'.[49]

The overt, public expression of grief was in contrast to its absence in reports of earlier disasters. The public reportage of such catastrophes as the Black Friday bushfires of January 1939 in Victoria; the Maitland floods in February 1955, the West Gate Bridge disaster in 1970, and even the tragedy of Cyclone Tracy in Christmas 1974, is devoid of the language of grief, anguish or emotional loss. The reports of these events are characterised by stories of stoic heroism, and survival against tragic circumstances.[50] They reflect what Kubler-Ross identified in her 1969 study as the taboo of death and grief in contemporary culture.[51]

The shift towards a more overt expression is evident when we consider the ways in which the anger, grief and sense of loss of the Vietnam veterans could, by the late 1980s, find public expression. This culminated in the ticker-tape parade in October 1987 in Sydney, which aimed to provide veterans with the public recognition they felt they had been denied. This event allowed them to grieve and mourn their losses openly. 'Vietnam Veterans Weep As Nation Says Thanks' read the headline of the Sydney *Sun-Herald*. Phil Holmes led the Third Cavalry Regiment in his wheelchair, the legacy of being blown up by a mine, and '[t]ears welled in his eyes behind dark glasses as he told his story' of neglect and rejection. Tim Whitelum, who lost several friends in Vietnam, 'was cheering louder than anybody else … [with] tears in his eyes'.[52] The emotionally charged procession attracted 30,000 servicemen and women and 'a crowd of more than 100,000, standing 10-deep in some places along the route'.[53] The parade to 'welcome home' veterans was, reported the *Australian* newspaper, 'also about tears'.[54] In more recent times, the media has become a means through which emotions, in particular grief, have been not only conveyed, but also commodified. The response to death of Princess Diana illustrates how, in the late twentieth century, grief has come to occupy a powerful place in the public arena.[55] The media has played a central role in collapsing the public and private spheres, with the role of the visual media in particular increasing in the daily reporting of trauma and tragedy, and so in publicising grief.[56]

Voltz's experience does not imply that all men could express themselves only through violence, nor that their wives responded in the same way. Nonetheless, the volatility of some veterans' moods affected their relationships, and many wives identified a discernible difference in their husbands' personalities.

Beryl Tuttle remembers the mood swings of her husband James, who served in both Korea and Vietnam. Like Voltz, she also met her husband at Young and Jackson's, when she was an employee at the hotel. He was a regular patron and would arrive for a drink when he was home from the army. Tuttle served in Korea, Borneo and Malaya, and then in Vietnam. The way that she recalled his erratic behaviour captures the tenuous relationships of many war widows where they were aware of the ways in which they became a target for their husband's anger:

> I used to just put up with him. Just these moods ... I used to say I was his whipping boy because he took it out on me. Not physically ... I sort of put up with it. In the whole [*sic*] he was a very good husband.[57]

Her husband's experience in Vietnam was, in her mind, a trigger for such behaviour. One of the soldiers during the war:

> got a machine gun and machine-gunned [the soldiers] all down. And my husband was never the same after that ... my husband hit the ground and there were only two out of the whole lot ... that survived ... [He] came in with a machine gun and just went berserk ... it was just on Christmas time ...[58]

The 'war' made sense of his volatile behaviour, and it justified his tempers and swings. How had Vietnam affected him? 'He was happy-go-lucky. He had a little drink. Then he got mood swings ...'. He would arrange for drinks to be 'continued after closing time and then suddenly would lock himself away and tell everyone to go. Then he would stop and ask where has everybody gone'. Another incident involved him throwing a cup of coffee and walking out after some milk had been spilt. She explained it; 'that's how he, I think, got rid of his anxieties or whatever you'd like to call them'. These actions, erratic and volatile, enabled a release of tension and anxiety, and were induced by the 'war'. Glenis Hargen explained her partner's drunkenness and his temper in terms of his experience in Vietnam. She also viewed his behaviour in terms of his personality: 'that was George' became a way of broadly 'explaining' his volatility, his depression and mood swings:

> he used to say, 'bloody Vietnam. I've never been the same since I went there. Never been the same. And I've never been the same again'. And I used to say to him, 'Get over it George, go and see somebody. Do something about it. Don't keep whingeing to me' ... They do not think that people will understand what they've gone through. But how can people understand what they've gone through if they don't know what they've gone through if you know what I mean.[59]

For other women, the relationship between the behaviour of their husbands and their experience in Vietnam was not so easily drawn. Rosie James confessed that when her husband, Robert, returned after serving,

> The trust wasn't there and he began to drink very heavily and smoked very heavily and not get on with people where he had previously. I can't necessarily attribute that to Vietnam ... interesting it changed during that period ... the changes in him did affect me. Now, whether I can attribute those to Vietnam or anything else I don't know ...[60]

She was also reluctant to blame the Vietnam War directly:

> I'd certainly say for some people ... I know there would be no doubt in my mind that the impact made a difference to those people and that it could be attributed to having been in Vietnam. But in my husband's case and in my own case I couldn't say it, because it was only a short period; [if necessary] he wasn't involved in any of those atrocities.[61]

James also confessed that her marriage had been difficult:

> We had a number of years of a really difficult time. From having a very good solid basis of a marriage in the first place and having regained that before he died, there was a period in the middle that was ... rather awful ... We actually went through a legal separation

... I guess the relationship was worth it to both of us to work on so we were fortunate enough to find some ... support groups that ... allowed us the opportunity for us to get back together again reluctantly I must admit, on my part ... We rode through [his personality changes] really extremely well, I guess, and came out on the other side better people and the relationship was even stronger.

For others, the war was remembered as 'wasted years' and the separation created strangers within a relationship. Noela Hatfield married her first husband, Robert McGregor, in 1955, and he joined the army five years later. The marriage had its 'downs' because of his absences. McGregor went to Vietnam in April 1968 and returned on 1 May 1969. He died from a massive stroke, eight years later. The physical injuries he sustained placed him in an enormous amount of pain. He came back with a:

terrible rash all over his chest. It used to nearly send him mad. He used to scratch all night. It was like scratching on a leather coat. It was terrible ... Every now and again it would go away but come back again. I don't think he ever got really clear of it, but I think that must have put a lot of strain on his blood pressure because he found out he had blood pressure three and a half years before he died and nobody knew what that rash was all about ... Nobody knew what that was all about, it was dreadful.[62]

But the man who returned was another person. 'You were just like two strangers after being separated all that time because the men are used to being with men for 13 months. That's what makes it so difficult, I think, and very tired.'[63] In addition, 'I think well that part of your married life was wasted and it's not fair on your kids'.

Not all marriages of returned men were characterised by violence, restlessness and volatility. Raftery and Schubert conclude in their study of fifty veterans returning from the war that '[t]here was often a tension between leaving the familiarity of military [life] and ... taking on their new roles', as only 'a small number of veterans appeared to have settled back into family and civilian life with no apparent difficulty'.[64] Wives who were forced to endure such instability related the story of their husband's return in different ways, but their response was to continue on and make do. Women shaped their identity through their marriages, yet these defied the expectation that they would conform to a particular suburban model of 'the family' or 'the housewife'.

In these accounts, the women choose to retell their stories as opportunities missed, and as tragedies which could have been avoided.

All of them have one motif in common: the 'battler' metaphor. In adopting the 'battler persona', their self-representation is one of survival against unbearable and insurmountable odds. By adopting this metaphor for their lives, women claim a role, and find a voice in articulating the nature of their sacrifices. The 'battler' image comes from traditions and stereotypes that have been identified within family histories. Within these narratives, it becomes a means by which some war widows conveyed their stoic endurance of hardship.

The self-identity of many of those women whose husbands were violent was that of the 'battler', and was used as a way of moving on and beyond grieving, while women who remember their marriages as less volatile construct their relationship as romantic although 'coping' is a motif for them as well. Those women for whom the army was a way of life present a different image of their men returning home and of the role of war in their lives. Their stories are informed by an acceptance of their predicament, rather than by the notion of the battler. The loss they endured was the loss of a former persona of their husbands – the man they had once known had gone – and another, who was less familiar, more restless and removed, had returned.

SOLDIERS' WIVES

As a group, the wives of soldiers have been under-researched by both feminist scholars and military historians. The wives of professional army men were different from wives whose husbands had been conscripted or had gone as volunteers. They tended to have a particular understanding of their husband's involvement, were more accepting and accommodating of their husbands' commitment. Even so, they had experiences that were specific to their status as army wives. Nevertheless, while these attitudes shaped the 'soldiers' wives' narrative, they were not critical of war. Their narrative is informed by a mourning of the man 'they once knew', who the 'war' had transformed.

Phyllis Muller's husband Keith served in the air force, in Korea and later Vietnam. As an air force wife, the pressures on Muller were often intense. Moving house became a lifestyle for these wives, and their lives were taken up with high mobility. Muller stressed that the men had no choice and it was just accepted that they would go wherever they were sent:

> They had no idea of the fact that when a man was in the air force
> if he was told to go he went ... when your husband's in the

permanent air force they've got to go, that's all there is to it and you just hope for the best.[65]

Loris Pini's husband Desmond joined the army in 1953 and in the early years of their marriage, they lived in five houses in two years. She was critical of the treatment army wives received. The expression 'army wives' was, in her opinion, a 'degrading' one: 'I felt I was an individual, not just the wife of a soldier – perhaps I was one of the early feminists. I really didn't like that expression'. The payment of soldiers' wives through the post office was symptomatic of their lowly status. Her pride was also important to her, in not wanting to publicly and openly queue for her payment: 'We were paid through the post office in those days ... the wives received a separate pension. I never received mine that way. I had mine put into a bank because I wasn't going to queue up.'[66]

Her own history had made her critical of the armed services:

> I was very anti-services [in early stages] ... in fact I wouldn't go out with him if he had come down in uniform to visit me ... What I really felt was I couldn't see the point in an Army when we weren't at war ... I have now ... I suppose in a way it was shutting out the fact that he could have been sent to war like my brothers had been so it was probably a reaction to them being away.[67]

Pini recognised that most army wives were apart from their husbands for much of the time, which meant they reared their families alone. The absences meant that 'perhaps you are not as close as two that have relied totally on each other throughout their marriage. It made me more independent.' With each new posting, the network of women gave her support. Desmond Pini remained in the army until 1974, when he was discharged, and found the transition to peacetime Australia was extraordinarily difficult. After his return from Vietnam, he was:

> a totally different man in the respect of tolerance and everything like that. For a long time he was edgy ... If I could see he was so terribly agitated ... I'd make sure the children were kept away. You learnt to protect him and them in that respect ...

The shift was dramatic and severe, and she felt a sense of loss for the former relationship:

> He never really settled after the time he came ... he was intolerant of things that would just have gone over his head before that. We weren't perhaps [as] close as we would have normally have been, but then again in a lot of ways you became protective of

him … When I went back to work you were living almost two separate lives …

Desmond Pini found employment very difficult indeed:

> He couldn't adjust to civilian life terribly well … he was under a psychiatrist by that time … because he had these panic attacks that were rather horrific for him and we realised the position he went into really didn't suit him … He was dealing with hiring and firing and the firing part didn't suit his nature at all … he then had quite a bad breakdown at that stage and had to resign from the job …[68]

The absence, in the end, had an impact and the 'battler' metaphor suggests moving beyond strains and difficulties:

> I would say in all cases, war and the fact that you are away from each other such a lot does put a great strain on the relationship but fortunately you are able to battle though it right to the end …[69]

The absences created very real difficulties when Pat Medaris' husband, Jack, was away: 'The eldest girl was born 12 months after we were married … Jack was sent away when she was eight months old'.[70] Her husband spent twenty-two and a half years in the navy. Medaris focused her energies on her children and rearing her family, despite these gaps.

Beverley Schmidt's husband Terence joined the army in 1959 and served in Vietnam. She felt that women's participation in assisting their men and the crucial role they played has been ignored. The veterans have had a lot of attention:

> but it's all for men. Nothing for us women … We don't exist. If [they] never [had] us wives they wouldn't have a damn army … we went through it back home not knowing but they should have something for us women.[71]

The support from other wives was important, because they 'understood one another, you knew what [she] was going through and whatever and you become mates'. The absence of husbands encouraged an independence, but with it came several domestic burdens as well:

> You get very, very independent … but what I didn't like was the fact that you had to be mother and father to the children … You were frightened of anything happening to the children because if anything happened to them … you're frightened that he was going

to come back and blame you ... You're a one man band ... very, very lonely, very lonely life ...[72]

Schmidt's comments reflect the difficulties and strains of the absence of a father and husband. The routine could be unsettled at any time, which was not always welcomed:

> One minute they're home and they're doing it all and all of a sudden ... you're left to do it all. And you get into a routine and a pattern and you feel, as if ... he's intruding on my turf ...[73]

Assuming the role of the head of the household, as well as rearing the children, gave many wives an independence and self-confidence, which could be undermined by the arrival of a husband.[74] The impact of the war was felt severely, and needed to be accommodated in the daily routine of domestic life: 'His body jumps a lot with nerves. He used to talk in his sleep ... the boy that got blown up on the mines that ... played tremendously on him.' Yet she enjoyed the excitement of being an army wife: 'I loved that ... I don't know why ... maybe it was just that I loved my husband ... I hated him at times but I enjoyed the life he gave me ...'.[75]

Other army wives similarly felt belittled by the treatment they received from the army. Jessie Morland recalls, with bitterness, that:

> On our day, when we married ... the men went off [and] we coped. You just go on with life and did what you could ... When the husbands joined the services the wives and family never counted. That's what they used to tell 'em ... your family don't count ... Now they go wherever they're posted ... In our days we weren't allowed to do things like that ...

The anguish of waiting and hoping they would return was alleviated by the fact that there was a community of people on the army base who would be supportive. The army community often provided women with a network of support which was of great assistance when they were experiencing difficulties and problems. Civilian wives, in contrast, had no such structural or formal support.

Another view of being an army wife is presented by Maureen Matthews, who believed that the separation the army provided was a positive thing,

> because I feel that it gives the woman time to herself and to cultivate her interests and it gives the husband time to himself and neither one sort of feels restricted ... It may not be for everybody but I felt in my case the separation was good. It didn't give us time to become sour with one another.[76]

Maureen and Robert Matthews, 3 July 1971

She too, had asserted her independence. 'I'm not really a very good army wife', she confessed, 'even though I like it on the barracks … I did participate with everything that was happening in as much that when they had a function or a dance or something like that'. When her husband returned from Vietnam, he was no longer the same man:

> I think Robert going to Vietnam put a strain on the marriage, a big strain because the person who went to Vietnam wasn't the same person who came back and you have to learn to live if you want to with a different personality and he had a different outlook on life. The person before he went to Vietnam was a very happy, bright, everything was wonderful but when he came back he was very cynical, rather depressed. I don't know why. And, as I say, a short fuse.[77]

She felt it was a disgrace that they were placed so quickly in civilian life, when they clearly were not equipped for it:

> [Robert] would probably say he was no different … from when he came home than when he went away. But I can assure you he was very different and in many ways. But I didn't dwell on them. I think anybody who has gone to war is different. Well, he had a very short fuse, very short fuse and he suddenly got … very, very short with the children. He felt that they were spoilt, that they had everything and that they didn't appreciate anything. And he got very aggressive … From being a very mild mannered sort of a chap … Robert would get enraged … he never touched them but there would be these, what I would call sessions at the table …[78]

In all of these testimonies, there is mourning for the man who will no longer return, a sentiment which was not articulated at the time. Some of this may be a romanticised nostalgia for the pre-war husband, the easy-going, casual personality that the wars killed off. But in many of these accounts, the sense of loss for the person left behind in the war zone is dramatic. Jessie Morland remembers how when her husband returned,

> [i]t was awful because you had to get used to their ways and everything like that. He used to drink a fair bit in those days. All servicemen did, like I think they used to drown their sorrows in their drink. Because I think a lot of them couldn't cope with what they used to do. He was in an engine room. His ship was torpedoed, went right through the engine room and things like that. That was in Korea.[79]

The mood swings were particularly difficult:

> You used to find their moods used to swing very badly … They never knew what was going to happen next … They used to keep it to themselves, unless he got really drunk. He used to say … really it wasn't very nice … A few of his friends committed suicide … who couldn't cope with life …[80]

Others claimed that they could not know how the war affected their husbands because they met their husbands after the war. As Jan McNeill states:

> It was hard to say because I didn't know him before and after and I only knew him after. He was a very peaceful sort of man so he probably didn't like it much … I think probably he didn't want to remember the war … really I can't say how it affected him because as I say I didn't know him before.

On reflection, she claims that the war affected the marriage in less direct ways. The illnesses her husband suffered meant that 'most of our married life he was not a hundred per cent well ... he had to take numerous tablets'. There was a strain in other more subtle ways, to do with the nature of her life:

> I suppose it affected my life in that I was told he had to have a calm life, a quiet life. How can you have a calm life bringing up a young family ... it was as calm as we could make it ... I took a lot of that on and had to make a lot of decisions and keep the calm.[81]

For others, the health and well-being of their spouses was a source of constant anxiety. Jean Davis' husband, Leonard, returned from the Second World War with malaria. Born one year apart – she in Windsor in 1922 and he in Geelong in 1923 – they were married in 1948. He joined the army at the age of 17 and had served in New Guinea. In the first few years of the marriage he 'was very sick', he 'didn't know when he was going to collapse.' But on reflection, 'at the time you just take it day by day, but when you go back over it and you think "gee anything could have happened to him"'.[82]

While most women recalled changes in their husband, others felt that the war had no impact on their marriage. Jeanette Connellan viewed her husband's experiences in a different light. Her husband served in New Guinea, and although he was 'very nervy, very nervous about everything he did', she didn't think his service had severely affected him. It:

> took two or three years out of his life, but that was probably a good part of his education; it was a good growing up process ... I don't think he had any regrets about it ... but he didn't really suffer a great indignity like the prisoners of war did.[83]

Ann Templar did not identify a radical shift in her husband. Her husband Wayne was happy for her to keep control and did not suffer the difficulties of readjustment that many conscripts endured:

> I suppose getting back to a normal life because I'd had to take charge of everything and he was quite happy for me to stay in charge ... he didn't have the problems that the conscripts had ... he went back to work. Life went on as normal; it didn't for the conscripts. They came home and they just were just left.[84]

In the memories of the wives of men who had gone to war, the men who returned were not the same men who had gone. In this experience, women suffered a grief and the loss of the men they once knew. The men they had married had gone forever. The ones who arrived anew were often changed. Wives dealt with this in a variety of ways. Some became active in politics, others perceived of themselves as 'battlers' in the way they handled the struggle in their marriage. Soldiers' wives were more likely to be accommodating of their husband's careers, although even the narrative of the 'soldier's wife' was not an uncritical one. The possibility of another life, unaffected by war, was an ideal that informed some of the memories of women whose husbands had returned from a war which left an indelible imprint.

CHAPTER EIGHT

DEATH, SOLITUDE, AND RENEWAL

> And then I began to learn what widowhood was all about and I don't think it's got much to do with whether your husband was killed in the army or not. Suddenly, an outcast.[1]

Some war widows remember the wave of relief which swept through them after the death of their husband. Gwen Robertson recalls how she felt when her husband had a heart attack in 1985, when she was 62 years of age:

> I stood beside his body on the floor ... and prayed that he was dead ... Oh god, take him, take him, we've all been through enough, all of us, we suffered enough ... I suppose I felt relief it was all over.

Given the nature of her relationship with her husband, this response is not surprising. Often, an unhappy marriage is followed by a sense of relief expressed by the widow.[2] Despite this evident alleviation, Robertson recalls how the period immediately after his death was extremely difficult for her. She went into a physical decline and was sustained by doses of Valium and Serepax. The strain was soon overcome, but it was as if the pain she endured was necessary to compensate for the guilt she felt for her husband's own hurt. She described her experience as being 'bombed out', but the overwhelming emotion was relief: 'I suppose I felt relief. It was all over', as there was 'peace at least'. Robertson began her road to recovery in 1988 through grief counselling, and she emerged from it with a powerful sense of renewal.[3]

Her memories of his death are now seen through another prism, that through which she has rebuilt her life. While traumatic at the time, she now recalls the event of death through a renewed identity. Although

164

she felt a sense of guilt about her relief, Robertson shared with many widows whose marriage became oppressive a feeling of relinquishment from the bounds of a difficult marriage.[4] With death came not only a personal release in her life, but also an analysis of her marriage, which was impossible while her husband was alive.[5] Robertson's journey points to what Di Giulio argues is the way in which relief may 'provide the widow with new insight into herself, as well as into the flows and burdens of her marriage ... relief by itself does not enable a widow to move beyond widowhood. Her identity must be rebuilt or reformulated'.[6]

In the literature on grief following the death of a spouse, it is claimed that the degree of mourning and loss depends on the nature of the widow's relationship with her husband. Some war widows were adamant that they have never been separated from their husbands; others felt that they experienced a renewed sense of themselves. As Raphael notes, the:

> more the identity of each partner relies on that bond, the roles it involves, and the sense of identity provided by the interactions with the other, the greater the loss of identity and threat to identity should a partner die.[7]

As these women came to accept the reality of death, their memories are shaped by a mixture of regret, guilt, anger and depression.[8]

The death of a spouse, it has been argued, can be 'one of the most emotionally devastating experiences that an individual can undergo, as evidenced by the fact that loss of a spouse is consistently rated as the most stressful of life events'.[9] As with the historical expression of loss and grief in general, the question of widowhood has increasingly come under scrutiny. Studies which detail the experience of widowhood and how to deal with it are now widely published.[10] This openness has come with an appreciation that grieving is legitimate, and can and should be experienced in a range of contexts.

How widows experience this loss and how they remember this period of their lives is the theme of this chapter. A paradox emerges: as time fades, and the memories of war recede, widows speak less of the significance of war in their lives. Yet, they remain attached to the identity of war widow, and continue to view themselves in these terms. Although their experience of grief may not be different to that of other widows, they do not readily relinquish their own identity as 'war widow'.

In the stories told by war widows who lost their husbands later in life, one of the major themes is their profound sense of renewal.

Their reflections on how they coped with death suggest how this particular generation of women faced life without their husbands. In now speaking openly about grief and in discussing it with the level of intimacy and depth not available to earlier generations, the second theme of this chapter is that there has been a shift during the lifetime of war widows in the ways grief has become publicly articulated in the late twentieth century. Mary Cooper, whose husband died suddenly when she was 74, believed that it was now important to tell her story of grief and loss. 'You can sit out and bawl and feel sorry for yourself', she claimed, 'but you can say to yourself, well, look, I'm left behind to tell the story and that's exactly what I'm doing'.[11]

Grief can take many routes. Rather than follow a rational, ordered progression as those who are committed to models of the 'stages' of grief believe, the stories which are narrated here suggest that grieving follows a less linear path. The pioneering 1969 work by Elisabeth Kubler-Ross,[12] who identified several stages of grieving, has since been revised. Interviews with war widows reflect what Littlewood characterises as 'wave after wave of violently contradictory emotional impulses'.[13] In the earlier phases of the grief and mourning, the lost partner is 'idealised' and the bereaved 'paints a picture of a perfect man, a perfect woman, a perfect love, a perfect relationship'.[14] Eventually, such sentiments subside, and there is a reviewing process, where the meaning of each memory is dissected and considered.[15] Support networks – which include the immediate family, and groups like the RSL and War Widows' Guild – play an important part in this process. The role of significant others in nurturing the bereaved through loss has been documented extensively.[16] The crisis, which often precipitates longer term adjustments by the widow to new roles, identities, and interactions, needs to be further understood and analysed historically.[17]

Shifts in attitudes to death and to ageing in western societies have had a significant influence on this adjustment process. Since the inter-war years, grieving practices have been dictated by the fact that 'a heavy silence has fallen over the subject of death',[18] and that contemporary society has been both ashamed and afraid of death.[19] As one commentator has noted of the American case, 'Americans have lost their intimacy with death'.[20] In the past, ritual practices have also facilitated the bereavement process, but rituals themselves can simply channel, rather than resolve tensions and anxieties. Littlewood has argued that 'the rites themselves facilitate an understanding of the ambiguity which often surrounds people who have recently been bereaved'.[21] It remains unclear how such rituals 'in themselves, could help to assuage the grief of the survivors'.[22] It is past memories, not only rituals, that need to be restructured in order for the new self to emerge.[23]

The shift towards a more open and frank expression of grief through memories is annunciated in these testimonies, as there emerges an articulation of the need to grieve. As we have seen, women who lost their husbands later in life articulate this loss with an expressiveness and openness not available to women whose husbands died during the war, or immediately afterwards. In this newer process, there has been within society, a move away from the 'pathological sheen often attributed to widowhood' to a model of growth.[24]

WIDOWS AND AGEING IN AUSTRALIA

The shifting perceptions of death are closely related to the social, cultural and historical experiences of ageing. The history of old age remains an under-researched field of research in Australia.[25] In other historical studies, the emphasis has been on the period prior to the Second World War.[26] Changing and multiple meanings of ageing and the aged need to be considered within their historical context when analysing the ways in which widows endure loss, and how society accommodates them.[27] The timing of widowhood is all-important, for it is framed by socio-economic, cultural and historical circumstances.[28] As Scadron argues,

> [w]hether widowhood occurs during a depression, during a period of economic growth, or during a time when welfare exists on a broad scale or not at all affect coping and outcome in a funda- mental way, as does the widow's past up to that point.[29]

The specific issues confronting women as they age has been the focus of several sociological studies. Lopata observes that ageism and sexism have operated to make women's transition to old age difficult.[30] Issues relating to increased poverty, discrimination in work and remarriage, increased burdens of care, and cultural stereotyping have been identi- fied as problems specific to older women.[31] As the membership of war widows' groups has aged so too have their shifting preoccupations and concerns. During the 1960s and 1970s the concerns of the War Widows' Guild and WWWMA began to be dictated by their ageing clientele.

In Australia, as in the western countries generally, the popu- lation has been ageing. Until the 1940s, the Australian age pension scheme had been little changed. Before the 1890s, care was provided by voluntary charitable relief organisations to those aged who lived in poverty. After the depression of the 1890s, when destitution among the aged increased, and relief agencies and benevolent asylums were stretched beyond their means, state intervention on behalf of the aged became an imperative. In 1908, the Commonwealth government introduced aged pension legislation for the 'deserving' poor to provide them with a minimum subsistence income, which would not 'discourage thrift or weaken individual self-reliance'. Successive governments have attempted to introduce social insurance schemes, but the most significant shifts since the 1940s have been in regard to the maximum pension income and the liberalising of the means test. The reforms introduced by the Curtin, Chifley and Menzies governments during the 1940s and 1950s included subsidised hospital care, the construction of homes for the aged and allowances for handicapped aged pensioners. During the 1960s and 1970s, nursing homes became the main form of accommodation for the aged, and subsidies were provided for them.[32] By the 1980s and 1990s, arguments about overburdening the welfare state have led to new doubts about public entitlements such as the aged pension. In the late twentieth century, according to Cole, society has 'turn[ed] its disappointments and anxieties into anger towards old age'.[33] He argues that 'the burden of an ageing population merge[s] with the fiscal and ideological crises of the welfare state' to create a strain on resources.[34]

Despite such recent trends, the war widows' pension continues to be the main source of income for war widows and a commitment to maintaining it remains. A 1994 report on compensation to veterans and to war widows, noted that the 'current value of the payments to war widows is fair and appropriate but this value should be maintained, in real terms'.[35] Apart from pensions, widows – both civilian and war widows – have had access to several welfare services.[36] Nevertheless, the campaign to improve assistance to war widows continued throughout the 1960s and 1970s as widows argued for an increase in the pension and services; concessions for travel and telephone use; and programmes for training and employment of widows.[37] This period also saw a new influx of younger war widows because of the Vietnam War, although the priorities of an older generation seem to continue to determine the agenda of the war widows' organisations.

Jean Aitken-Swan's study of widows in Sydney is one of the few studies to consider the condition of older women, and of widows in Australia. In 1962 she documented their experiences and how they coped as sole parents, and she offers several important insights into how widows have been perceived during the post-war period. One marked characteristic of widows is the way their identity sits rather uneasily within a society that feels uncomfortable about women without men. 'Society's ambivalent attitude to women without men', Aitken-Swan asserts, 'must be borne in mind when considering what it is prepared to do for widows'.[38] It was significant that her study did not take the psychology of grief among war widows as a major concern, and in not doing so she reflected the reticence researchers adopted in regard to such matters at the time. The absence of grief and emotional experiences is a general characteristic of empirical research. Historians have eschewed engaging with what Scadron describes as the 'psychological components of widowhood'. As she argues, that which 'distinguishes widowhood from many other life course experiences' can only be fully understood through an 'examination of the psychological stress of bereavement and individual coping strategies'.[39] These 'coping strategies' include the ways in which women tell their stories and the motifs and symbols they use for conveying their emotional states and expression.

The connection between history and gerontology, notes David G. Troyanky, is that both 'share an interest in the passage of time'. To consider them together is to consider historical change through the experience of ageing individuals. An examination of the narratives of widows explains the diversity of grieving and mourning. In particular, in articulating grief in these terms, these testimonies reflect a late twentieth century shift to emphasising the importance of the *need* to grieve.[40]

MEMORIES OF DEATH

When a partner is lost, suggests one psychiatrist, 'all meanings of the marriage, all its memories, will be thrown into relief'.[41] How death is understood will be related to the history of the relationship, 'past experience and present fantasies'.[42] After the death of their husbands, widows remember them and their experiences in many and varied ways. For some, there is a preoccupation with past memories and past images, often to the point of idealising the deceased.[43] This reviewing of the relationship takes place over a period of time and the shifting identities which widows experience in this process are fundamental to the grieving process.[44] These transitions are characterised by an openness and expressiveness which have recently become more common in articulating emotions of grief and mourning.

Death as a welcome relief, as expressed by Robertson, is not an unusual sentiment for war widows. The memories of Verna Phillips were similarly not that of trauma but of relief. She recalled with an openness that she felt:

> relief in one way because he'd been sick … At least he's not suffering any more. It was a relief then. When it happens it's more relief when they're been sick than it is sorrow … because he was so ill … I'm not sad about him going. I'm not really sad …

With the solitude came a sense of isolation:

> Until the funeral is over and everyone goes, all of a sudden it dawns on you, 'Oh my God, I'm on my own'. Married 34 years and have nobody to talk to. The hard part is that: you can go out in the day time and walk around, and occupy your mind, but when you go back inside. You want to tell somebody what you've seen, or you want to tell somebody what somebody said to you … and when you walk in the door there's no one to tell. That's the hard part of being on your own.

Phillips never slept again in the same bed as she had during her marriage. She was not superstitious, but in a succinct comment about the chill of absence and the coldness of death, she rationalised to herself that 'it would be too cold in there anyway'.[45]

Maureen Matthews' husband died very suddenly, when she was only 46 years of age. Initially she felt a deep sensation of guilt:

> The doctors insisted that no help could have saved him, they said, 'never feel guilty' … because you know you tend to think I wonder if I missed something should I have got the ambulance earlier, should I have done this. But looking back, no, I think everything would have still been exactly the same. But it's still a shock.

The suddenness of absence was difficult to deal with:

> The shock was that he was not coming home again. You tend to think at first … that they are going to come back … and then one day it sort of dawns on you … [that] this is the way it is … I think it's shock, the big shock because there is no lead up to it … I found [the suddenness of it] a real big shock. And I think a real big shock, too … suddenly [I didn't have him].

The response from others was not as supportive as she had hoped and she experienced an overwhelming sense of disappointment on recognising that:

people are more interested in getting on with their lives ... it's life. Nobody is really interested in you. The only person really that's interested in you is you and that's a fact. People can be supportive to a point but then after that, they've got their own life.[46]

Her response to her husband's death left her extremely vulnerable and fearful:

I feel that perhaps after Robert died I may have in a way had a slight breakdown. I don't know ... When I look back now, I think underneath I was in a lot of turmoil ... in a way being a bit petrified. Because the world is a big place.[47]

On reflection, Isobel Ford also felt there was more that she could have done, when her husband died, when she was 53 years of age. Narrating her story in philosophical terms and accepting 'things as they come' allowed her to absolve herself of too much guilt. Death:

was traumatic ... You know that this is going to happen but you don't realise how it is going to affect you ... [I went to a] bereavement course ... I had problems for a while. I started to think about all the things that I had done wrong. I don't know whether I did or not but I think this is all part of the grieving process that I really got out of my system ... I felt guilty that I probably hadn't been patient enough and I should have done this and I should have done that ... By nature I'm fairly philosophical. I accept things as they come ...[48]

In a marriage which lasted fifty years, Mary Cooper spoke of her relationship in romantic terms, and fondly recalled the times when she went out dancing and when her husband would kiss her on the dancefloor. In her case, the retrenchment of her husband was more traumatic than the war, and this was the real tragedy of his life:

That was when I saw a change in my Des ... Said he'd been sacked. Not wanted any more, it did break his heart. He started to do peculiar things. He went out in the front and started to lay a course of bricks ... He [was] in shock ... I wouldn't believe it ... [he] was never the same person ever, ever, and I used to try and get him motivated ... He looked like a broken man. That was harder than any wartime experience.[49]

The irony was that he died on the day he was finally going to put in for a pension. She never intends to remarry and, yearning in a way that is common among widows, she still feels for him physically: 'I still feel in the bed for him'.

Having lost her husband only very relatively recently, Jean Davis remembers him in a romantic way. She met her husband Leonard, she recalls, on 'one enchanted evening', across a room. 'I just knew then there could never be anybody else'. They were married in 1948 and spent 'a beautiful life together'. She considered Len as 'that beautiful special person that I chose the first time, nobody could ever take his place'. Davis relies on particular memories of her life with her husband to sustain her. These memories give her a comfort and a solace that she once had with her relationship with her husband:

> the things we have got are memories. And you could be sitting there ... and ... you may be looking at a picture and then all these beautiful memories will come flooding back ... You think you're very clever and very brave but you're not. Because all of a sudden your eyes are full of tears. But the memories are really gorgeous and that's what we thrive on ... and that's what we survive on.

Widowhood did not come easily to her. It was 'sheer terror', she recalled: 'you really have to tell yourself it's you against the world'. She also speaks of those who offered her assistance – such as Legacy and the Guild – as offering her support. At both organisations, there were a lot:

> of sisters, a lot of wonderful people who can teach you what it's all about. Their beautiful attitude and their lovely friendliness to each other ... They're like having a lot of beautiful sisters. Because that's what they are there for ... you're all in the same boat ... they teach you how to live on your own. By example they show you that it can be done. And it can be done. I'm here to tell you. I'm a different person altogether.[50]

As this study has suggested, this generation of women drew assistance from these networks rather than from grief professionals. Davis claims that: 'those Legacy people and the Guild people they show you what the meaning of strength is ... they are so wonderful ... they teach you the meaning of strength ... they teach you that it's not impossible to do that'.[51] Despite perceiving themselves as war widows, the war was not a topic of conversation for them: 'that's all behind ... that means sadness to them. The war means sadness to them, and the loss of their loved ones. And they live for the present which is all we've got left'.

A recent death makes the presence more immediate. The distinctions between war widows did not seem apparent to her. 'We are all equal', Davis claims. 'We're all on our own. We've all raised a family. We've all lost our husbands. We are equal [and] try to be sisters to each other, not anything else.'[52] Legacy and the War Widows' Guild offered support for many of these women. As Phyllis Muller, who was 65 when she was widowed in 1980, noted:

> It helped me from the point of view that I was among a lot of other ladies in exactly the same position as I was in. We are all in the same position, all on the same level ... and it's ... a happy club ... everyone gets on very well ...[53]

These new relationships replaced the old.

The positive memories were important to Lorna Higgenbotham:

> it's hard to think back and the happy days; you'd think all sadness ... he had a bit of life when he came back but ... he could have more. Every day was a special day with Bill. He was just a lovely person. That's all I can remember.

She would visualise him in the house, but she was not sad to leave it because it was sad being reminded of his illness: 'You were lonely. You visualise your life and you'd go through it and try to think of the happy days'. She 'never really enjoyed life after the war'.[54] Conversation between war widows did not centre on the war, although the understanding of themselves as 'war widows' was not jettisoned because of their common experience of widowhood:

> you don't hear many widows talking about the war ... I think they'd rather hear of the time you're living ... You don't want to bring sadness into your life all the time ... Now all we talk about is our aches and pains as we [are] growing old ... none of them talk about the war, they just talk about present day things ...[55]

There is a feeling of resentment when death occurs. 'Why did it happen, why did it happen to me?', recalled Myra Davies who was left a widow at the age of 52. 'Panic as to how you are going to cope. Sadness that the time you had wasn't better ... You get angry and sometimes bitter. You're got to pick up the pieces and start somewhere ...'. The cemetery was not the place to put all your energies: 'I've got a thing about cemeteries. It's a wasteless effort. I'd prefer to remember them as they are were ... It's too upsetting emotionally'. She recalled the songs they shared, and started 'seeing people who look like him'. Remarriage simply conjured yet another life of caring for someone. She was 'too afraid of being hurt again maybe too afraid that if they got married they'd die'. This was apparent because she had lost her father and her husband, both of whom she was very close to, and so feared intimacy again.[56]

Loris Pini, whose husband died in 1992, when she was 64, remembered her husband as a loving man:

> he was a very loving father. He idolised his children. He really loved them and even when he came back from Vietnam and there were times when he was rather angry, he was very angry at times, but love'd show through ... I supposed I remember him much as a loving man ... He brought flowers and things like that and remembered birthdays perhaps better than I ever did ...

She also remembers:

> his angry turns, too, as the children will remember them. They probably remember that I protected them a lot [and] got them out of the road. I could see he really was in a depressed state because he ... used to get into quite a bit of depression and coming out of a depression he would often be very very angry but no I think I remember him as a loving man. All he wanted to do was be loved.[57]

She found support and nurture from relatives, and from those in the War Widows' Guild and the RSL. In her memory of his death, other objects took on significance when she retold the story. The family cat remained at the centre of her story:

> He had a pet cat and do you think we could get the cat off his bed: no way he would not leave the bed ... the day he died it was on the end of the bed and it would not get off. It put up a real fight ...[58]

The memory of the dead is revived and sustained in other ways. Isobel Ford's husband, James, devised a macabre method of celebrating their anniversary:

> The year after Keith died ... he always forgot our wedding anniversary ... on the December after he died a bouquet of flowers came wishing me happy anniversary from him. He'd made arrangements with the florist. That sort of blew me a bit ... He died in the May. He made arrangements the year before and said [to the florist] look I always forget every year on the 29th, send these flowers, so they did ...

This was an unsettling experience for her as if he retained a presence after his death, as if the past could never be relinquished. Others like Beverley Schmidt were angry at her husband for dying and the anniversaries of their death ignited feelings of grief and pain. She recalls in anger, that 'I've cursed him to blazes [since he died]. We were mates ... I miss him tremendously'. She recalls that 'two to three weeks prior' to the anniversary of his death,

> I'm very teary, very down and as it actually comes to the day, I'm
> fine. And I've spoken to other widows and that's quite common ...
> You're teary, you're moody, you get irritable, cranky and whatever,
> and then all of a sudden the day arrives and you say happy birthday,
> happy anniversary, Terry. We were happy just to be home ... In all
> the times he was away I never got interested in anybody else and
> never been interested in nobody else since ... there was only one
> Terry, there could never be another.[59]

She remembered him as a 'tease' and a 'likeable, loveable man', who
was very caring, a 'rogue and a flirt'. The children 'loved him to death'.
Schmidt kept his clothes which she treasured as items with which she
could remember him by and which brought her closer to his memory.[60]

One woman who resisted sentimentality and coped by keeping
busy was Claire Dunstan whose husband died in 1985, when she was
64 years. She was not a 'weepy type of person. You just want to think
positive.' Her approach was to put aside such emotions, and she joined
the Country Women's Association (CWA) rather than the Guild, because the latter was not her 'cup of tea'. 'You don't have to be sad ...
[or just spend time] sitting around feeling miserable.'[61]

Jeanette Connellan, whose husband died in 1988 when she was
aged 71, also resisted dwelling on her husband's memory. 'I'm not
given to visiting graves ... [being a widow] not my favourite pastimes
... . It's a silly expression, "lost your husband". I know exactly where
he is. He didn't pass away, he died'. She doesn't believe in ongoing
grieving, because there is no point: 'what would you grieve for? ...
what would you want? That they come back again?' It's the memories
that are important: 'You are thankful for the years you got. You can't
say I'm going to grieve for the rest of my life ... I say thank you for the
fabulous things ...'.[62] Being a war widow was not that important to her
although she retained the label:

> I don't have the right attitude, I realise that ... We have all benefited
> in the honour and glory of being a war widow. We have benefited
> by being cared for by Vet. Affairs ... and it annoys me when people
> behave as if they are poverty-stricken ... I think we expect too
> much.[63]

These varying motifs – of relief, romance, guilt and resentment –
represent the myriad ways women responded to the grief. In the late
twentieth century, these sentiments have been articulated in ways not
available to widows of earlier generations. An acceptance of an explicit
and overt expression of these emotions signifies a historical shift over

the past two decades. Paradoxically, while the war is not often raised in these reflections, the identity of 'war widow' remains significant to this group of widows.

REMARRIAGE

The resistance to remarriage was almost universal among the group of war widows who were interviewed. Remarriage did not inspire positive thoughts for Isobel Ford. She believed she would find it difficult to relinquish the independence she had acquired since her husband's death. Ford did not want to perform the same role as she once had in her former marriage:

> now I would have been landed with that and for various reasons I thought I didn't want to be tied down to ironing shirts and cooking and being there when a man comes home. A lot of that's gone. I'm not suggesting it hasn't, but ... I was sick of it. I think I had a belly full of it ...

She was under no illusions about falling in love with somebody else: 'I'm not stupid enough to say, "well, of course, I could never fall in love" because you don't know ... I wouldn't say that because [I would be] a liar'. She was not so bound by the past that she would not allow herself to be open to other possibilities. He 'would have expected me to have got married. He wouldn't have wanted me to be on my own.' Ford continued to conduct conversations with her deceased husband and she still feels his presence, at times intimately:

> Sometimes I don't think about him for weeks and months ... then a couple of nights ago I was having a conversation with him. Then I woke up [and thought] 'how stupid, he wouldn't be like that now'. So it must still be there.[64]

Sustaining conversations with the deceased is not uncommon among war widows. This sort of connectedness is another way in which widows can deal with the absence of the deceased.[65]

Others who did not feel it appropriate to remarry felt an awkwardness about it and a sense of betrayal in remarriage. Marie Hill, who was left a widow in 1985, aged 58, had met other men, but 'you never forget ... I have gone out with other men and had a few marriage proposals, no, no, I couldn't. I suppose, I don't know, it wouldn't be the same, I don't know.'[66]

Alice Lockwood focused her energies on joining her husband rather than on forging another identity with another man. 'No, No, No.

Remarry? Never entered me head. Oh, no. I had a good mate. I couldn't do that. I never thought of it. One day time will come and I'll join him'.[67] He still remained a part of her and she could not shed that feeling. The material evidence which remained of her husband provided meaning, as well as a sense of continuity in her changing circumstances: 'My photos are all up here … It's just that I'm still part of him.'

Dorothy Hutton believed that she still felt the 'pressure' of his hand on her shoulder, after her husband died in 1985, when she was 65. Her husband was a constant companion, and friend: 'I suppose it's a loss of a mate, a loss of a husband, a loss of a friend … George was my mate, my lover …' The particular nature of their relationship, she maintained, would preclude her from remarriage:

> George was my first love and my only love. We were married for 43 and a half years … Strange to say on the 6 June … it would have been the 56th anniversary … I suppose it's uncanny really, but that's I suppose when I get fidgety … it comes around anniversaries. I just get sort of uptight, just a bit uptight and I usually just have a glass of wine or something and settle my nerves down …

Eating on her own was another reminder of her singular status, and her solitary life. But in conversation, war widows did not dwell on the past, and this was an important way of moving forward: 'we are all one of the same … to make the most of what we have got … you've got to live with it … and what you've got left …'.[68] Hutton dealt with it by travelling, joining organisations, but it's just 'something that you've got to accept … you've got to accept … I'm a great believer in fate … I think our lives are just cut out. When my time comes it just comes …'[69]

For Phyllis Muller remarriage was not really a possibility: 'Perhaps you've felt that the life you've had has been satisfying. You just don't feel you want to share intimate life again with anybody else.' However, the view of the widow can be an ambivalent one, with Phyllis claiming several times that other people would not always welcome women on their own in their homes.[70] Pearl Reiman made a similar claim, stating that after her husband died, she lost all her friends: 'they were frightened you might be after them or something'.[71] Claire Dunstan adopted a stoic, tight-lipped approach, and was not interested in remarriage because she wanted to 'do [my] own thing'.[72]

Another common theme that many women, like Barbara Potter, note is that, 'it doesn't get any easier, and the worst part is the loneliness. Still no better. Someone to talk to, love, companion. That's all you need. You don't need anything else, just someone to talk to.' She was interested in a companion, and while she had dated, she had never remarried. The status of widow is a difficult one: 'I went to an 80th birthday on Saturday night and I would have liked somebody to dance with ... Or someone to take you out to dinner occasionally.'[73]

Loris Pini similarly did not see her future in terms of remarriage. Instead, she perceived a new sense of life and freedom emerging on her own after her husband's death. She had not:

> considered [remarriage] at all ... I am [an] independent person and ... I like my independent lifestyle and I don't think I could share myself again to the degree you have to really in a marriage. You have to give and take so much and I'm not prepared to do it again. I don't think. It was lovely while it was the one you really chose in the first place, but as [you] get older I think you like to be on your own a bit.

She did not envisage a future with another partner because she would lose that part of herself which was immersed in the identity of her husband:

> I promised Jack I never would ... I don't think I'll get that [sort of marriage] again ... It's a feeling that if I remarried I've lost a part of what was always mine, always part of me. You meet your husband when you're young. You have your family when you're young. Your children grow up. That's not replaced. It would only be a makeshift companionship. It would never ever be the real thing ... Perhaps we were brought up in a different era and marriage ... it was a very binding thing ...

And she concludes by saying that:

> Well, what would I want to get married again for? I've got my family, I've got my grandchildren. I've got my home. All my memories are here. I'm never lonely ... Why do I need to complicate my life?[74]

For Jean Thomas, remarriage was not a consideration, partly because it was difficult for her to replace her husband:

> I just don't think I want anybody to take Bill's place ... You know even though we fought and carried on a bit I don't think there would be anybody to take his place in my life ... I'm certainly not looking.

This came after a lifetime of an intense marriage, when emotional expression was not encouraged. Despite the fact that they were:

both brought up tough … I know he loved me. He really really did. He wouldn't come up and say 'I love you'. Nothing like that. Because we didn't know. We didn't know that sort of talk. We were never taught to say I love you.[75]

For this generation of women, marriage was understood to be an enduring and life-long commitment that was never broken, even in death. During the 1950s and 1960s when most of them were married, women's personal fulfilment was to be attained through marriage and motherhood.[76] Widowhood, and the reluctance to marry, was a way of honouring the memory of their husbands and of upholding a respect for their marriage. These widows felt that the memory of their husbands' connection with the war imposed a particular responsibility and honour upon them though such commitment to the memory of their marriage characterised most widows of this generation.

OBJECTS OF DESIRE

Mementoes symbolised much about loss, and meanings associated with the relinquishing death are projected onto these objects. Like photographs, material objects offer a connectedness and continuity, even a sense of nostalgia with the past. Norma Jones reflected that:

When I left the house he always sat in one chair and when I said to [her daughter] 'you know when we leave this house we will be breaking off all ties with dad'. That was the hard part … that was dad's chair there and he always sat there and I could still see him sitting there. And that's what I said, we're breaking all ties now because we're moving out of the place and he's never been in this house …

Houses are central to memories of death. They figure prominently in women's recollections and are central to how women negotiated their memories of their husbands. Nancy Murrell has kept her husband's shoes on the back verandah since her husband died in 1990 when she was 60 years old. Metaphorically, it was a way of keeping him alive, and literally not allowing him to walk away. His presence is very real in the house and becomes more prominent on special occasions:

I've left his shoes where he left them on the back verandah and will not allow them to be touched. In the back of my mind he's still coming back … On special occasions he has come back … he's coming in that door. It's just a feeling … On special occasions

I know he came through that door … he was still in his pyjamas
and dressing gown … Christmases I have just woke up and I just
automatically look across and he'll say 'Merry Xmas darling' …
Just as we start to eat, it's just so vivid … they [the children] feel
it just as I do …

For others, the familial home could be a reminder of vulnerability,
and not a place of solace. Pearl Reiman remembered the fear she
experienced of her own home after her husband died in 1989, when she
was 53:

The house was the hardest thing. I couldn't stay in the house
on weekends … I had to get out on weekends … I was frightened
of the house I think. Sometimes if I came in during the day, I'd
check every room … And I'd check under the beds when no-one
could have got under a bed … Then … I'd go for another walk but
when I'd come back again I did the same thing and I did that for
a long time.[77]

She felt crazy checking where people could not hide, in cupboards and
under beds. She continues to sustain conversation with her husband
which keeps their relationship alive. 'I always talk to me husband … If
I need something or that, I still talk to me husband and say to him, "do
you think I'm all right with this" … and it seems to help me.'[78] It helps
to talk to him, she claims:

If I need to ask him something I think he'll be able to help me. He
doesn't tell me what to do. I'll say to him, 'I've invested me
money' and I got so much and I say, 'Do you think that was good?'.
Then I go to bed and I could worry about it. But next morning I
think, 'yes, I've done the right thing now'. I think he tells me you
know that I've done the right thing with the money. I talk to just the
whole room. But the lamp will go on during the day and I'll just
say to him, 'is it too dark in here for you Terry to read today? Open
the blinds'.[79]

She could never remarry because she 'had one good husband and
I don't think I could … get a second one … Terry gave me everything I wanted'.[80] Peg Pollock felt it difficult to handle her husband's
car, because 'I couldn't get rid of [it] quickly enough … he used to
take me to work every day'. She felt shunned as a war widow: 'people
stand back from you especially if they are a couple … they would take
a step back … you are not any more'.[81] She did not join any war-
related support groups because, in her view, 'war was over, forget all
about it'.

Truda Naylor avoided her home after her husband's death. Initially she thought she would not be able to confront the outside world, but in fact, she had the contrary experience of constantly wanting to leave the house:

> I went out every day, all day and … sometimes I'd get right to the gate and I couldn't come into the house. I'd walk around the block until it became ridiculous … It was the emptiness … into an empty evening … So I went out incessantly.

In contrast, Jean Thomas was not inspired to get involved in external activities, but she still found living in the house difficult.

> It was [difficult] being in the same house as the one he died in … It was hard there for a while, I wouldn't do anything. I wouldn't dust. I wouldn't vacuum the floor for a month. I just didn't want to touch anything. I didn't even want to be in the house. But I stayed. Probably that's what's helped me. If I'd gone out and around about … I might never have wanted to come back at all. But I stayed. It's sorta hard to put into words how different people feel …[82]

Jean Davis was also unsettled by remaining in the same house. She re-arranged the lounge in order to exorcise the presence of her husband. 'I took everything out of the lounge', she recalled, 'because that's where all the sadness and pain was and I changed all of it … completely changed that room where the sadness and the pain was … it was like a different room'.

Gardening was 'wonderful therapy', and she sentimentalised one particular part of it associated with her husband. His presence was symbolised by a rose:

> There's one particular rose that my daughter gave my husband for Father's Day … wild horses couldn't make me leave because that rose is there and it's his … and it blooms unbelievably … and that's his symbol I've got … that's a good reason why I didn't want to leave my house, because he is there …

The projection of grief and mourning onto material objects became a part of the grieving process for some widows. These expressions of mourning were privatised, as the domestic space is the arena where emotional attachments were initially formed and indeed continue to shape the nature of their grieving process. But in articulating these expressions of loss beyond the private, these widows were making their most intimate and emotional experiences public, and thus claiming a public legitimacy for their grief.

EXPRESSIONS OF EMOTION

After her husband's death in 1992, when she was 62 years old, Beryl Tuttle recalls how her husband remained an important part of her life and like other widows, continued to have conversations with him. This was a way of maintaining the comfort of another's ongoing presence.[83]

> I used to come in of a night time and be in all darkness and I'd think to myself and I could hear Jim saying to me, 'where the heck have you been?' Because I'd be that long away. All day ... for months and months I'd heard him say, 'where the heck have you been?'.[84]

She used to go to the cemetery and abuse him, feeling her abandonment, 'because he shouldn't have left me ... [I'd] ... really get up and really go to town on him ... swearing and everything. He had no right to leave me ...'. She can remember nothing about the funeral service, or taking off the bed sheets and her wedding ring: 'It was really trauma that day'.[85] She also recalls being told off for reading in bed, and 'I think of that all the time'. Her response has been to withdraw: 'you can shut your mind and don't worry about things ... I've always been one of those people that bury their head in the sand.'[86]

Some widows gave graphic details of the circumstances surrounding her husband's death and the mementos left by their husbands became important in their narratives. Roma Pressley talked about the heat of the night her husband died: 'It was very hot. It was May. It must have been March. It was very very hot ... he looked a bit red. It was the heat. It was very hot'.[87] On his death bed, he left her a card, which read, 'thank you for 31 happy and wonderful years and Merry Xmas'. He also left her a ring, which has never been taken off since.

Evelyn Peterson, whose husband died in 1991, aged 73, found it difficult to suddenly be alone. Reflecting the restraint and stoicism which was demanded of her generation, she admitted it was important for her to restrain the tears:

> I'm not a one for tears. It's more inside me than tears. I think that probably comes from my mother. That you don't cry about things. I think that's been drummed into me all my life. That you don't cry so the feeling is inside, not on show ... mother had always ruled us with the iron hand.[88]

After Margery Wittig's husband died in 1989, when she was 69 years, Margery claimed a difference in coping during the day and during the night:

You don't get over it. It's all right of a daytime you can cope. But once you get in that bed of a night then you lay there thinking. And I never sleep on his side of the bed. Now don't ask me why because I can't answer that question for myself, but if I find I'm over near his side of the bed, I roll back to my side so fast, it's a wonder I don't roll over ... I can't [give?] you the answer.

To move beyond grief, Wittig attempted to jettison and repress memories, but found she couldn't: 'threw out a lot of stuff when he died. Got rid of everything, everything he owned ... I didn't want memories. But you can't get rid of memories as I know ...'. It doesn't get easier, and she wouldn't want another relationship, claiming it would be difficult not to expect another man would live up to her husband, and be like him:

I don't think [it gets easier], I don't really think so. Maybe if you flighted around ... maybe yes ... But as I say ... if I was to pick up with a chap ... it wouldn't be fair to him because I'd be thinking now are you the same as the one I've lost? Now that wouldn't be fair to that man or I don't think it would. You'd be down on him ... I no more go out with anybody because I wouldn't treat them fair in my heart, that's what I think ... Because we had a helluva life with one another and I sure don't want it with another ...[89]

Jean Rayner whose husband died in 1996, when she was 58 years, found the process of being alone somewhat more confronting. Her husband died unexpectedly after an illness of about seven months. The initial period she recalls as most unsettling, and she channelled her energies into busy activity:

I came in here and I worked ... doing housework until late [at] night and then during [the] early morning. Then [I] went out into the garden, from 7 o'clock in the morning until 5 o'clock at night, for weeks on end ... I ... [couldn't settle] ... I hated being inside the house. I wanted to be outside. I used to go down to the shops and I would go in and I'd put half a dozen things in the basket and something would trigger me off and I'd just walk away and leave the basket and come home ...

It remained important for her to stay in the house, where she felt secure rather than go to the cemetery where she did not feel bonded to her husband. The house offered her a form of retreat and a fortress away from the stresses and difficulties of coping with the outside world:

The main thing is to stay in your own house until you feel you could cope away ... I'm still happier here than I am anywhere.

> I very rarely go to the cemetery because I don't feel close to him
> there. You know he's here with me … that's the way I look at it.
> He's here, he's not over at the cemetery.

She remembers it as a 'good life' and never forgets him: 'At one time
… I used to talk to him'.

The fantasy of her husband's possible return haunts Isabelle
Bradford who was 51 years of age when her husband died in 1959:
'You're always waiting at night for them to come home and they never
do. That's the hard time … you're lonely.' Remarriage was not a
possibility: 'I had opportunities but I didn't worry about it really …
[Men I met] didn't appeal to me at all … [being alone]. You got used
to it after many years … it was a very lonely life though …'.

In death, other relatives had to be considered. Rosie James recalls
how she had to deal with her mother-in-law's grief. She found it
difficult:

> dealing with her grief, and her anger which was projected my way
> … it would be the most terrible terrible thing to lose your child,
> particularly an only child but to lose your child at any age and to be
> so far away and for it to be so sudden and she has got to feel angry.
> She has to have this anger … She really wasn't angry with me, she
> was just … going through those stages you have to go through, that
> denial of guilt and anger … I had more resources than she had
> … It wasn't my son. It was my husband and that's a different
> relationship … it was really really hard dealing with her grief
> from so far away …[90]

Her loss was not as traumatic as losing a close son: 'I lost him but I
didn't lose me … Some people in relationships live perhaps through
each other and one without the other just can't function and that wasn't
the case.'[91] James refused to place her husband on a pedestal and
romanticise their relationship unlike other widows might do:

> You know what widows are like. There goes this fellow and he
> comes up on [a] pedestal somehow and … then you match all the
> others up and you say … nowhere near that … Anybody else stands
> a pretty poor chance, don't they? They'd come off second best.

James valued her independence, and this she believed would be difficult to give up, for in any relationship there have to be compromises.[92]

The particular relationship with mothers-in-law was often one
way in which some women coped with, and shared the difficulty of
losing their husbands. Sylvia Brown remembers the courage and
stoicism shown by her mother-in-law. She lost two sons, 'with dignity',

during the Second World War and her behaviour remained a role model for her:

> When I was crying for my husband one day and she said, 'Sylvia, the *Renown* has just gone down ... with a thousand men and there must be at least 500 or 700 widows from that ship'. I said, 'yes, but they're not all grieving for Johnnie Brown like I am', and she said, 'what do you think I feel?'[93]

Brown felt that her own grief was placed in some sort of perspective.

These strategies for survival were often shaped by the role women assumed as carers of ailing husbands in their later years. It is well documented that women have been, historically, the carers of the dying. Indeed, in the recent past, argues Sheila Adams, the social management of death was transferred from the private sphere of the home, to the public sphere of the hospital and funeral director. In the process, the informal care organised by women was superseded by professional, scientific training dominated by male doctors.[94] Jean Thomas recalls that she nursed her husband for fourteen months when he contracted bone cancer: 'by the time it was finished I was walking like a crab, I was so exhausted'.[95] Truda Naylor spent the last ten years of her husband's life caring for him. This could be restricting on her behaviour and her activities:

> He'd become very apprehensive. He didn't like me out of his sight ... he used to time my time away from him ... He'd say you can have an hour [to shop] ... I couldn't get done what I wanted to in an hour so I had to pelt home to reassure him and calm him down and then have another little leave to do the rest of the shopping.[96]

In caring for the ill, women bore much of the burden of this role, even when they themselves were elderly. Naylor recalls: 'Towards the last he became very nervous and frightened. Everything worried him and frightened him ... I think it was really fear of dying but he didn't express it of course and I think it must have been that.' When he died, she was glad he was out of his misery:

> I mean he was a hopeless case ... mentally anguished ... so I was glad. I've talked to another war widow since and she said she was glad. It gets to the stage where it's inevitable. All you wish is for peace, and it's [an] awful and terrible thing to say.

Initially, she was shocked and couldn't believe what had happened. The readjustments were significant and profound:

You know it's a strange thing, that I practically never slept … in a room by myself all my life because we were a big family and I slept in my room with my sister. Then I went to boarding school … then I got married … It was strange being in a room by myself … Being in the bedroom at night by myself … I still thought he was there. Even now, sometimes I'll think he's just there … Not in the house but just in the bedroom … Sometimes I wake up at two in the morning and I hear him breathing … he'll never leave me …

The different experiences of war widows are evident in these testimonies, but highlighting the differences between war widows, she believed, was a futile exercise. There was a difference, to be sure, 'but it's not worth making a difference', because…

There are swift deaths and there are slow deaths. And if you lost them overseas, it was a swift death and if you nursed them for years … that is a slow death … Some women have had twenty or thirty years or more of looking after sick men who are not themselves. Very trying and on the children. In fact I almost think they've had the worst of it … You can't draw comparisons.

How women filled the gap and processed this grief varied considerably among widows. Jessie Moreland, aged 59 in 1993 when her husband passed away, remembers how she put on weight, was driven to pills and became reliant on sleeping tablets, as a way of dealing with her grief. She travelled around Australia on her own, and through this found herself, and a new identity, returning after six and a half months a different person.[97]

Others found solace in group activities. Violet Bourke who was 71 when she was widowed in 1992, became active in a number of activities. After about sixteen months she could get involved and became president of the RSL ladies. The moment hit when she had to move on an impulse to do something:

I was sitting on the fence waiting for something to happen … I've got to go out and I've got something to do … I'm just sitting on the fence here waiting and marking time sort of thing and then all of a sudden, I felt yes, I've got to do these sorts of things so I did.

She found support in the group: 'That was a great help to me because they were all widows and they were just as badly off as I was emotionally and so I think that was the start of it … we're all widows …'. Time does not heal:

I think as it goes on it gets worse … I think it gets lonelier and things are so different … Everyone says the same and some of them have been ten and fifteen years. It gets worse … it just gets a bigger void or something that he is gone for good. It took me a long time to realise that I couldn't come to grips with that, that I would never see him again and I think that was one of the hardest things.[98]

RENEWAL

The shift to a new identity can be a liberating experience for widows, once they have moved beyond the period of grief and bereavement. Only a handful of the women we interviewed had moved through this process through remarriage. Most of them claimed that the identity of their husbands was still a part of their own and to remarry would create a shift that they were not interested in, or prepared to make. While some women suffer the displacement of having to face the future without their husbands, and can never perceive themselves as separate from them, others evolve a new identity, different from their past self. Widows, it has been argued, often feel they have lost 'not only a spouse but a part of themselves'.[99] For some women, the identity of widow becomes a new identity which allows a freedom and liberation. In the case of others, it has been a time of continuing a relationship between the past and the present, where their husbands remain with them and their memories shape their sense of identity. The interaction between the past and the present is fundamental when discussing shifts in identity. As Littlewood has argued, the 'relationship between the person bereaved and the dead person is located within a broader network of social relationships in the past, present and future'.[100]

Gwen Robertson's road to recovery was through counselling and defining a new sense of self, which others did not altogether accept. She began to remember who she was before she was married, and she relied on existential explanations. She accepted that she could learn from what she had gone through. But she believes that others found her strength and the change in herself very difficult to deal with because it suited them that she was vulnerable. It was difficult for them to accept her new identity:

> They began to see that I was changing and they couldn't accept the change; they preferred to think of me as being sick … somebody that they had to help. They couldn't accept the fact that I had got on top of it all. People are like that, especially women. So this year I have been myself.

One way in which she has moved to a stronger position has been through an involvement with clubs and societies. She is a member of a number of clubs. But in the journey towards a new sense of herself, she needed to separate from her husband. 'I'm quite happy to be me', she claimed, 'because I know who I am ... and to live the life that I'm living'.

It was through dreams and apparitions that she expressed many of her emotions, including a sense of guilt about her feelings towards her husband:

> It was in the house on the ... farm where we lived for 29 years ... and in the dream I dreamt that I had left him and I walked into the house and the house was in such a muck ... and he was just about to walk out of the house to go and get a meal ... and ... I remember feeling, 'Oh, he's got to get a meal for himself. I'm not here to cook it for him.' And I felt regret that he was having to go and find his own meal.

As we have seen in chapter 6, apparitions are a part of her healing.

Jean McNeill believed that after the death of her husband, she just kept on going, 'you had to'. The methods of dealing with grief have become excessive and point to a difference with her generation. 'That's another thing that amazes me these days. You have to have all this counselling for everything. Whatever happens you've got to go to counselling. We just got on with it.' She joined the War Widows' Guild to help other war widows: 'I was ... probably arrogant enough to think I didn't need help'. This is not to say that she didn't feel the death of her husband, because once left alone, 'Nobody seems to need you ...' A form of companionship would be great:

> I think when you get older, it would be harder to adapt to living with somebody. I have a friend and I agree with her entirely. She'd like a friend who ... would take her out when she wanted and afterwards she could hang him up in the cupboard. Next time she wanted him she could dust him off and take him out again. Yes, we can tend to become a little selfish.

For all of the difficulties associated with being alone, 'you get lonely and yes, you get tired talking to ladies only. I suppose you'd like a man's point of view ... but then on the other hand you don't have to wash their dirty socks ...'. Her memories of her husband are not concentrated on certain days, but she remembers him 'all the time'. 'Anniversaries were no worse that other days: I can't say those days are any worse than any other days.' The Guild showed how people could move forward in their life, and 'create a new life – a different life'. The first two lines of the War Widows' motto encapsulated this for McNeill: 'We all belong to each other/We all need each other'.

The distinctions between those war widows whose husbands had died in war service, who had died but not overseas, and those who returned, she thought unfair:

> if your husband died it really shouldn't matter whether he died due to war service or whether he died from being in the services … It wasn't his fault that he didn't go overseas and it certainly wasn't his fault that he didn't get hit or hurt or injured. That was just in the luck of the draw. That's an anomaly that sort of worries me a bit.

For Truda Naylor, the grief does pass, because at 94 years of age, she doesn't 'think about it much. And I don't think about him much now. I've made my own life … I don't feel any grief now. You get over it … I don't think I could conjure up any grief now.'[101] Norma Jones was cynical about remarriage and life with another man. She replied to her daughter when asked, that 'I'm 60. And I said a fella of 60, if he's got money, he wants a thirty year old. And if he hasn't got any money, I don't want him.' 'These fellas', she rather cynically responded, just get married, 'for someone to do their washin' and their cookin'. I don't want that sort of thing. I'm quite happy with my life. It wouldn't enter my head to get married again.' To think of what life would have been like if her husband had not been in the war, is to speculate about the unknown and what may have been:

> You can't say what might have been. Because you don't know what might have been. Who knows? I might have left him! If he hadn't have gone to the war. You don't know … Things weren't like that in those days. You had nowhere to go. The government didn't pay you to leave your husband … I wouldn't have done anything like that but you just can't say what you would have done or how life would have been because nobody can tell. You live your life as it is as you go along, don't you?[102]

The initial shock was difficult for Jean Thomas to cope with:

> I had the screaming heeby jeebies and I was crying. I cried every day and all night I think. Starting to come good now … I was … throwing things around and everything. You just don't know what ya gonna do until it happens to you … I just picked myself up and dusted myself down and thought, 'Well, this is stupid girl. You've just got to keep on going. You're either going to die or bring yourself out of it. One or the other.' And I love livin' too much.[103]

It took her three and a half years 'to come good'. She would stay home and cry:

> probably thinking of all rotten hard times I've had all my life and now when we're old enough to enjoy ourselves he gets up and died on me. See he's done the wrong thing again. You know life was just starting to come good for the pair of us and we were enjoying ourselves ... Things were starting to pick up and look good for us and he up and carks it. I'll never forgive him for that. And I just dropped me bundle I suppose.

The loss was dramatic and real: 'you lose something out of your life that's been there forever. It leaves a big hole'.

Paula Voltz was unusual in this study, as she channelled her energies in the Vietnam Veterans' Association and was a major force behind its organisation after her husband died in 1985 when she was 40 years old. She would go to the homes of veterans and assist the veterans' wives, girlfriends and family. This did help her, although her own children suffered and she took in veterans into her own home. You need to:

> think of the good times. The only time I even kind of spoke the bad times is when I'm doing something like this ... or if I'm [talking] to a vet who thinks he's the only one on earth who's suffering all this kind of stuff and then I'll just talk and say about what happened with us so he doesn't think that he's the only one in the world. Because I know we used to think like that way.[104]

Remarriage is not a consideration 'because I think you're lucky if you find true love once and I'd never push the issue, plus at the moment I'm very independent, I must underline that ...'.[105]

The oral testimonies in this chapter reflect the intersections between the past and the present, and a new identity shaped through grief. These stories point to the fact that there is not a break with the past for some widows and that the deceased remains a part of their lives. Many claimed that they spoke to their husbands, and that they continued to sustain an intimate bond with them. Others lived out their loss through their dreams, their connection to objects and routines which assisted them to forge their new identities, and through an attachment to, and a distance from, the loved one as they attempted to create a new sense of themselves.[106] The ways in which these women have discussed their experiences suggests a shift to a more open, articulate and expressive way of living with the past. The expression of loss and grief, and the recognised need to share these sentiments form a defining characteristic of these narratives. Significantly, these testimonies find expression at the end of the twentieth century, when sentiments of grief have become more legitimated in public, and are not to be repressed. Although 'the war' does not figure in these accounts, and the grieving process itself appears generic, these widows continue to understand themselves as 'war widows'.

CHAPTER NINE

CONCLUSION

> I very rarely show my emotions publicly ... I've always been a
> person who does what has to be done.[1]

In *The Public Emotions: From Mourning to Hope*, Graham Little
exhorts his readers to learn about the importance of 'emotional literacy,
about becoming better at recognising what's happening emotionally
both to us personally and in the public world around us'.[2] In exploring
the place of emotions in contemporary society, Little articulates two
phenomena which, I have argued, characterise the late twentieth century in relation to grieving. First, the recognition of the need to express
one's emotions, recognise our feelings, and that it is desirable to do so,
has been articulated more fully in recent times. 'Emotional literacy', he
argues, 'requires us to reverse the habit of avoiding, and voiding our
feelings ... and begin using them to enlarge our sense of who we are
and what we do'.[3] Second, the relationship between the public and
private emotions has become blurred as, in his words, the 'boundaries
of public and private affairs [have been] tested in both directions'.[4] In
this book, I have suggested that these developments have evolved
distinctively throughout the late twentieth century. Although these
mirror the public and open expression of death during the nineteenth
century, the more recent phenomena differ in that they have shed the
rituals and ceremony of the earlier period as society has become more
secularised in its cultural practices.

These historical shifts have been explored by considering the
experiences of Australian war widows, and thus juxtaposing 'lifetime
and historical time'.[5] By using oral history and examining how they

have made personal meaning through their memories, I have attempted to consider these oral testimonies not as markers of 'facts',[6] but as ways in which women have understood their identity as 'war widow' through their memories. It is a contested category, and the means by which women have come to understand themselves in these terms is varied and complex, historically contingent and occurs in relation to shifting circumstances. 'A life story', writes Peter G. Coleman, 'is the particular construction of an individual person in a particular context'.[7] The different meanings given to 'war widow' is a theme throughout this book, one which is in large part defined by the context of whether the widow's husband died during or after the war and to what extent his death was a result of the war.

During the immediate post-war period, with the memory of war fresh and alive in their minds, war widows remembered their husbands with a pride and patriotism which ironically meant they became critical of military authorities for not giving them the respect they believed they were due. They wore the label 'war widows' with honour, but it was an honour borne of loss and anguish. In articulating their grief through anger, they challenged the prevailing expectations of the day that women would be passive and that grief was to be expressed privately. Rituals and a sense of community were central in defining their own sense as 'war widows'. In attempting to highlight their loss, war widows were questioning existing mores which did not allow a space for such expressions of grief. This denial would continue throughout the 1950s and 1960s.

Since then, women have remembered the wars in a greater variety of ways. One striking characteristic of these narratives has been the ways in which women have internalised their husbands' own feelings of neglect. In doing so, they have highlighted the ways in which their own contribution to war – through forbearance or absence and emotional support of their men – has been left unacknowledged. In conflating their own sense of neglect with that of their husbands, widows carried a lack of recogntion for both husband and wife.

The memories of those women who lost their husbands in battle are imbued with particular images of nostalgia, lost opportunities, hopes left unrealised and a disavowal of grief, of a longing of a world devoid of loss. In sustaining a hope of their husband's return, they often retained a romantic memory of their deceased husbands and of perfection which could not be matched by any other. The paradox is that in remaining loyal to the memory of their deceased husbands, they have negated the possibility of creating new opportunities or forging new relationships.

For many widows, it is the 'battler' metaphor that is used as an empowering and strengthening motif in telling their life stories. Those widows whose husbands died during the war drew on it to convey the difficulties of being a single mother in a less than sympathetic climate. For others whose husbands did return, it becomes a mechanism for coping with and articulating the psychological burdens they endured. In both cases, describing oneself in terms of a 'battler' also has the effect of conveying the need to move on and beyond grief. For this generation of women, to be a 'battler' is to endure, but not to dwell on the loss, nor on the expression of grief, which is often seen as a form of 'weakness'. The loss expressed by these widows is the loss of the easy-going, casual men they believed they had known, taken from them – through death or personality change – by war.

A lack of expression of loss was compounded by the silence which greeted the wives of the men who returned. Men were not expected to openly grieve their losses. Their wives were encouraged to be complicit in this silence, by accepting it as a fact of the war experience, and by keeping silent about their own anguish. These silences have been punctuated in recent times through memoirs and autobiographies, which suggests a shift to a more public openness and discussion as well as acknowledgement of the trauma and impact of war.

How war widows remembered and dealt with this trauma in their stories is suggestive. Those women who spoke about domestic violence and living with the stresses of men who returned affected by war, did so in terms of 'war' as a coherent explanatory category that gave meaning to their husband's behaviour. In documenting these sentiments in their testimonies, there remains a need for 'trauma' to be more broadly defined, and for it to incorporate the experiences of women that have remained 'secret'. Internalising their husband's own guilt and aggres-siveness is one way in which women were affected by living their domestic lives with returned men.

The most compelling oral history not only tells us about the ways in which people remember their experiences, but also can offer new interpretations of historical accounts. The underlying theme of this collection of memories is how these stories can confront us in the ways in which the experience of war and trauma can be revised and written. The residue of war is one of the key themes throughout the book. War widows challenge the sharp dichotomies that are drawn between the war and post-war period, and highlight the ways in which women who lived with returned men experienced and internalised a form of trauma themselves. This process of internalising trauma and feeling guilt is a powerful motif in these narratives. In this way, the shadows of war remain psychologically embedded and played out in post-war Australia. These accounts challenge the representations of the 1950s and 1960s as a tranquil and harmonious period, with the rise of suburbia offering a quiet retreat. Marital discord is a dominant theme in these testimonies, and women make sense of it through the coherent and all-encompassing term, 'the war'. The story was very different for women who lost their husbands at the time of war. For these women, their memories are filled with a sense of missed opportunities, of nostalgia and regret.

Another example of internalising is that of wartime rhetoric about war. Many of the women remember the anguish associated with Vietnam and absorb the negative associations with that war. In the case of the Korean War, the question of forgetting becomes a source of anger and resentment. These issues pose problems regarding definitions of 'trauma' and how what arises in the private sphere has so often been denied that status of 'trauma' in wartime narratives. As a part of this, the loss endured by war widows of the 'men they once knew' is also a common motif.

These issues need further consideration, and a growing literature among psychologists and other health workers addresses the residue of war for the families who endured its impact after the Second World War. The children of fathers who went to war is another area where recent and fruitful research is being undertaken, as is the experience in general of children of war.[8] The residue of wartime experience remains a significant gap in Australian history, especially in relation to the impact war has on the waves of immigrants who settled in Australia after the war.[9]

All memories reflect on the present. As Donna Merwick notes, it:

> is not really the case that memory is short or long or kept alive or dead. The act of remembering, like the act of forgetting is a maneuver. A family, community or nation answers a present need by endowing some event or person of the past with significance.[10]

This study shows how the significance war widows placed on these memories reflects their present negotiation with the past – whether it be the negotiation of nostalgia, regret, renewal or as survivors and witnesses of trauma. In offering a coherent narrative along these lines, war widows created comfort and solace – once attained in their relationship – which both sustained a continuity with the past, and accommodated the change of the future.[11] In doing so, this study continues the broader project of insisting that grief and loss have a history, defined by circumstances of time and place. In recognising that these are historical categories of analysis, an examination of these testimonies has sought to widen this understanding and recognise that emotional life is an important, and ever changing, part of our social and cultural history.

Notes

CHAPTER 1: INTRODUCTION

1 Interview with Pat Medaris, 3 March 1998.
2 Alessandro Portelli, *The Battle of Valle Giulia: Oral History and the Art of Dialogue*, Wisconsin, University of Wisconsin, 1997, p. 5.
3 Peter G. Coleman, 'Ageing and Life History: The Meaning of Reminiscence in Late Life', in Shirley Dex (ed.), *Life and Work History Analyses: Qualitative and Quantitative Developments*, Routledge, London, 1991, p. 121.
4 Luisa Passerini, *Fascism in Popular Memory: The Cultural Experience of the Turin Working Class*, Cambridge, Cambridge University Press, 1987, p. 8.
5 See Joan Sangster, 'Telling Our Stories: Feminist Debates and the Use of Oral History', *Women's History Review*, vol. 3, no. 1, 1994, pp. 5–28.
6 Selma Leydesdroff, 'Gender and the Categories of Experienced History', in Dex (ed.), *Life and Work History Analyses*, pp. 180–1.
7 Luisa Passerini, 'Women's Personal Narratives: Myths, Experiences and Emotions', in Personal Narratives Group (eds), *Interpreting Women's Lives: Feminist Theory and Personal Narratives*, Bloomington, Indiana University Press, 1989, p. 194.
8 Alessandro Portelli, 'The Death of Luigi Trastulli: Memory and the Event', in Alessandro Portelli, *The Death of Luigi Trastulli and Other Stories: Form and Meaning in Oral History*, Albany, State University of New York, 1991, p. 26.
9 Alessandro Portelli, 'The Peculiarities of Oral History', *History Workshop Journal*, no. 12, Autumn, 1981, p. 99.
10 Alessandro Portelli, 'Time of My Life: Functions of Time in Oral History', in Portelli, *The Death of Luigi Trastulli*, p. 61.
11 Portelli, *The Battle of Valle Giulia*, p. 4.
12 Graham Greene, *A Sort of Life*, London, Bodley Head, 1971, p. 31.

13 Emily Hong, 'Getting to the Source: Striking Lives Oral History and the Politics of Memory', *Journal of Women's History*, vol. 9, no. 1, 1997, p. 140. See also Susan Geiger, 'What's So Feminist About Doing Women's Oral History?', in Cheryl Johnson-Odim and Margaret Strobel (eds), *Expanding the Boundaries of Women's History*, Bloomington, Indiana University Press, 1992, pp. 305–18; Kristina Minister, 'A Feminist Frame for the Oral History Interview', in Sherna Gluck and Daphne Patai (eds), *Women's Words: The Feminist Practice of Oral History*, New York, Routledge, 1991, pp. 27–41.

14 Quoted in Adam Phillips, *On Flirtation*, London, Faber and Faber, 1994, p. 73.

15 Kathryn Anderson and Dana C. Jack, 'Learning to Listen: Interview Techniques and Analyses', in Gluck and Patai (eds), *Women's Words*, p. 11.

16 Joan Wallach-Scott, 'Introduction', in Luisa Passerini, *Autobiography of a Generation: Italy 1968*, translated by Lisa Endberg, Connecticut, Wesleyan University Press, 1996, p. xii.

17 Paul Antze and Michael Lambek, 'Introduction: Forecasting Memory', in Paul Antze and Michael Lambek (eds), *Tense Past: Cultural Essays in Trauma and Memory*, London, Routledge, 1996, pp. xi–xxxviii.

18 Adam Phillips, 'Freud and the Uses of Forgetting', *On Flirtation*, p. 22.

19 Wallach-Scott, 'Introduction', in Passerini, *Autobiography of a Generation: Italy, 1968*, p. xii.

20 Karl Figlio, 'Oral History and the Unconscious', *History Workshop Journal*, no. 26, Autumn, 1988, p. 128.

21 I wish to thank Stuart Macintyre for generously offering his important insights regarding this argument.

22 See Jonathan Dollimore, *Death, Desire and Loss in Western Culture*, London, Allen Lane, 1998, pp. 119–27.

23 Philippe Airès, *The Hour of Our Death*, translated by Helen Weaver, New York, Alfred A. Knopf, 1981, p. 580.

24 ibid., p. 578.

25 ibid., p. 613.

26 Dollimore, *Death, Desire and Loss*, p. 122.

27 See 'Old Age and Death', in Graeme Davison, J.W. McCarty and Ailsa Leary (eds), *Australians 1888*, Sydney, Fairfax, Syme and Weldon, 1987, pp. 323–41.

28 Mark Seltzer, 'Wound Culture: Trauma in the Pathological Public Sphere', *October* 80, Spring 1997, pp. 3–26.

29 Hilary M. Carey, *Believing in Australia: A Cultural History of Religions*, Sydney, Allen & Unwin, 1996, pp. 172–77.

30 See Pat Jalland, *Death in the Victorian Family*, Oxford, Oxford University Press, 1997.

31 Several studies have attempted to address this, most notably, Nicole Ann Dombrowski (ed.), *Women and War in the Twentieth Century: Enlisted With and Without Consent*, New York, Garland Publishing, 1999.

32 John R. Gillis (ed.), *Commemorations: The Politics of National Identity*, New Jersey, Princeton University Press, 1994, p. 20.

33 There is a vast medical and psychological literature on the effects of wars
   on the families and children of returned men. Some of the most useful for
   this study include Zahava Soloman et al., 'From Front Line to Home Front:
   A Study of Secondary Traumatization', *Family Process*, 31, September
   1992, pp. 289–302; Malcolm Kidson, John C. Douglas and Brendan J.
   Holwill, 'Post-Traumatic Stress Disorder in Australian World War II
   Veterans Attending a Psychiatric Outpatient Clinic', *Medical Journal of
   Australia*, vol. 158, April 1993, pp. 563–66; Laurie Leydic Harkness,
   'Transgenerational Transmission of War-Related Trauma' in John P.
   Wilson and Beverley Raphael (eds), *International Handbook of Traumatic
   Stress Syndrome*, New York, Plenum Press, 1993, pp. 635–43.
34 See Stephen Garton, *The Cost of War: Australians Return*, Melbourne,
   Oxford University Press, 1996; Judith Allen, *Sex and Secrets: Crimes
   Involving Women Since 1880*, Melbourne, Oxford University Press, 1990;
   Joan Beaumont, 'Gull Force Comes Home: The Aftermath of Captivity',
   Journal of the Australian War Memorial, no. 14, April 1989, pp. 43–52;
   Hamilton I. McCubbin, Edna J. Hunter and Barbara B. Dahl, 'Residuals of
   War: Families of Prisoners of War and Servicemen Missing in Action',
   Journal of Social Issues, vol. 31, no. 4, 1975, pp. 95–109.
35 John Murphy, *Imagining the Fifties: Private Sentiment and Political
   Culture in Menzies' Australia*, Sydney, University of New South Wales
   Press, 2000, p. 8.
36 For the use of oral testimonies, see Peter Read, *Returning to Nothing:
   The Meaning of Lost Places*, Cambridge, Cambridge University Press,
   1996; Paula Hamilton, 'Memory Remains: Ferry Disaster, Sydney, 1938',
   History Workshop Journal, issue 47, Spring 1999, pp. 193–210; Lucy
   Taska 'The Masked Disease: Oral History, Memory and the Influenza
   Pandemic, 1918–1919' and Glenda Sluga, 'Bonegilla and Migrant
   Dreaming', in Kate Darian-Smith and Paula Hamilton (eds), *Memory and
   History in the Twentieth Century*, Melbourne, Oxford University Press,
   1994, pp. 77–91; 195–209; John Murphy, 'The Voice of Memory: History,
   Autobiography and Oral Memory', *Historical Studies*, vol. 22, no. 87,
   1986, pp. 157–75; Alistair Thomson, 'Anzac Memories: Putting Popular
   Memory Theory into Practice in Australia', *Oral History*, vol. 18, no. 1,
   1994, pp. 25–31; Chris Healy, 'Meatworkers' Memories: The Mnemonics
   of the Nose', in Donna Merwick (ed.), *Dangerous Liaisons: Essays in
   Honour of Greg Dening*, Parkville, University of Melbourne, 1994; Janet
   McCalman, *Journeyings: The Biography of A Middle-Class Generation*,
   Melbourne, Melbourne University Press, 1993; Greg Langley (ed.), *A
   Decade of Dissent: Vietnam and the Conflict on the Australian Homefront*,
   Sydney, Allen & Unwin, 1992; Libby Connors et al. (eds), *Australia's
   Frontline: Remembering the 1939–1945 War*, St Lucia, Queensland
   University Press, 1992; Shurlee Swain with Renata Howe, *Single Mothers
   and Their Children: Disposal, Punishment and Survival in Australia*,
   Cambridge, Cambridge University Press, 1995.
37 Betty Peters, 'The Life Experiences of Partners of Ex-POWs of the
   Japanese', *Journal of the Australian War Memorial*, issue 28, April 1996,
   pp. 1–11, and John Raftery and Sandra Schubert, *A Very Changed Man:*

Families of World War Two Veterans Fifty Years After War, Adelaide, School of Human Resource Studies, University of South Australia, n.d.; Sandy Gilman, '"Widowhood Remembered" – An Analysis of the Oral Testimony of War Widows as An Illustration of the Human Consequences of the Second World War', BA Honours Thesis, Department of History, University of Melbourne, 1989.

38 Alistair Thomson, *Anzac Memories: Living With the Legend*, Melbourne, Oxford University Press, 1994.

39 John Barrett, *We Were There: Australian Soldiers of World War II Tell Their Stories*, Melbourne, Viking, 1987.

40 Kate-Darian Smith, 'Remembering Romance: Memory, Romance and World War Two', in Joy Damousi and Marilyn Lake (eds), *Gender and War: Australians at War*, Cambridge, Cambridge University Press, 1995, pp. 117–29.

41 See Penny Summerfield, *Reconstructing Women's Wartime Lives: Discourse and Subjectivity in Oral Histories of the Second World War*, Manchester, Manchester University Press, 1998.

42 Heather Goodall, 'Telling Country: Memory, Modernity and Narratives in Rural Australia', *History Workshop Journal*, issue 47, Spring 1999, p. 187.

43 See Peter Read, *A Rape of the Soul So Profound: The Return of the Stolen Generations*, Sydney, Allen & Unwin, 1999; Peter Read and Coral Edwards, *The Lost Children*, Sydney, Doubleday, 1989; Stuart Rintoul, *The Wailing: A National Black Oral History*, Melbourne, Heinemann, 1993; A. Jackomos and D. Fowell, *Living Aboriginal History: Stories in the Oral Tradition*, Cambridge, Cambridge University Press, 1991; Heather Goodall, 'Colonialism and Catastrophe: Contested Memories of Nuclear Testing and Measles Epidemics in Eenabella', in Darian-Smith and Hamilton (eds), *Memory and History*, pp. 55–76; Deborah Bird Rose, 'Remembrance', *Aboriginal History*, vol. 13, no. 2, 1989, pp. 135–148; Bain Attwood, A Life Together, *A Life Apart: A History of Relations Between Europeans and Aborigines*, Melbourne, Melbourne University Press, 1994.

44 This area of study is now substantial. See Dominick La Capra, *History and Memory After Auschwitz*, Ithaca, Cornell University Press, 1998; Lawrence Langer, *Holocaust Testimonies: The Ruins of Memory*, New Haven, Yale University Press, 1991; Dominick La Capra, *Representing the Holocaust: History, Theory, Trauma*, Ithaca, Cornell University Press, 1994; Geoffrey H. Hartman (ed.), *Holocaust Remembrance: The Shapes of Memory*, Oxford, Blackwell, 1994; Eric L. Santner, *Stranded Objects: Mourning, Memory and Film in Postwar Germany*, Ithaca, University Press, 1990; Saul Friedlander, *Memory, History and the Extermination of the Jews in Europe*, Bloomington, Indiana University Press, 1993; Saul Friedlander, *Probing the Limits of Representation: Nazism and the Final Solution*, Cambridge, Harvard University Press, 1992; Andrea Liss, *Trespassing Through Shadows: Photography, Memory and the Holocaust*, Minneapolis, University of Minnesota Press, 1998; Barbie Zelizer, *Remembering to Forget: Holocaust Memory through the Camera's Eye*, Chicago, University of Chicago Press, 1998; Efraim Sicher (ed.), *Breaking

Crystal: Writing and Memory After Auschwitz, Chicago, University of Illinois Press, 1998.

CHAPTER 2: WAR WIDOWS REMEMBER

1 Interview with Jean Davis, 3 April 1998.
2 War Widows' Guild, Circular no. 28, 1954–1955, Melbourne Branch.
3 ibid.
4 ibid.
5 ibid.
6 ibid.
7 Ken Inglis, *Sacred Places: War Memorials in the Australian Landscape*, Melbourne, Miegunyah Press, 1998, p. 362.
8 ibid., p. 241.
9 ibid., pp. 239–41.
10 War Widows' Guild Circular, 29 April 1954.
11 War Widows' Guild, Minutes, 28 April 1955, Tasmanian Branch.
12 ibid., 28 April 1957.
13 ibid., 29 May 1958.
14 *Remembrance*: Newsletter of the Widows' and Widowed Mothers' Association of Victoria (hereafter, *Remembrance*), November 1953.
15 Inglis, p. 375.
16 ibid., p.207.
17 *Argus*, 8 November 1954, p. 9.
18 Adrian Gregory, *The Silence of Memory: Armistice Day 1919–1946*, Oxford, Berg Publishers, 1994, p. 128.
19 ibid., p. 215.
20 War Widows' Guild, Circular no. 30, c. 1954–1955, Melbourne Branch.
21 ibid.
22 War Widows' Guild, Circular no. 31, c. 1954–1955, Melbourne Branch.
23 'Widows Assailed on Dedication Stand: Anzac "Boycott" Echo', War Widows' Scrapbook, NSW Branch, n.d.
24 ibid.
25 'They'll Be at the Shrine', War Widows' Scrapbook, NSW Branch, 22 March 1955.
26 *Remembrance*, March 1954.
27 ibid.
28 ibid.
29 See Joy Damousi, *The Labour of Loss: Mourning, Memory and Wartime Bereavement*, Cambridge, Cambridge University Press, 1999, pp. 26–45.
30 *Remembrance*, April 1954.
31 ibid.
32 *Herald*, 2 October 1945.
33 *Argus*, 22 March 1955.
34 ibid.
35 *Argus*, 23 March 1955.
36 Patricia Grimshaw, Marilyn Lake, Ann McGrath and Marian Quartly, *Creating A Nation: 1788–1990*, Melbourne, McPhee/Gribble, 1994, p. 273.

37 John Murphy, *Imagining the Fifties: Private Sentiment and Political Culture in Menzies' Australia*, Sydney, University of New South Wales Press, 2000, p.48.
38 *Herald*, 31 July 1947.
39 ibid.
40 T. Howard Crago, *When We Are Bereaved*, Melbourne, Clifford Press, 195–?, p. 5.
41 Granger E. Westberg, *Good Grief: A Constructive Approach to the Problem of Loss*, Church Education Press, Melbourne, 1966, p. 28.
42 Circular no. 3, May 1946.
43 ibid.
44 War Widows' Guild, Annual Report 1950–51, Melbourne Branch.
45 ibid.
46 ibid.
47 ibid.
48 Letter from Vasey, 'Protest from War Widows', n.d., War Widows' Scrapbook, NSW Branch.
49 ibid.
50 War Widows' Guild, Annual Report 1953–54, Melbourne Branch.
51 ibid.
52 ibid.
53 Bertam J,. Cohler, 'Aging, Morale and Meaning: The Nexus of Narrative', in Thomas R. Cole, W. Andrew Achenbaum, Patricia L. Jakobi and Robert Kastenbaum (eds), *Voices and Visions of Aging: Toward A Critical Gerontology*, New York, Springer Publishing Company, 1993, p. 108.
54 War Widows' Guild, Circular no. 31, c. 1954–1955, Melbourne Branch.
55 Stephen Garton, *Out of Luck: Poor Australians and Social Welfare: 1788–1988*, Sydney, Allen & Unwin, 1990, pp. 144–5.
56 Nico H. Frijida, 'Commemorating', in James W. Pennebaker, Dario Paez and Bernard Rime (eds), *Collective Memory in Political Events: Social Psychological Perspectives*, New Jersey, Lawrence Erlbaum, 1997, p. 109.
57 ibid, p. 119.
58 ibid., pp. 119–20.
59 Paul Connerton, *How Societies Remember*, Cambridge, Cambridge University Press, p. 45.
60 ibid., pp. 120–3.
61 John R. Gillis, 'Memory and Identity: The History of a Relationship', in John R. Gillis (ed.), *Commemorations: The Politics of National Identity*, Princeton, Princeton University Press, 1994, pp. 3–5.
62 Guglielmo Belleli and Mirella A. C. Amatulli, 'Nostalgia, Immigration and Collective Memory', in Pennebaker, Paez and Rime (eds), *Collective Memory of Political Events*, p. 217.
63 Donna Bassin, 'Maternal Subjectivity in the Culture of Nostalgia: Mourning and Memory', in Donna Bassin, Margaret Honey and Meryle Mahrer Kaplan (eds), *Representations of Motherhood*, New Haven, Yale University Press, 1994, p. 168.
64 Mavis Thorpe Clark, *No Mean Destiny: The Story of the War Widows' Guild of Australia, 1945–1985*, Melbourne, Hyland House, 1986.

65 Stephen Garton, 'Changing Minds', in Ann Curthoys, Tim Rowse and A.W. Martin (eds.), *Australians From 1939*, Sydney, Fairfax, Syme and Weldon, 1987, p. 349.

66 *Sun*, 1 October 1947, in War Widows' Scrapbook, NSW Branch.

67 Mary Smith, 'War Widows: The Forgotten Victims of War', *Journal of the Australian War Memorial*, no. 5, October 1984, p. 10.

68 War Widows' Craft Guild, Circular no. 8, February 1948, Melbourne Branch.

69 ibid.

70 War Widows' Guild, Circular, August 1948.

71 *Sydney Morning Herald*, 14 June 1956, Women's Section, p. 7.

72 See Jean Aitken-Swan, *Widows in Australia: A Survey*, Sydney, Council of Social Service of New South Wales, 1962.

73 Jill Roe, 'Chivalry and Social Policy in the Antipodes', *Historical Studies*, vol. 22, no. 88, April 1987, pp. 398–409.

74 Lorraine Wheeler, 'War, Women and Welfare', in Richard Kennedy (ed.), *Australian Welfare: Historical Sociology*, Melbourne, Macmillan, 1989, p. 187.

75 ibid.

76 ibid.

77 Commonwealth of Australia, *Parliamentary Debates* (Hansard), Session 1946–47. First Session of the Eighteenth Parliament (Second Period), vol. 190, p. 2980.

78 ibid.

79 ibid.

80 ibid.

81 ibid., p. 2911.

82 ibid., p. 520.

83 Quoted in Jill Roe, 'The End is Where We Start From: Women and Welfare Since 1901', in Cora Baldock and Bettina Cass (eds), *Women, Social Welfare and the State*, Sydney, Allen & Unwin, 1983, p. 12.

84 ibid., p. 11.

85 ibid., p. 12.

86 ibid., p. 12.

87 Minutes of the Second Committee meeting War Widows' Craft Guild 9 August 1946.

88 War Widows' Guild, Circular, August 1949, Melbourne Branch.

89 Interview with Marjory Miller, 2 April 1997.

90 War Widows' Guild, Circular no. 11, November 1948, Melbourne Branch.

91 ibid.

92 War Widows' Guild, Circular no. 13, August 1949, Melbourne Branch.

93 ibid.

94 ibid.

95 *Sydney Morning Herald*, 17 May 1951, p. 12.

96 *Sydney Morning Herald*, 10 June 1954, p. 3.

97 War Widows' Guild, Circular no. 13, August 1949.

98 Smith, 'War Widows', p. 14.

99 War Widows' Guild, Minutes of the First Annual meeting of the War Widows' Craft Guild in NSW, 30 September 1947.

100 War Widows' Scrapbook, 9 July 1947, n.d., 'Widows Demand the Basic Wage', NSW War Widows' Guild Branch.

101 'Australia's War Widows Must Not Be Forgotten, Says Guild President', in *The Farmer and Settler*, 3 October 1947, in War Widows' Scrapbook.

102 War Widows' Guild, Minutes at the Second Annual Meeting, 18 May 1949, Minute book, 17 December 1947 – 31 March 1956, NSW Branch.

103 War Widows' Guild, Minutes, Executive Committee, 16 May 1951, NSW Branch.

104 War Widows' Guild, Minutes, Executive Committee, 21 May 1952, NSW Branch.

105 Jessie Vasey to Mrs Graham, October 1945.

106 *Herald*, 2 July 1947, p. 3.

107 *Herald*, 22 September 1947.

108 War Widows' Guild, Circular, no. 24, n.d.

109 *Sydney Morning Herald*, 14 June 1956, Women's Section, p. 7.

110 *Sydney Morning Herald*, 31 August 1945, p. 6.

111 War Widows' Guild, Minutes of the Third Annual Meeting of the Council, 31 May 1950, NSW Branch.

112 War Widows' Guild, Minutes of Executive Committee, Entries for 15 November 1950, NSW Branch.

113 Garton, *Out of Luck*, p. 137.

114 ibid., p. 139.

115 War Widows' Guild, Minute Book of Annual Council and Executive Committee Meetings, 24 January 1957 – 11 December 1958, Entry for 17 October 1957, NSW Branch.

116 Minutes of the 13th Annual Public Meeting, 15 June 1960, NSW Branch.

117 War Widows' Guild, Circular no. 13, 13 August 1949, Melbourne Branch, War Widows' Guild.

118 Mark Lyons, *Legacy: The First Fifty Years*, Melbourne, Lothian, 1978, p. 154.

119 *Remembrance*, February 1954.

120 *Remembrance*, August 1953.

121 *Remembrance*, November/December 1951.

122 Annual Conference, 18 March 1953, in Executive Minutes, 4 May 1953 – 7 February 1956, WWWMA Records.

123 Conference, 1 April 1963, Minute Books, 19 June 1961 – 13 April 1964, WWWMA.

124 Annual Conference 1970, State Executive Council, 13 March 1968 – 13 December 1991, WWWMA.

125 Constitution Committee Meeting, 23 August 1968, State Executive Council, 13 March 1968 – 13 December 1991, WWWMA.

126 State Council Committee Meeting, 9 December 1963, Minute Books, 19 June 1961 – 13 April 1964, WWWA.

127 Annual Conference, 6 April 1965, Executive Council Minutes, 16 March 1964 – 15 December 1965, WWWMA.

128 Annual Meeting, November 1951, Minutes of General Meeting, 10 November 1948 – 12 July 1954, WWWMA.

129 See for instance, ibid., Annual Meeting, 1949.
130 General Meeting, 8 May 1967, Minutes, State Council, 25 January 1966 – 12 February 1968. WWWMA.
131 Minutes of General Meeting of WWWMA, 13 July 1949, 10 November 1948 – 12 July 1954.
132 *Remembrance*, December 1955 – January 1956.
133 State Executive Round Table Conference, Minutes, State Council, 25 January 1966, 25 January 1966 – 12 February 1968. WWWMA.
134 Minutes of General Meeting of WWWMA, October 1951, 10 November 1948 – 12 July 1954.
135 Minutes of General Meeting of WWWMA, February 1953.
136 *Remembrance*, January 1960.
137 *Remembrance*, September 1951.
138 Annual Conference. 3 September 1956, Minute Book, 4 April 1956 – 8 May 1961, WWMA.
139 *Remembrance*, September 1957.
140 ibid.
141 Aitken-Swan, *Widows in Australia*, p. 1.
142 Quoted in Joan Clarke, *Just Us: A History of the Association of Civilian Widows of Australia*, Sydney, Hale and Iremonger, 1988, p. 20.
143 ibid., p. 32.
144 ibid., p. 36.
145 War Widows' Scrapbook, Report of Annual Conference in Melbourne 1955 (p. 22 of notes), NSW Branch.
146 See War Widows' Guild, Minutes of the Executive Committee, 13 April 1950, Minute Book, 17 December 1947, NSW Branch.
147 ibid., pp. 54–6.
148 ibid., p. 84.
149 'Widows' Pensions Bill', *NSW Parliamentary Debates*, Sessions 1925–26, Legislative Assembly, Sydney, Government Printer, 1926, p. 2766.
150 ibid.
151 Desma Jean Guthrie, 'Widows and Welfare in Victoria in the 1920s and 1930s', MA Thesis, University of Melbourne, 1984, p. 11.
152 *Interim Report* from the Joint Committee on Social Security, 24 September 1941, Government Printer, n.d., pp. 5–6.
153 ibid., p. 13.
154 ibid., p. 15.
155 ibid., p. 16.
156 T. H. Kewley, *Social Security in Australia 1900–1972*, Sydney, Sydney University Press, 1965/1973, p. 212.
157 ibid., p. 215.
158 ibid., p. 215.
159 ibid., p. 223.
160 Clarke, *Just Us*, p. 54.

CHAPTER 3: THE WARS

1 Janet Sayers, *The Man Who Never Was: Freudian Tales*, London, Chatto and Windus, 1995, p. 141.

2 See Kate Darian-Smith, 'Remembering Romance' in Joy Damousi and Marilyn Lake (eds), *Gender and War: Australians at War*, Cambridge, Cambridge University Press, pp. 117–29; Sue Hardisty (ed.), *Thanks Girls and Goodbye: The Story of the Australian Women's Land Army, 1942–1945*, Melbourne, Viking/O'Neil, 1990.

3 Ann Curthoys, 'Mobilising Dissent: The Later Stages of Protest', and Peter Cochrane, 'At War At Home: Australian Attitudes During the Vietnam Years', in Gregory Pemberton (ed.), *Vietnam Remembered*, Sydney, Weldon Publishing, 1990, pp. 138–63; 165–85 respectively.

4 See for instance, Ken Inglis, *Sacred Places: War Memorials in the Australian Landscape*, Melbourne, Miegunyah Press, 1998.

5 Geoffrey Bolton, *The Oxford History of Australia, Volume 5: 1942–1988*, Melbourne, Oxford University Press, 1990, pp. 3–26.

6 Stuart Macintyre, *A Concise History of Australia*, Cambridge, Cambridge University Press, 1999, p. 188.

7 Interview with Lorna Higginbotham, 4 June 1998.

8 Interview with Mary Hopper, 26 March 1998.

9 *Sydney Morning Herald*, 27 December 1944, p. 7.

10 Interview with Norma Jones, 3 April 1998.

11 Hamilton I. McCubbin, Edna J. Hunter and Barbara B. Dahl, 'Residuals of War: Families of Prisoners of War and Servicemen Missing in Action', *Journal of Social Issues*, vol. 31, no. 4, 1975, p. 106.

12 ibid., pp. 100–7.

13 Marilyn Lake, 'Female Desires: The Meaning of World War II', in Damousi and Lake (eds), *Gender and War*, pp. 60–80.

14 Interview with Mary Cooper, 7 May 1998.

15 ibid.

16 ibid.

17 Richard White, 'War and Australian Society', in M. McKernan and M. Browne (eds), *Australia: Two Centuries of War and Peace*, Sydney, Allen & Unwin/Australian War Memorial, 1988, p. 13.

18 Andrea S. Walsh, *Women's Film and Female Experience, 1940–1950*, New York, Praeger, 1984, p. 168.

19 Interview with Margery Wittig, 19 May 1998, in possession of the author.

20 Interview with Trudar Naylor, 20 July 1998.

21 ibid.

22 Gavan McCormack, *Cold War, Hot War: An Australian Perspective on the Korean War*, Sydney, Hale and Iremonger, 1983, p. 15.

23 ibid., p. 17.

24 See Jack Gallaway, *The Last Call of the Bugle: The Long Road to Kapyong*, St Lucia, University of Queensland Press, 1994; Norman Bartlett, *With the Australians in Korea*, Canberra, Australian War Memorial, 1954/1960.

25 One of the few collections of letters is American: Dorothy G. Horwitz (ed.), *We Will Not Be Strangers: Korean War Letters Between a MASH Surgeon and His Wife*, Chicago, University of Illinois Press, 1997.

26 This line of inquiry is being pursued in 'Remembering Korea', by Richard Trembath, unpublished paper for Australian Historical Association Conference, July 1998.

27 Peter Dennis et al., 'Korean War', *The Oxford Companion to Australian Military History*, Melbourne, Oxford University Press, 1995, p. 333.

28 ibid.

29 Interview with Olwyn Green, 5 July 1996.

30 Interview with Jean Rayner, 17 March 1998.

31 Interview with Jean McNeill, 12 March 1998.

32 Interview with Jean Nelson, 3 April 1999.

33 Interview with Jessie Moreland, 8 May 1988.

34 ibid.

35 Interview with Joyce Richards, 8 April 1998.

36 See Peter Edwards, *A Nation at War: Australian Politics, Society and Diplomacy during the Vietnam War 1965–1975*, Sydney, Allen & Unwin/ Australian War Memorial, 1997; Peter Edwards with Gregory Pemberton, *Crisis and Commitments: The Politics and Diplomacy of Australia's Involvement in South East Asian Conflicts 1948–1965*, Sydney, Allen & Unwin/Australian War Memorial, 1992; Greg Pemberton, *All the Way: Australia's Road to Vietnam*, Sydney, Allen & Unwin, 1987.

37 Pemberton, *All the Way*, pp. 41–6.

38 Jock McCulloch, *The Politics of Agent Orange: The Australian Experience*, Melbourne, Heinemann, 1984, p. 51.

39 Barry York, 'Power to the Young', in Verity Burgmann and Jenny Lee (eds), *Staining the Wattle: A People's History of Australia Since 1788*, Melbourne, Penguin, 1988, p. 230.

40 Dennis et al., *The Oxford Companion to Australian Military History*, p. 620.

41 See Robin Gerster and Jan Bassett, *Seizures of Youth: 'The Sixties' and Australia*, Melbourne, Hyland House, 1991, p. 5; Ann Curthoys, '"Vietnam": Public Memory of An Anti-War Movement', in Kate Darian-Smith and Paula Hamilton (eds), *Memory in Twentieth Century Australia*, Melbourne, Oxford University Press, 1994, pp. 114–31; Ann Curthoys, 'Mobilising Dissent: The Later Stages of Protest', in Pemberton (ed.), *Vietnam Remembered*, pp. 138–63; Peter Cochrane, 'At War at Home: Australian Attitudes During the Vietnam Years', in Pemberton, *Vietnam Remembered*, pp. 165–85; Peter Pierce, '"Never Glad Confident Morning Again": Australia, the Sixties and the Vietnam War', in Jeffrey Grey and Jeff Doyle (eds), *Vietnam War: Myth and Memory*, Sydney, Allen & Unwin, 1992, pp. 70–9. See also, Greg Langley (ed.), *A Decade of Dissent: Vietnam and the Conflict on the Australian Homefront*, Sydney, Allen & Unwin, 1992.

42 Jeffrey Grey, 'Vietnam, Anzac and the Veteran', in Jeffrey Grey et al. (eds), *Vietnam Days: Australia and the Impact of Vietnam*, Melbourne, Penguin, 1991, p. 78.

43 ibid.

44 The one exception to this is the oral testimony recorded in Siobhan McHugh, *Minefields and Miniskirts: Australian Women and the Vietnam War*, Sydney, Doubleday, 1993. See also Jan Green, 'A Soldier's Wife's Story', in Keith Maddock and Barry Wright (eds) *War: Australia and Vietnam*, Sydney, Harper and Row, 1987, pp. 118–31.

45 Ann Curthoys, '"Vietnam": Public Memory of An Anti-War Movement', p. 124.
46 *Sydney Morning Herald*, 27 April 1968, p. 5.
47 Ann Curthoys, 'Vietnam', p. 130.
48 ibid., p. 131.
49 Interview with Olwyn Green, 5 July 1996.
50 Interview with Noela Hatfield, 12 March 1998.
51 ibid.
52 Interview with Ann Templar, 24 February 2000.
53 Interview with Glenis Hargen, 25 February 2000.
54 Barry York, 'Power to the Young', in Burgmann and Lee (eds), *Staining the Wattle*, pp. 230–1.
55 Interview with Josephine Betts, 21 March 2000.
56 Interview with Loris Pini, 13 March 1998.
57 ibid.
58 Interview with Rosie James, 23 March 1998.
59 Interview with Beverley Schmidt, 23 March 1998.
60 Interview with Pat Medaris, 3 March 1998.
61 ibid.
62 Interview with Phyllis Muller, 8 April 1998.
63 Interview with Maureen Matthews, 14 August 1998.
64 Interview with Paula Voltz, 19 May 1998.
65 For a further discussion of absence, see McCubbin et al., 'Residuals of War', pp. 95–109.
66 Interview with Noela Hatfield, 12 March 1998.
67 Interview with Ann Templar, 24 February 2000.
68 Interview with Loris Pini, 13 March 1998.
69 Interview with Ann Templar, 24 February 2000.
70 Interview with Beverley Schmidt, 23 March 1998.
71 Interview with Pat Medaris, 3 March 1998.
72 Interview with Roma Pressley, 13 May 1998.

CHAPTER 4: MEMORIES OF DEATH

1 Christopher Bollas, *Cracking Up: The Work of the Unconscious Experience*, London, Routledge, 1995, p. 119.
2 ibid., p. 188.
3 ibid.
4 Interview with Mary Ellen Simpson, 6 March 1998.
5 ibid.
6 Interview with Eve Harris, 3 April 1997.
7 Adam Phillips, *On Flirtation*, London, Faber and Faber, 1995, p. xx.
8 Bollas, *Cracking Up*, p. 117; p. 119; Wendy Wheeler, 'After Grief? What Kind of Inhuman Selves?', *New Formations*, 25, Summer 1995, p. 87.
9 Wheeler, 'After Grief?, p. 82.
10 See Sigmund Freud, 'Mourning and Melancholia' (1917), in *On Metapsychology: The Theory of Psychoanalysis*, vol. 11, Penguin Freud Library, London, Penguin, 1991, pp. 251–68.

11 Jonathan Rutherford, *Men's Silences: Predicaments in Masculinity*, London, Routledge, 1992, p. 125.
12 ibid., p. 127.
13 ibid.
14 Roderick Peters, 'Reflections on the Origin and Aim of Nostalgia', *Journal of Analytical Psychology*, vol. 30, no. 2, 1985, p. 137.
15 Donna Bassin, 'Maternal Subjectivity in the Culture of Nostalgia: Mourning and Memory', in Donna Bassin, Margaret Honey and Meryle Mahrer Kaplan (eds), *Representations of Motherhood*, New Haven, Yale University Press, 1994, p. 168.
16 Susan Stewart, *On Longing: Narratives of the Miniature, the Gigantic, the Souvenir, the Collection*, Baltimore, Johns Hopkins University Press, 1985, p. 138.
17 ibid.
18 David Lowenthal, 'Nostalgia Tells It Like It Wasn't', in Christopher Shaw and Malcolm Chase (eds), *The Imagined Past: History and Nostalgia*, Manchester, Manchester University Press, 1989, p. 21.
19 Jean Pickering, 'Remembering D-Day: A Case Study in Nostalgia', in Jean Pickering and Suzanne Kehde (eds), *Narratives of Nostalgia, Gender and Nationalism*, London, Macmillan, 1997, p. 189.
20 Guglielmo Bellelli and Mirella A.C. Amatulli, 'Nostalgia, Immigration, and Collective Memory', in James Pennebaker et al. (eds), *Collective Memory of Political Events: Social Psychological Perspectives*, New Jersey, Lawrence Erlbaum, 1997, p. 218.
21 Bollas, *Cracking up*, p. 119.
22 Beverley Raphael, *The Anatomy of Bereavement*, New York, Basic Books, 1983, p. 178.
23 Letter from Jean Fry to the author, 27 June 1996. In possession of the author.
24 Interview with Jean Fry, 6 July 1996.
25 Interview with Shirley Tilley, 29 July 1998.
26 Adam Phillips, *Terrors and Experts*, London, Faber and Faber, 1995, p. 66.
27 Interview with Marjory Miller, 3 April 1997.
28 Interview with Eve Harris, 3 April 1997.
29 Raphael, *The Anatomy of Bereavement*, p. 41.
30 Interview with Shirley Tilley, 29 July 1998.
31 Raphael, *The Anatomy of Bereavement*, p. 36.
32 *Random Harvest* [1942] directed by Mervyn LeRoy, starring Ronald Colman and Greer Garson, tells the story of a shell-shocked First World War veteran who is saved from oblivion by the compassion of a music hall entertainer. (Mick Martin and Marsha Porter, *Video Movie Guide*, New York, Ballantine Books, 1997, p. 876.)
33 Interview with Shirley Tilley, 29 July 1998.
34 Raphael, *The Anatomy of Bereavement*, p. 43.
35 Interview with Shirley Tilley, 29 July 1998.
36 Interview with Virginia Gerrett, 7 July 1996.

37 ibid.
38 Interview with Mary Hopper, 26 March 1998.
39 ibid.
40 Interview with Sylvia Brown, 23 July 1998.
41 Letter from Pearl Sutton to the author, 28 June 1996.
42 ibid.
43 ibid.
44 ibid.
45 Interview with Olwyn Green, 5 July 1996.
46 Olwyn Green, *The Name's Still Charlie: A Remarkable Story of Courage and Love*, St Lucia, University of Queensland Press, 1993, pp. 3–4.
47 ibid., p. 5.
48 ibid., p. 293.
49 ibid.
50 ibid., p. 215.
51 ibid., p. 5.
52 Letter from Faye Longmore to Olwyn Green, 21 December 1999.
53 Interview with Lois Murphy, 21 March 2000.
54 ibid.
55 ibid.
56 Patricia Grimshaw, Marilyn Lake, Ann McGrath and Marian Quartly, *Creating A Nation: 1788–1900*, McPhee/Gribble, Melbourne, 1994, p. 273.
57 Stephen Garton, *The Cost of War: Australians Return*, Melbourne, Oxford University Press, 1996, pp. 201–7.
58 Letter from Jean Fry to the author, 27 June 1996.
59 Interview with Olwyn Green, 5 July 1998.
60 Letter from Pearl Sutton to the author, 28 June 1996.

CHAPTER 5: THE QUESTION OF SILENCE

1 Interview with Glenis Hargen, 25 February 2000.
2 Paul Fussell, *The Great War and Modern Memory*, Oxford, Oxford University Press, 1975, p. 170.
3 Elaine Showalter, 'Rivers and Sassoon: The Inscription of Male Gender Anxieties', in Margaret Higgonet et al. (eds), *Behind the Lines: Gender and the Two World Wars*, New Haven, Yale University Press, 1987, p. 64.
4 Adrian Gregory, *The Silence of Memory: Armistice Day, 1919–1946*, Oxford, Berg Publishers, 1994, p. 11.
5 ibid., p. 222.
6 Inga Clendinnen, *Reading the Holocaust*, Melbourne, Text Publishing, 1998, p. 38.
7 ibid., p. 41.
8 ibid., p. 57.
9 See Patsy Adam-Smith, *Prisoners of War: From Gallipoli to Korea*, Melbourne, Viking, 1992.

10 See John Raftery and Sandra Schubert, *A Very Changed Man: Families of World War Two Veterans Fifty Years after the War*, Adelaide, School of Human Resource Studies, University of South Australia, n.d., p. 65.
11 Joanna Bourke, *An Intimate History of Killing: Face to Face Killing in 20th Century Warfare*, New York, Basic Books, 1999.
12 Interview with Trudar Naylor, 20 July 1998.
13 Interview with Pat Medaris, 3 March 1998.
14 Interview with Jan McNeill, 12 March 1998.
15 Interview with Jean Davis, 3 April 1998.
16 ibid.
17 Interview with Doris White, 7 April 1998.
18 ibid.
19 Interview with Nancy Murrell, 7 April 1998.
20 ibid.
21 Interview with Lorna Higgenbotham, 4 June 1998.
22 Interview with Jessie Moreland, 8 May 1998.
23 ibid.
24 Interview with Nell Durnford, 7 May 1998.
25 Interview with Verna Phillips, 12 December 1998.
26 Interview with Olwyn Green, 5 July 1996.
27 ibid.
28 Interview with Jean Rayner, 17 March 1998.
29 Interview with Beverley Schmidt, 23 March 1998.
30 Interview with Phyllis Muller, 8 April 1998.
31 Interview with Glenis Hargen, 25 February 2000.
32 ibid.
33 Interview with Loris Pini, 13 March 1998.
34 Interview with Lorna Higgenbotham, 4 June 1998.
35 Interview with Noela Hatfield, 12 March 1998.
36 John Kingsmill, *No Hero: Memoirs of a Raw Recruit in World War II*, Sydney, Hale and Iremonger, 1994; Fred Airey, *The Time of The Soldier*, Fremantle, Fremantle Arts Centre Press, 1991; Leonard L. Barton, *The Desert Harassers: Memoirs of 450 (RAAF) Squadron*, Mosman, Astor Publications, 1991; Cam Bennett, *Rough Infantry: Tales of World War II*, Warrnambool, Warrnambool Institute Press, 1985; Ted Coates, *Lone Evader: The Escape From France of RAAF Sergeant Pilot Ted Coates 1942–1943*, Loftus, Australian Military History Publications, 1995; Peter James Jones, *The Reluctant Volunteer in Service with the Ninth Division 1940–1945*, Loftus, Australian Military History Publications, 1997; Peter Medcalf, *War in the Shadows: Bouganville 1944–1945*, Canberra, Australian War Memorial, 1986.
37 Medcalf, *War in the Shadows*, p. 25.
38 See for instance, Barton, *The Desert Harassers*.
39 See for instance, Jones, *The Reluctant Volunteer*.
40 John Kingsmill, *No Hero: Memoirs of a Raw Recruit in World War II*, Sydney, Allen & Unwin, 1994, p.172.
41 Roland Griffiths-Marsh, *I Was Only Sixteen*, Sydney, Harper Collins, 1990, p. 362.

42 Philippe Airès, *The Hour of Our Death*, trans. by Helen Weaver, New York, Alfred A. Knopf, 1981, pp. 580, 578.
43 The exception to this are texts like Rohan D. Rivett, *Behind Bamboo*, Melbourne, Penguin, 1973 (first published 1946).
44 See Beverley Raphael, *The Anatomy of Bereavement*, New York, Basic Books, 1983.
45 See Betty Riordan, *Living Well with Grief*, Sydney, Hale and Iremonger, 1995; Thomas Attig, *How We Grieve: Relearning the World*, New York, Oxford University Press, 1996; Gerard Dowling, *Growing Through Grief: From Anguish to Healing: Coping with Death, Suicide and Trauma*, Melbourne, Spectrum, 1998.
46 *Age*, 11 June 1994.
47 *Grief Education* 99, Newsletter, February–July 1999, Centre for Grief Education; *Grief Matters: The Australian Journal of Grief and Bereavement*, no. 1, vol. 2, May 1999.

CHAPTER 6: MARRIAGE WARS

1 Robert S. Laufer, 'The Serial Self: War Trauma, Identity and Adult development', in John P. Wilson, Zev Harel and Boaz Kahana (eds), *Human Adaptation to Extreme Stress: From the Holocaust to Vietnam*, New York, Plenum Press, 1988, p. 41.
2 Richard White, 'War and Australian Society', in M. McKernan and M. Browne (eds), *Australia: Two Centuries of War and Peace*, Sydney, Allen & Unwin/Australian War Memorial, 1988, p. 415.
3 Interview with Gwen Robertson, 8 July 1998.
4 ibid.
5 Michael Lambek and Paul Antze, 'Introduction: Forecasting Memory', in Paul Antze and Michael Lambek (eds), *Tense Past: Cultural Essays in Trauma and Memory*, London, Routledge, 1996, p. xxv.
6 Beverley Raphael, *The Anatomy of Bereavement*, New York, Basic Books, 1983, p. 181.
7 ibid., p. 187.
8 See Joan Scott, 'The Evidence of Experience', *Critical Inquiry*, vol. 17, no. 4, Summer, 1991, p. 782; Luisa Passerini, *Fascism in Popular Memory: The Cultural Experience of the Turin Working-Class*, Cambridge, Cambridge University Press, pp. 61–2.
9 For a discussion of the historical concept of selfhood, see Lynn Hunt, 'Psychoanalysis, the Self, and Historical Interpretation', *Common Knowledge*, Fall 1997, vol. 6, no. 2, pp. 10–19.
10 Interview with Gwen Robertson, 8 July 1998.
11 Kali Tal, *Worlds of Hurt: Reading the Literature of Trauma*, Cambridge, Cambridge University Press, 1996, p. 6.
12 Janet McCalman, *Journeyings: The Biography of a Middle-Class Generation 1920–1990*, Melbourne, Melbourne University Press, 1993, p. 208.
13 Stephen Garton, *The Cost of War: Australians Return*, Melbourne, Oxford University Press, 1996, pp. 199–200.

14 Judith A. Allen, *Sex and Secrets: Crimes Involving Women Since 1880*, Melbourne, Oxford University Press, 1990, pp. 183–8.

15 Betty Peters, 'The Life Experience of Partners of ex-POWs of the Japanese', *Journal of the Australian War Memorial*, Issue 28, April 1996, p. 1–11.

16 Zahava Soloman et al., 'Front Line to Home Front; A Study of Secondary Traumatization', *Family Process*, 31, September 1992, pp. 289–302.

17 ibid., p. 289.

18 ibid., p. 291.

19 ibid., p. 299.

20 Sarah Fishman, *We Will Wait: Wives of French Prisoners of War, 1940–1945*, New Haven, Yale University Press, 1991.

21 See Raymond Evans, 'A Gun in the Oven: Masculinism and Gendered Violence', in Kay Saunders and Raymond Evans (eds), *Gender Relations in Australia*, Sydney, Harcourt, Brace and Jovanovich, 1992, pp. 199–200.

22 Laura S. Brown, 'Not Outside the Range: One Feminist Perspective on Psychic Trauma', in Cathy Caruth (ed.), *Trauma: Explorations in Memory*, Baltimore, Johns Hopkins University Press, 1995, p. 102.

23 Cathy Caruth, *Unclaimed Experience: Trauma, Narrative and History*, Baltimore, Johns Hopkins University Press, 1996, p. 8.

24 See for instance, Joel Osler Brende and Erwin Randolph Parson, *Vietnam Veterans: The Road to Recovery*, New York, Plenum Press, 1985, p. 118.

25 Robert J. Lifton, 'Understanding the Traumatized Self: Imagery, Symbolization and Transformation', in Wilson et al. (eds), *Human Adaptation to Extreme Stress*, pp. 9–10, 20–1.

26 Tom Williams, 'Diagnosis and Treatment of Survivor Guilt: The Bad Penny Syndrome', in Wilson et al. (eds), *Human Adaptation to Extreme Stress*, p. 323.

27 Lifton, 'Understanding the Traumatized Self', p. 20.

28 ibid., p. 26.

29 Laufer, 'The Serial Self', pp. 49–50.

30 ibid., p. 38.

31 Lifton, 'Understanding the Traumatized Self', p. 27.

32 Robert Di Giulio, *Beyond Widowhood: From Bereavement to Emergence and Hope*, Free Press, New York, 1989, p. 23.

33 ibid., p. 32.

34 ibid., p. 26.

35 Interview with Gwen Robertson, 8 July 1998.

36 Reverend W.G. Coughlan, 'Marriage Breakdown', in A.P. Elkin (ed.), *Marriage and Family in Australia*, Sydney, Angus & Robertson, 1957, p. 120.

37 ibid., p. 120.

38 ibid., p. 123.

39 ibid.

40 ibid.

41 John Murphy, *Imagining the Fifties: Private Sentiment and Political Culture in Menzies' Australia*, Sydney, University of New South Wales Press, 2000, p. 20.

42 Charlie Fox and Marilyn Lake (eds), *Australians At Work: Commentaries and Sources*, Melbourne, McPhee/Gribble, 1990, p. 147.

43 See Shurlee Swain and Renata Howe, *Single Mothers and Their Children*, Cambridge, Cambridge University Press, 1995.

44 Allen, *Sex and Secrets*, p. 233.

45 Garton, *The Cost of War*, p. 198.

46 Allen, *Sex and Secrets*, p. 233.

47 *Sydney Morning Herald*, 27 March 1940, p. 13.

48 *Sydney Morning Herald*, 23 January 1942, p. 4.

49 David Hilliard, 'Church, Family and Sexuality in Australia in the 1950s', in John Murphy and Judith Smart (eds), 'The Forgotten Fifties: Aspects of Australian Society and Culture in the 1950s', Special Issue, *Australian Historical Studies*, no. 109, October 1997, p. 137.

50 Sol Encel, 'The Family', in A.F. Davies and S. Encel (eds), *Australian Society: A Sociological Introduction*, Melbourne, Cheshire, 1970, p. 275.

51 ibid.

52 Patricia Grimshaw, Marilyn Lake, Ann McGrath and Marian Quartly, *Creating a Nation: 1788–1990*, Melbourne, McPhee/Gribble, 1994, p. 276; Kim Humphery, *Shelf Life: Supermarkets and the Changing Cultures of Consumption*, Cambridge, Cambridge University Press, 1998, pp. 91–6.

53 Judith Brett, *Robert Menzies' Forgotten People*, Melbourne, Macmillan, 1992, p. 46.

54 *Sydney Morning Herald*, 4 August 1957, p. 29.

55 *Sydney Morning Herald*, 21 December 1952, p. 18.

56 *Sydney Morning Herald*, 2 February 1958, p. 79.

57 Grimshaw et al., *Creating a Nation*, p. 270.

58 W.D. Borrie, 'Australian Family Structure: Demographics Observations', in Elkin (ed.), *Marriage and Family in Australia*, p. 18.

59 Murphy, *Imagining the Fifties*, p. 48.

60 Nicholas Brown, *Governing Prosperity: Social Change and Social Analysis in Australia in the 1950s*, Cambridge, Cambridge University Press, 1995, p. 195; p. 198.

61 Hilliard, 'Church, Family and Sexuality', p. 139.

62 Kerreen Reiger, 'The Coming of the Counsellors: The Development of Marriage Guidance in Australia', *Australian and New Zealand Journal of Sociology*, vol. 23, no. 3, November 1987, p. 378.

63 Hilliard, 'Church, Family and Sexuality', p. 139.

64 See *Sydney Morning Herald*, 11 February 1947, p. 10; 29 April 1947, p. 14.

65 *Sydney Morning Herald*, 5 February 1947, p. 3.

66 *Sydney Morning Herald*, 29 May 1948, p. 7.

67 Reiger, 'The Coming of the Counsellors'; Brown, *Governing Prosperity*.

68 *Sydney Morning Herald*, 31 May 1960, p. 6.

69 *Sydney Morning Herald*, 31 August 1960, p. 20.

70 *Sydney Morning Herald*, 18 January 1961, p. 21.

71 *Sydney Morning Herald*, 26 March 1949, p. 2.

72 Murphy, *Imagining the Fifties*, pp. 28–9.

73 Coughlan, 'Marriage Breakdown', p. 139.

74 Interview with Joyce Richards, 8 April 1998.
75 ibid.
76 Murphy, *Imagining the Fifties*, p. 17.
77 ibid.
78 Olwyn Green, *The Name's Still Charlie: A Remarkable Story of Courage and Love*, St Lucia, University of Queensland Press, 1993, p. 214.
79 ibid., p. 219.
80 ibid., p. 226.
81 Olwyn Green and Isobel Russell (see later in this chapter) were the only other women in this study who sought counselling after their husbands' deaths.
82 Interview with Gwen Robertson, 8 July 1998.
83 ibid.
84 See Jane Littlewood, *Aspects of Grief: Bereavement in Adult Life*, London, Routledge, 1992, p. 47 for a discussion of the role of hallucinations.
85 Interview with Isobel Russell, 30 July 1998.
86 Laurence J. Kirmayer, 'Landscapes of Memory: Trauma, Narrative and Dissociation', in Antze and Lambek (eds.), *Tense Past*, p. 182.
87 Janet Sayers, *The Man Who Never Was: Freudian Tales*, London, Chatto and Windus, 1995, p. 169.
88 Interview with Margery Wittig, 19 May 1998.
89 Interview with Jean Thomas, 1 April 1998.
90 ibid.
91 ibid.
92 ibid.
93 Interview with Lorna Higgenbotham, 4 June 1998.
94 Garton, *The Cost of War*, pp. 181–9.
95 John Raftery and Sandra Schubert, *A Very Changed Man: Families of World War Two Veterans Fifty Years After War*, Adelaide, School of Human Resource Studies, n.d., p. 22.
96 R.S. Ellery, *Psychiatric Aspects of Modern Warfare*, Melbourne, Reed and Harris, 1945, p. 49.
97 ibid., p. 151.
98 ibid., p. 152.
99 *Medical Journal of Australia*, 20 January 1945, p. 50.
100 ibid., p. 54.
101 Garton, *The Cost of War*, p. 199.
102 See Garton, *The Cost of War*; Sonya Michel, 'Danger on the Home Front: Motherhood, Sexuality, and the Disabled Veterans in American Postwar Films', *Journal of the History of Sexuality*, vol. 3, no. 1, 1992, pp. 109–28.
103 W.M. O'Neil, *A Century of Psychology in Australia*, Sydney, Sydney University Press, 1987, p. 89.
104 Brown, *Governing Prosperity*, pp. 195, 197.
105 Ellery, *Psychiatric Aspects of Modern Warfare*, p. 156.
106 ibid.
107 ibid., p. 157.

108 Murphy, *Imagining the Fifties*, pp. 22–3, 59–60.
109 *Medical Journal of Australia*, 29 June 1946, p. 911.
110 ibid., p. 912.
111 *Medical Journal of Australia*, 6 July 1946, p. 2.
112 ibid., p. 4.
113 *Medical Journal of Australia*, 29 June 1946, p. 913.
114 ibid., p. 915.
115 Malcolm Kidson, John C. Douglas and Brendan J. Holwill, 'Post-traumatic Stress Disorder in Australian World War II Veterans Attending a Psychiatric Outpatient Clinic', *Medical Journal of Australia*, vol. 158, April 1993, p. 563.
116 Interview with Lorna Higgenbotham, 4 June 1998.
117 Interview with Myra Davies, 26 May 1998.
118 ibid.
119 ibid.
120 Interview with Barbara Potter, 27 May 1998.
121 Kirmayer, 'Landscapes of Memory', p. 193.

CHAPTER 7: 'OVERLOOKED'

1 Interview with Paula Voltz, 19 May 1998.
2 *Sydney Morning Herald*, 27 July 1950, p. 2.
3 *Sydney Morning Herald*, 29 July 1950, p. 2.
4 *Sydney Morning Herald*, 30 July 1950.
5 *Age*, 27 July 1950, p. 2.
6 *Sydney Morning Herald*, 29 July 1950, p. 2.
7 Jack Gallaway, *The Last of the Bugle: The Long Road to Kapyong*, Brisbane, University of Queensland Press, 1994/1999, p. xii.
8 Interview with Jean Nelson, 3 April 1999.
9 Interview with Mary McLeod, 19 March 1998.
10 ibid.
11 ibid.
12 ibid.
13 Christopher Tennant, Jeffrey H. Streimer and Helen Temperly, 'Memories of Vietnam: Post-Traumatic Stress Disorders in Australian Veterans', *Australian and New Zealand Journal of Psychiatry*, vol. 24, no. 1, March 1990, pp. 29–36; Bruce Bowman, 'The Vietnam Veteran Ten Years On', *Australian and New Zealand Journal of Psychiatry*, vol. 16, no. 3, pp. 107–27; J.A.M. Cugley and R.D. Savage, 'Cognitive Impairment and Personality Adjustment in Vietnam Veterans', *Australian Psychologist*, vol. 19, no. 2, July 1984, pp. 205–16. For studies in the American context, see Joel Osler Brende and Erwin Randolph Parson (eds), *Vietnam Veterans: The Road to Recovery*, New York, Plenum Press, 1985; Charles Fidgely (ed.), *Stress Disorders Among Vietnam Veterans: Theory, Research and Treatment*, New York, Brunner/Mazel, 1978; Herbert Hendin and Ann Pollinger Haas, *Wounds of War: The Psychological Aftermath of Combat in Vietnam*, New York, Basic Books, 1984.

14 Jeffrey Grey, 'Memory and Public Myth', in Jeffrey Grey and Jeff Doyle (eds), *Vietnam, War, Myth and Memory*, Sydney, Allen & Unwin, 1992, p. 143.

15 Jeffrey Streimer and Christopher Tennant, 'Psychiatric Aspects of the Vietnam War: The Effects on Combatants', in Kenneth Maddock and Barry Wright (eds), *War: Australia and Vietnam*, Sydney, Harper and Row, 1987, pp. 231, 236.

16 ibid., p. 239.

17 ibid., p. 238.

18 Bowman, 'The Vietnam Veteran Ten Years On', pp. 113–14.

19 ibid., pp. 114–15.

20 ibid., p. 120.

21 Tennant, Streimer, and Temperly, 'Memories of Vietnam', p. 29.

22 Streimer and Tennant, 'Psychiatric Aspects of the Vietnam War', p. 235.

23 ibid., p. 245.

24 ibid., p. 246.

25 ibid., p. 249.

26 ibid.

27 ibid., p. 250.

28 Glenn C. Boxshall, 'The Development and Evaluation of the Vietnam Veterans Counselling Service, Country Outreach Programme', Master of Social Work, University of Melbourne, 1993, pp. 7–9.

29 Graham Walker, 'The Vietnam Veterans Association of Australia', in Maddock and Wright (eds), *War: Australia and Vietnam*, pp. 206–29.

30 A.F. Davies and Sol Encel (eds), *Australian Society: A Sociological Introduction*, Melbourne, Cheshire, 1970, p. 275.

31 Brende and Parson (eds), *Vietnam Veterans*, p. 44.

32 Interview with Paula Voltz, 19 May 1998.

33 Streimer and Tennant, 'Psychiatric Aspects of the Vietnam War', p. 238.

34 Brende and Parson (eds), *Vietnam Veterans*, p. 72.

35 ibid.

36 Streimer and Tennant, 'Psychiatric Aspects of the Vietnam War', pp. 245–6.

37 In the Australian case, see, Bowan, *The Vietnam Veteran*, p. 117.

38 ibid., p. 114. For detailed analysis of dreams and nightmares of Vietnam veterans, see, Harry A. Wilmer, 'The Healing Nightmare: War Dreams of Vietnam Veterans', in Deirdre Barrett (ed.), *Trauma and Dreams*, Cambridge, Harvard University Press, 1996, pp. 85–99.

39 John Raftery and Sandra Schubert, *A Very Changed Man: Families of World War Two Veterans Fifty Years after the War*, Adelaide, School of Human Resource Studies, University of South Australia, n.d., p. 25.

40 Interview with Paula Voltz, 19 May 1998.

41 ibid.

42 ibid.

43 *Sydney Morning Herald*, 22 January 1977, p. 4.

44 *Sydney Morning Herald*, 21 January 1977, p. 4.

45 *Sydney Morning Herald*, 24 February 1977, p. 4.

46 *Age*, 1 May 1996, p. A4.

47 ibid., p. A5.

48 *Age*, 2 May 1996, p. 1.
49 *Age*, 3 May 1996, Liftout, Epilogue, p. 4.
50 See *Sydney Morning Herald*, 25 January 1939; *Sydney Morning Herald*, 17 March 1955; *Age*, 16 October 1970; *Age*, 28 December 1974.
51 Elisabeth Kubler-Ross, *On Death and Dying*, New York, Macmillan, 1969, p. 6.
52 *Sun-Herald*, 4 October 1987, p. 3.
53 *Age*, 5 October 1987, p. 16.
54 *Australian*, 5 October 1987, p. 3.
55 Ien Ang (ed.), *Planet Diana: Cultural Studies and Global Mourning*, Sydney, Research Centre in Intercommunication Studies, University of Western Sydney, 1997.
56 See Graham Little, *The Public Emotions: From Mourning to Hope*, Sydney, ABC Books, 1999, p. 11; Mark Seltzer, 'Wound Culture: Trauma in the Pathological Public Sphere', *October* 80, Spring 1997, pp. 3–26.
57 Interview with Beryl Tuttle, 7 May 1998.
58 ibid.
59 Interview with Glenis Hargen, 25 February 2000.
60 Interview with Rosie James, 23 March 1998.
61 ibid.
62 Interview with Noela Hatfield, 12 March 1998.
63 ibid.
64 Raftery and Schubert, *A Very Changed Man*, pp. 51, 53.
65 Interview with Phyllis Muller, 8 April 1998.
66 Interview with Loris Pini, 13 March 1998.
67 ibid.
68 ibid.
69 ibid.
70 Interview with Pat Medaris, 3 March 1998.
71 Interview with Beverley Schmidt, 23 March 1998.
72 ibid.
73 ibid.
74 See Hamilton I. McCubbin, Edna J. Hunter and Barbara B. Dahl, 'Residuals of War: Families of Prisoner of War and Servicemen Missing in Action', *Journal of Social Process*, vol. 31, no. 4, 1975, pp. 95–109.
75 ibid.
76 Interview with Maureen Matthews, 14 August 1998.
77 ibid.
78 ibid.
79 Interview with Jessie Moreland, 8 May 1988.
80 ibid.
81 Interview with Jean McNeill, 12 March 1998.
82 Interview with Jean Davis, 3 April 1998.
83 Interview with Jeanette Connellan, 12 June 1998.
84 Interview with Ann Templar, 24 February 2000.

CHAPTER 8: DEATH, SOLITUDE, AND RENEWAL

1 Interview with Olwyn Green.
2 Robert Di Giulio, *Beyond Widowhood: From Bereavement to Emergence and Hope*, New York, Free Press, 1989, p. 40.
3 Interview with Gwen Robertson, 8 July 1998.
4 Di Giulio, *Beyond Widowhood*, pp. 33–4.
5 ibid., p. 33.
6 ibid., p. 40.
7 Beverley Raphael, *The Anatomy of Bereavement*, New York, Basic Books, 1983, p. 180.
8 ibid., p.180.
9 L. Eugene Thomas, Robert C. Di Giulio and Nancy W. Sheehan, 'Identity, Loss and Psychological Crisis in Widowhood: A Re-evaluation', *International Journal of Aging and Human Development*, vol. 26, no. 3, 1988, p. 225.
10 Tangea Tansley, *For Women Who Grieve: Twelve Steps to Life After the Death of Your Partner*, Melbourne, Lothian, 1995; Deborah Sheldon, *Where to Now? The Practical Advice for Australian Widows*, Melbourne, Mandarin, 1996.
11 Interview with Mary Cooper, 7 May 1998.
12 See Elisabeth Kubler-Ross, *On Death and Dying*, New York, Macmillan, 1969.
13 Jane Littlewood, 'Widows' Weeds and Women's Needs: The Re-Feminisation of Death, Dying and Bereavement', in Sue Wilkinson and Celai Kitzinger (eds), *Women and Health: Feminist Perspectives*, London,Taylor and Francis, 1994, p. 171.
14 Raphael, *The Anatomy of Bereavement*, p. 187.
15 ibid., p. 188.
16 George Hagman, 'The Role of the Other in Mourning', *Psychoanalytic Quarterly*, LXV, 1996, pp. 327–52.
17 Raphael, *The Anatomy of Bereavement*, p. 228.
18 Philippe Airès, *The Hour of Our Death*, New York, Alfred A. Knopf, trans. by Helen Weaver, 1981, p. 614.
19 Jane Littlewood, *Aspects of Grief: Bereavement in Adult Life*, London, Routledge, 1992, p. 2.
20 John Canine, *The Psychosocial Aspects of Death and Dying*, Stamford, Connecticut, Appleton and Lange, 1996, p. 4.
21 Littlewood, *Aspects of Grief*, p. 23.
22 ibid., p. 31.
23 Helen Znaniecka Lopata, *Current Widowhood: Myths and Realities*, California, Sage, 1996, pp. 120–2.
24 Thomas, Di Guilio and Sheehan, 'Identity, Loss and Psychological Crisis in Widowhood', p. 225.
25 For recent work in this field, see David Walker with Stephen Garton (eds), *Ageing: Australian Cultural History*, no. 14, 1995.

26 See Margaret Pelling and Richard M. Smith (eds), *Life, Death, and the Elderly: Historical Perspectives*, London, Routledge, 1991; David I. Kertzer and Peter Laslett (eds), *Aging in the Past: Demography, Society and Old Age*, Berkeley, University of California Press, 1995.

27 See Paul Johnson, 'Historical Readings of Old Age and Ageing', in Paul Johnson and Pat Thane (eds), *Old Age from Antiquity to Post-Modernity*, London, Routledge, 1998, pp. 2–5.

28 Arlene Scadron, 'Letting Go: Bereavement Among Selected Southeastern Anglo Widows', in Arlene Scadron (ed.), *On Their Own: Widows and Widowhood in the American Southwest, 1848–1939*, Chicago, University of Illinois Press, 1988, pp. 244–65; Bettina Bradbury, 'Surviving as a Widow in 19th Century Montreal', *Urban History Review*, vol. xvii, no. 3, pp. 148–60.

29 Scadron, 'Introduction', in Scadron, *On Their Own*, pp. 1–2.

30 Lopata, *Current Widowhood*, p. 209.

31 Cherry Russell, 'Ageing As A Feminist Issue', *Women's Studies International Forum*, vol. 10, no. 2, 1987, p. 129; Sara Arber and Jay Ginn, *Gender and Later Life: A Sociological Analysis of Resources and Constraints*, London, Sage, 1991, pp. 36–43.

32 John Dixon, *Australia's Policy Towards the Aged, 1890–1972*, Canberra, Canberra College of Advanced Education, 1977, pp. 161–70.

33 Thomas R. Cole, *The Journey of Life: A Cultural History of Aging in America*, Cambridge, Cambridge University Press, 1992, p. 235.

34 ibid.

35 Peter Baume, Richard Bomball and Robyn Layton, *Fair Go: Report on Compensation for Veterans and War Widows*, Canberra, Department of Veterans' Affairs, 1994, p. 105.

36 See *Information for Widows in Victoria*, Melbourne, Victorian Council of Social Service, 1967, pp. 13–23; *War Widows' Benefits*, Canberra, Repatriation Department, 1974.

37 See *Sydney Morning Herald*, 3 July 1969, p. 7; 2 June 1972, p. 6; 4 September 1972, p. 6; 6 January 1969, p. 1.

38 Jean Aitken-Swan, *Widows in Australia: A Survey*, Sydney, Council of Social Service of New South Wales, 1962, p. 2.

39 Scadron, *On Their Own*, p. 7.

40 David G. Troyansky, 'Historical Research into Ageing, Old Age and Older People', in Anne Jamieson, Sarah Harper and Christian Victor (eds), *Critical Approaches to Ageing and Later Life*, Buckingham, Open University Press, 1997, p. 49.

41 Raphael, *The Anatomy of Bereavement*, p. 181.

42 ibid., p. 182.

43 ibid., p. 187.

44 ibid., p. 182.

45 Interview with Verna Phillips, 12 December 1998.

46 Interview with Maureen Matthews, 14 August 1998.

47 ibid.

48 Interview with Isobel Ford, 30 July 1998.

49 Interview with Mary Cooper, 7 May 1998.

50 Interview with Jean Davis, 3 April 1998.

51 ibid.
52 Interview with Nancy Murrell, 7 April 1998.
53 Interview with Phyllis Muller, 8 April 1998.
54 Interview with Lorna Higgenbotham, 4 June 1998.
55 ibid.
56 Interview with Myra Davies, 26 May 1998.
57 Interview with Loris Pini, 13 March 1998.
58 ibid.
59 Interview with Beverley Schmidt, 23 March 1998.
60 ibid.
61 Interview with Claire Dunstan, 26 May 1998.
62 Interview with Jeanette Connellan, 12 June 1998.
63 ibid.
64 Interview with Isobel Ford, 30 July 1998.
65 Littlewood, *Aspects of Grief*, p. 50.
66 Interview with Marie Hill, 15 May 1998.
67 interview with Alice Lockwood, 10 June 1998.
68 Interview with Dorothy Hutton, 4 June 1998.
69 ibid.
70 Interview with Phyllis Muller, 8 April 1998.
71 Interview with Pearl Rieman, 9 April 1998.
72 Interview with Claire Dunstan, 26 May 1998.
73 Interview with Barbara Potter, 27 May 1998.
74 Interview with Pat Medaris, 13 March 1998.
75 Interview with Jean Thomas, 1 April 1998.
76 John Murphy, *Imagining the Fifties: Private Sentiment and Political Culture in Menzies' Australia*, Sydney, University of New South Wales Press, 2000, p. 43.
77 Interview with Pearl Rieman, 9 April 1998.
78 ibid.
79 ibid.
80 ibid.
81 Interview with Peg Pollock, 27 May 1998.
82 Interview with Jean Thomas, 1 April 1998.
83 Littlewood, *Aspects of Grief*, p. 47.
84 Interview with Beryl Tuttle, 7 May 1998.
85 ibid.
86 ibid.
87 Interview with Roma Pressley, 13 May 1998.
88 Interview with Evelyn Peterson, 15 May 1998.
89 Interview with Margery Wittig, 19 May 1998.
90 Interview with Rosie James, 23 March 1998.
91 ibid.
92 ibid.
93 Interview with Sylvia Brown, 23 July 1998.
94 Sheila Adams, 'A gendered history of the social management of death in Foleshill, Coventry, during the inter-war years', in David Clark (ed.), *The Sociology of Death: Theory, Culture, Practice*, London, Blackwell, 1993, pp. 149–65.

95 Interview with Jean Thomas, 1 April 1998.
96 Interview with Trudar Naylor, 20 July 1998.
97 Interview with Jessie Moreland, 8 May 1998.
98 Interview with Violet Bourke, 15 May 1998.
99 Di Giulio, *Beyond Widowhood*, p. 51.
100 Littlewood, *Aspects of Grief*, p. 68.
101 Interview with Trudar Naylor, 20 July 1998.
102 Interview with Norma Jones, 3 April 1998.
103 Interview with Jean Thomas, 1 April 1998.
104 Interview with Paula Voltz, 19 May 1998.
105 ibid.
106 See Robert Gaines, 'Detachment and Continuity: The Two Tasks of Mourning', *Contemporary Psychoanalysis*, vol. 33, no. 4, 1997, pp. 549–71.

CHAPTER 9: CONCLUSION

1 Interview with Ann Templar, 24 February 2000.
2 Graham Little, *The Public Emotions: From Mourning to Hope*, Sydney, ABC Books, 1999, p. 4.
3 ibid.
4 ibid., p. 59.
5 David G. Troyansky, 'Historical Research into Ageing, Old Age and Older People', in Anne Jamieson, Sarah Harper and Christian Victor (eds), *Critical Approaches to Ageing and Later Life*, Buckingham, Open University Press, 1997 p. 49.
6 Susan Geiger, 'What's So Feminist About Women's Oral History?', *Journal of Women's History*, vol. 2, no. 1, Spring, pp.13–15.
7 Peter G. Coleman, 'Ageing and Life History: The Meaning of Reminiscence in Late Life', in Shirley Dex (ed.), *Life and Work History Analyses*, London, Routledge, 1991, p. 121.
8 This absence is also noted by Stephen Garton, *The Cost of War: Australians Return*, Melbourne, Oxford University Press, 1996, p. 242. For work in this area, see, Laurie Lydia Harkness, 'Transgenerational Transmission of War-related Trauma', in John P. Wilson and Beverley Raphael (eds), *International Handbook of Traumatic Stress Syndrome*, New York, Plenum Press, 1993, pp. 635–43; John Raftery and Sandra Schubert, *A Very Changed Man: Families of World War Two Veterans Fifty Years after the War*, Adelaide, School of Human Resources Studies, University of South Australia, n.d.
9 Esther Faye, 'Missing the Real' Trace of Trauma: How the Second Generation Remembers the Holocaust, Unpublished conference paper, Frontiers of Memory Conference, London, 17–19 September 1999.
10 Donna Merwick, *Death of A Notary: Conquest and Change in Colonial New York*, Ithaca, Cornell University Press, 1999, p. 180.
11 See Bertram J. Cohler, 'Aging, Morale and Meaning: The Nexus of Narrative', in Thomas R. Cole et al. (eds), *Voices and Visions of Aging: Toward a Critical Gerontology*, New York, Springer Publishing Company, 1993, p. 120.

Bibliography

PRIMARY SOURCES

Interviews
Josephine Betts (21 March 2000), Francine Bartsch (2 September 1998), Violet Bourke (15 May 1998), Sylvia Brown (23 July 1998), Jean Connellan (12 June 1998), Mary Cooper (7 May 1998), Myra Davies (26 May 1998), Jean Davis (3 April 1998), Claire Dunstan (26 May 1998), Nell Durnford (7 May 1998), Isobel Ford (30 July 1998), Jean Fry (6 July 1996), Virginia Gerrett (7 July 1998), Olwyn Green (5 July 1996), Eve Harris (3 April 1998), Glenis Hargen (25 February 2000), Noela Hatfield (12 March 1998), Lorna Higgenbotham (4 June 1998), Marie Hill (15 May 1998), Mary Hopper (26 March 1998) Dorothy Hutton (4 June 1998), Rosie James (23 March 1998), Norma Jones (3 April 1997), Alice Lockwood (10 June 1998), Olive Maclennan (28 August 1998), Maureen Matthews (14 August 1998), Pat Medaris (13 March 1998), Mary McLeod (19 March 1998), Jean McNeil (12 March 1998), Marjory Miller (2 April 1997), Jessie Moreland (8 May 1998), Phyllis Muller (8 April 1998), Nancy Murrell (7 April 1998), Trudar Naylor (20 July 1998), Jean Nelson (3 April 1999), Evelyn Peterson (15 May 1998), Verna Phillips (12 December 1998), Loris Pini (13 March 1998), Barbara Potter, (27 May 1998), Peg Pollock (27 May 1998), Roma Pressley (13 May 1998), Jean Rayner (17 March 1998), Joyce Richards (8 April 1998), Pearl Rieman (9 April 1998), Gwen Robertson (8 July 1998), Bronwen Rowan (23 March 1998), Beverley Schmidt (23 March 1998), Mary Simpson (6 March 1998), Pearl Sutton (28 June 1996), Ann Templar (24 February 2000), Jean Thomas (1 April 1998), Shirley Tilley (29 July 1998), Beryl Tuttle (7 May 1998), Paula Voltz (19 May 1998), Doris White (7 April 1998), Margery Wittig (19 May 1998).

Correspondence
Pearl Sutton   Jean Fry

Documents

War Widows' Guild
Victorian Branch: Circulars: 1948–1949; 1954–1955
    Annual Reports: 1950–1951
NSW Branch: Minutes, Annual Meetings: 1947–1956
    Council and Executive Minutes: 1957–1958
Tasmanian Branch Minutes: 1953–1955

War Widows' and Widowed Mothers' Association
Executive Minutes: 1953–1956
State Executive Council Minutes: 1963–1964; 1968–1991
State Council Minutes: 1966–1968
Minutes, Annual General Meetings 1948–1954
*Remembrance: Newsletter of the Widows' and Widowed Mothers' Association
of Victoria*

Parliamentary debates/government publications
Commonwealth Parliamentary Debates, 1946–1947
NSW Parliamentary Debates, 1925–1926
Interim Report from the Joint Committee on Social Security, 1941
Baume, Peter et al., *Fair Go: Report on Compensation for Veterans and War
    Widows*, Department of Veterans' Affairs, Canberra, 1974.
Information for Widows in Victoria, Melbourne, Victorian Council of Social
    Service, 1967
War Widows' Benefits, Repatriation Department, Canberra, 1974

Pamphlets/newsletters
Cago, T. Howard, *When We are Bereaved*, Melbourne, Clifford Press, 195–?
Grief Education 99
Grief Matters: The Australian Journal of Grief and Bereavement
Westberg, Granger E., *Good Grief: A Constructive Approach to the Problem
    of Loss*, Melbourne, Church Education Press, 1966.

Newspapers/journals
Age
Argus
Australian
Herald
Medical Journal of Australia
Sun-Herald
Sydney Morning Herald

SECONDARY SOURCES
This list includes material that pertains directly to the topic of war widows'
experience and memories; it does not include material on allied topics, e.g.
Holocaust literature, which is cited in the chapter references.

Airès, Philippe, *The Hour of Our Death*, trans. by Helen Weaver, New York,
  Alfred A. Knopf, 1981.
Airey, Fred, *The Time of the Soldier*, Fremantle, Fremantle Arts Centre Press,
  1991.
Aitken-Swan Jean, *Widows in Australia: A Survey*, Sydney, Council of Social
  Service of New South Wales, 1962.
Allen, Judith, *Sex and Secrets: Crimes Involving Women Since 1880*, Mel-
  bourne, Oxford University Press, 1990.
Ang, Ien (ed.), *Planet Diana: Cultural Studies and Global Mourning*,
  Sydney, Research Centre for Intercommunications Studies, University
  of Western Sydney, 1997.
Antze, Paul and Michael Lambek (eds), *Tense Past: Cultural Essays in
  Trauma and Memory*, London, Routledge, 1996.
Arber, Sara and Jay Ginn, *Gender and Later Life: A Sociological Analysis
  of Resources and Constraints*, London, Sage, 1991.
Attig, Thomas, *How We Grieve: Relearning the World*, New York, Oxford
  University Press, 1996.
Attwood, Bain, *A Life Together, A Life Apart: A History of Relations Between
  Europeans and Aborigines*, Melbourne, Melbourne University Press,
  1994.
Baldock Cora and Bettina Cass (eds), *Women, Social Welfare and the State*,
  Sydney, Allen & Unwin, 1983.
Barrett, Deirdre (ed.), *Trauma and Dreams*, Cambridge, Harvard University
  Press, 1996.
Barrett, John, *We Were There: Australian Soldiers of World War Two Tell Their
  Stories*, Melbourne, Viking, 1987.
Bartlett, Norman, *With the Australians in Korea*, Canberra, Australian War
  Memorial, 1954/1960.
Barton, Leonard, L. *The Desert Harassers: Memoirs of (450) RAAF
  Squadron*, Mosman, Astor Publications, 1991.
Bassin, Donna, Margaret Honey, and Meryle Mahrer Kaplan (eds) *Rep-
  resentations of Motherhood*, New Haven, Yale University Press,
  1994.
Beaumont, Joan, 'Gull Force Comes Home: The Aftermath of Captivity',
  Journal of the Australian War Memorial, no. 14, April 1989.
Bennett, Cam, *Rough Infantry: Tales of World War II*. Melbourne,
  Warrnambool Press Institute, 1985.
Bollas, Christopher, *Cracking Up: The Work of the Unconscious Experience*,
  London, Routledge, 1995.
Bolton, Geoffrey, *The Oxford History of Australia, Volume 5: 1942–1988*,
  Melbourne, Oxford University Press, 1990.
Bourke, Joanna, *An Intimate History of Killing: Face to Face Killing in
  Twentieth Century Warfare*, New York, Basic Books, 1999.

Bowman, Bruce, 'The Vietnam Veteran: Ten Years On', *Australian and New Zealand Journal of Psychiatry*, vol. 16, no. 3.

Bradbury, Bettina, 'Surviving as a Widow in Nineteenth Century Montreal', *Urban History Review*, xvii, no. 3, February 1989.

Brende, Joel Osler, and Erwin Randolph Parson (eds), *Vietnam Veterans: The Road to Recovery*, New York, Plenum Press, 1985.

Brett, Judith, *Robert Menzies' Forgotten People*, Melbourne, Macmillan, 1992.

Brown, Nicholas, *Governing Prosperity: Social Change and Social Analysis in the 1950s*, Cambridge, Cambridge University Press, 1995.

Burgmann, Verity and Jenny Lee (eds), *Staining the Wattle: A People's History of Australia Since 1788*, Melbourne, Penguin, 1988.

Canine, John, *The Psychosocial Aspects of Death and Dying*, Stamford, CT, Appleton and Lange, 1996.

Carey, Hilary, *Believing in Australia: A Cultural History of Religions*, Sydney, Allen & Unwin, 1996.

Caruth, Cathy, *Unclaimed Experience: Trauma, Narrative and History*, Baltimore, Johns Hopkins University Press, 1996.

Caruth, Cathy (ed.), *Trauma: Explorations in Memory*, Baltimore, Johns Hopkins University Press, 1995.

Clark, David, *The Sociology of Death: Theory, Culture and Practice*, London, Blackwell, 1993.

Clarke, Joan, *Just Us: A History of the Association of Civilian Widows in Australia*, Sydney, Allen & Unwin, 1988.

Clendinnen, Inga, *Reading the Holocaust*, Melbourne, Text Publishing, 1998.

Coates, Ted, *Lone Invader: The Escape from France of RAAF Sergeant Pilot Ted Coates, 1942–1943*, Loftus, Australian Military History Publications, 1995.

Cole, Thomas R., *The Journey of Life: A Cultural History Aging in America*, New York, Cambridge University Press, 1992.

Cole, Thomas R., W. Andrew Achenbaum, Patricia L. Jakobi, and Robert Kastenbaum (eds), *Voices and Visions of Aging: Toward a Critical Gerontology*, New York, Springer Publishing Company, 1993.

Connerton, Paul, *How Societies Remember*, Cambridge, Cambridge University Press, 1982.

Cugley, J.A.M and R.D. Savage, 'Cognitive Impairment and Personality Adjustment in Vietnam Veterans', *Australian Psychologist*, vol. 19, no. 2, July 1984.

Curthoys, Ann, Tim Rowse, and A.W. Martin, (eds), *Australians from 1939*, Sydney, Fairfax, Syme and Weldon, 1987.

Damousi, Joy, *The Labour of Loss: Mourning, Memory and Wartime Bereavement*, Cambridge, Cambridge University Press, 1999.

Damousi, Joy and Marilyn Lake (eds), *Gender and War: Australians at War*, Cambridge, Cambridge University Press, 1995.

Darian-Smith, Kate and Paula Hamilton (eds), *Memory and History in Twentieth Century Australia*, Melbourne, Oxford University Press, 1994.

Davies, A.F., and Sol Encel (eds), *Australian Society: A Sociological Introduction*, Melbourne, Cheshire, 1970.

Davison, Graeme, J.W. McCarty and Alisa McLeary (eds), *Australians 1888*, Sydney, Fairfax, Syme and Weldon, 1987.

Dennis, Peter et al., *The Oxford Companion to Australian Military History*, Melbourne, Oxford University Press, 1995.

Dex, Shirley (ed.), *Life and Work History Analyses: Qualitative and Quantitative Developments*, Routledge, London, 1991.

Di Giulio, Robert, *Beyond Widowhood: From Bereavement to Emergence and Hope*, New York, Free Press, 1989.

Dixon, John, *Australia's Policy Towards the Aged, 1890–1972*, Canberra, Canberra College of Advanced Education, 1977.

Dollimore, John, *Death, Desire and Loss in Western Culture*, London, Allen Lane, 1998.

Dombrowski, Nicole Ann (ed.), *Women and War in the Twentieth Century: Enlisted With and Without Consent*, New York, Garland Publishing, 1999.

Dowling, Gerard, *Growing Through Grief: From Anguish to Healing. Coping with Death Suicide and Trauma*, Melbourne, Spectrum, 1998.

Edwards, Peter, *A Nation at War: Australian Politics, Society and Diplomacy During the Vietnam War, 1965–1975*, Sydney, Allen & Unwin/ Australian War Memorial, 1997.

Edwards, Peter with Gregory Pemberton, *Crisis and Commitments: The Politics and Diplomacy of Australia's Involvement in the South East Asia Conflict, 1948–1965*, Sydney, Allen & Unwin/Australian War Memorial, 1992.

Elkin, A.P. (ed.), *Marriage and Family in Australia*, Sydney, Angus and Robertson, 1957.

Ellery, R., *The Psychiatric Aspects of Modern Warfare*, Sydney, Reed and Harris, 1945.

Fidgely, Charles (ed.), *Stress Disorders Amongst Vietnam Veterans: Theory, Research and Treatment*, New York, Brunner/Mazel, 1978.

Figilo, Karl, 'Oral History and the Unconscious', *History Workshop Journal*, no. 26, Autumn, 1988.

Fishman, Sarah, *We Will Wait: Wives of French Prisoners of War, 1940–1945*, New Haven, Yale University Press, 1991.

Fox, Charlie and Marilyn Lake (eds), *Australians at Work: Commentaries and Sources*, Melbourne, McPhee/Gribble, 1990.

Freud, Sigmund, *On Metapsychology: The Theory of Psychoanalysis*, vol. 11, Penguin, 1991.

Fussell, Paul, *The Great War and Modern Memory*, Oxford, Oxford University Press, 1975.

Gaines, Robert, 'Detachment and Continuity: Two Tasks of Mourning', *Contemporary Psychoanalysis*, vol. 33, no. 4, 1997.

Gallaway, Jack, *The Last Call of the Bugle: The Long Road to Kapyong*, St Lucia, University of Queensland Press, 1994.

Garton, Stephen, *Out of Luck: Poor Australians and Social Welfare*, Sydney, Allen & Unwin, 1990.

Garton, Stephen, *The Cost of War: Australians Return*, Melbourne, Oxford University Press, 1996.

Gerster, Robyn, and Jan Bassett, *Seizures of Youth: 'The Sixties' in Australia*, Melbourne, Hyland House, 1991.

Gillis, John R. (ed.), *Commemorations: The Politics of National Identity*, Princeton, Princeton University Press, 1994.

Gluck, Sherna and Daphne Patai (eds), *Women's Words: The Feminist Practice of Oral History*, New York, Routledge, 1991.

Goodall, Heather, 'Telling Country: Memory, Modernity and Narratives in Rural Australia, *History Workshop Journal*, Issue 47, Spring 1999.

Green, Olwyn, *The Name's Still Charlie: A Remarkable Story of Courage and Love*, St Lucia, University of Queensland Press, 1993.

Greene, Graham, *A Sort of Life*, London, Bodley Head, 1971.

Gregory, Adrian, *The Silence of Memory: Armistice Day, 1919–1946*, Oxford, Berg Publishers, 1994.

Grey, Jeffrey, Peter Pierce, Jeff Doyle (eds), *Vietnam Days: Australia and the Impact of Vietnam*, Melbourne, Penguin, 1991.

Grey, Jeffrey and Jeff Doyle (eds), *Vietnam, War, Myth and Memory*, Sydney, Allen & Unwin, 1992.

Griffiths-Marsh, Roland, *I Was Only Sixteen*, Sydney, Harper Collins, 1990.

Grimshaw Patricia, Marilyn Lake, Ann McGrath and Marian Quartly, *Creating A Nation: 1788–1990*, Melbourne, McPhee/Gribble, 1994.

Hagman, George, 'The Role of the "Other" in Mourning', *Psychoanalytic Quarterly*, LXV, 1996.

Hardisty, Sue, *Thanks Girls and Goodbye: The Australian Women's Land Army*, Melbourne, Viking/O'Neil, 1990.

Hendin, Herbert and Ann Pollinger Haas, *Wounds of War: The Psychological Aftermath of Combat in Vietnam*, New York, Basic Books, 1984.

Higgonet, Margaret, Jane Jenson, Sonya Michel, and Margaret Collins Weitz (eds), *Behind the Lines: Gender and the Two World Wars*, New Haven, Yale University Press, 1987.

Hilliard, David, 'Church, Family and Sexuality in the 1950s', in John Murphy and Judith Smart (eds), *Forgotten Fifties, Special Issue, Australian Historical Studies*, no. 109, October 1997.

Hong, Emily, 'Getting to the Source: Striking Lives, Oral History and the Politics of Memory, *Journal of Women's History*, vol. 1, no. 9, 1997.

Humphery, Kim, *Shelf Life: Supermarkets and the Changing Cultures of Consumption*, Cambridge, Cambridge University Press, 1998.

Hunt, Lynn, 'Psychoanalysis, the Self and Historical Interpretation', *Common Knowledge*, vol. 6, no. 2, Fall 1997.

Inglis, Ken, *Sacred Places: War Memorials in the Australian Landscape*, Melbourne, Miegunyah Press, 1998.

Jalland, Pat, *Death in the Victorian Family*, Oxford, Oxford University Press, 1997.

Jamieson, Anne, Sarah Harper, and Christina Victor (eds), *Critical Approaches to Ageing and Later Life*, Buckingham, Open University Press, 1997.

Johnson, Paul and Pat Thane (eds), *Old Age from Antiquity to Post-Modernity*, London, Routledge, 1998.

Johnson-Odim, Cheryl and Margaret Strobel (eds), *Expanding the Boundaries of Women's History*, Indiana, Bloomington University Press, 1992.

Jones, James Peter, *The Reluctant Volunteer in Service with the Ninth Division, 1940–1945*, Loftus, Australian Military Publications, 1997.

Kennedy, Richard (ed.), *Australian Welfare: Historical Sociology*, Melbourne, Macmillan, 1989.

Kertzer, David and Peter Laslett (eds), *Aging in the Past: Demography, Society and Old Age*, Berkeley, University of California Press, 1995.

Kewley, T.H., *Social Security in Australia, 1900–1972*, Sydney, Sydney University Press, 1965/1973.

Kidson, Malcolm A., John C. Douglas and Brendan J. Holwill, 'Post-Traumatic Stress Disorder in Australian World War Two Veterans Attending a Psychiatric Outpatient Clinic', *Medical Journal of Australia*, vol. 158, 19 April 1993.

Kingsmill, John, *No Hero: Memoirs of a Raw Recruit in World War II*, Sydney, Allen & Unwin, 1994.

Kubler-Ross, Elisabeth, *On Death and Dying*, New York, Macmillan, 1969.

Little, Graham, *The Public Emotions: From Mourning to Hope*, Sydney, ABC Books, 1999.

Littlewood, Janet, *Aspects of Grief: Bereavement in Adult Life*, London, Routledge, 1992.

Lopata, Helen Znaniecka, *Current Widowhood: Myths and Realities*, California, Sage, 1996.

Lyons, Mark, *Legacy: The First Fifty Years*, Melbourne, Lothian, 1978.

McCalman, Janet, *Journeyings: The Biography of a Middle-Class Generation*, Melbourne, Melbourne University Press, 1993.

McCollough, Jock, *The Politics of Agent Orange: The Australian Experience*, Melbourne, Heinemann, 1984.

McCormack, Gavan, *Cold War: Hot War: An Australian Perspective on the Korean War*, Sydney, Allen & Unwin, 1983.

McCubbin, Hamilton I., Edna J., Hunter and Barbara B. Dahl, 'Residuals of War: Families of Prisoners of War and Servicemen Missing in Action', *Journal of Social Process*, vol. 31, no. 4, 1975.

Maddock, Kenneth and Barry Wright (eds), *War: Australia and Vietnam*, Sydney, Harper and Row, 1987.

McHugh, Siobhan, *Minefields and Miniskirts: Australian Women and the Vietnam War*, Sydney, Doubleday, 1993.

Metcalfe, Peter, *War in the Shadows: Bougainville, 1944–1945*, Canberra, Australian War Memorial, 1986.

Michel, Sonya, 'Danger on the Home Front: Motherhood, Sexuality, and Disabled Veterans in American Postwar Films', *Journal of the History of Sexuality*, vol. 3, no. 1, 1992.

Murphy, John, *Imagining the Fifties: Private Sentiment and Political Culture in Menzies' Australia*, Sydney, University of New South Wales Press, 2000.

O'Neill, W.M., *A Century of Psychology in Australia*, Sydney, Sydney University Press, 1987.

Passerini, Luisa, *Fascism in Popular Memory: The Cultural Experience of the Turin Working-Class*, Cambridge, Cambridge University Press, 1987.

Passerini, Luisa, *Autobiography of a Generation: Italy 1968*, trans. by Lisa Endberg, Connecticut, Wesleyan University Press, 1996.

Pelling, Margaret and Richard M. Smith (eds), *Life, Death and the Elderly: Historical Perspectives*, London, Routledge, 1991.

Pemberton, Gregory, *All the Way: Australia's Road to Vietnam*, Sydney, Allen & Unwin, 1987.

Pemberton, Gregory (ed.), *Vietnam Remembered*, Sydney, Weldon Publishing, 1990.

Pennebaker, James W., Dario Paez and Bernard Rime (eds), *Collective Memory in Political Events: Social Psychological Perspectives*, Malawah, NJ, Lawrence Erlbaum, 1997.

Personal Narratives Group (eds), *Interpreting Women's Lives: Feminist Theory and Personal Narratives*, Bloomington, Indiana University Press, 1989.

Peters, Betty, 'The Life Experiences of Partners of Ex-POWs of the Japanese', *Journal of the Australian War Memorial*, Issue 28, April 1996.

Peters, Roderick, 'Reflections on the Origin and Aim of Nostalgia', *Journal of Analytical Psychology*, vol. 30, no. 2, 1985.

Phillips, Adam, *On Flirtation*, London, Faber and Faber, 1994.

Phillips, Adam, *Terrors and Experts*, London, Faber and Faber, 1995.

Pickering, Jean and Kehde, Suzanne (eds), *Narratives of Nostalgia, Gender and Nationalism*, London, Macmillan, 1997.

Portelli, Alessandro, 'The Peculiarities of Oral History', *History Workshop Journal*, no. 12, Autumn 1981.

Portelli, Alessandro, *The Death of Luigi Trastulli and Other Stories: Form and Meaning in Oral History*, Albany, State University of New York, 1991.

Portelli, Alessandro, *The Battle of Valle Giulia: Oral History and the Art of Dialogue*, Wisconsin, Wisconsin University Press, 1997.

Raftery, John and Schubert, Sandra, *A Very Changed Man: Families of World War Two Veterans Fifty Years after the War*, Adelaide, School of Human Resource Studies, University of South Australia, n.d.

Raphael, Beverley, *The Anatomy of Bereavement*, New York, Basic Books, 1983.

Read, Peter, *Returning to Nothing: The Meaning of Lost Places*, Cambridge, Cambridge University Press, 1996.

Read, Peter, *A Rape of the Soul So Profound: The Return of the Lost Generation*, Sydney, Allen & Unwin, 1999.

Read, Peter and Coral Edwards, *The Lost Children*, Sydney, Doubleday, 1989.

Reiger, Kerreen, 'The Coming of the Counsellors: The Development of Marriage Counselling in Australia', *Australian and New Zealand Journal of Sociology*, vol. 23, no. 3, November 1987.

Rintoul, Stuart, *The Wailing: A National Black Oral History*, Sydney, Heinemann, 1993.

Riordan, Betty, *Living Well with Grief*, Sydney, Hale and Iremonger, 1995.

Rivett, Rohan D., *Behind Bamboo*, Melbourne, Penguin, 1946/1973.

Roe, Jill, 'Chivalry and Social Policy in the Antipodes', *Historical Studies*, vol. 22, no. 88, April 1987.

Rose, Deborah Bird, 'Remembrance', *Aboriginal History*, vol. 13, no. 2, 1989.

Russell, Cherry, 'Ageing As A Feminist Issue', *Women's Studies International Forum*, vol. 10, no. 2, 1987.

Rutherford, Jonathan, *Men's Silences: Predicaments in Masculinity*, London, Routledge, 1992.

Sangster, Joan, 'Telling Our Stories: Feminist Debates and the Use of Oral History', *Women's History Review*, vol. 3, no. 1, 1994.

Saunders, Kay and Raymond Evans, *Gender Relations in Australia*, Sydney, Harcourt, Brace, Jovanovich, 1992.

Sayers, Janet, *The Man Who Never Was: Freudian Tales*, London, Chatto and Windus, 1995.

Scadron, Arlene (ed.), *On Their Own: Widows and Widowhood in the American Southwest, 1848–1939*, Chicago, University of Illinois Press, 1988.

Scott, Joan, 'The Evidence of Experience', *Critical Inquiry*, vol. 17, no. 4, Summer 1991.

Seltzer, Mark, 'Wound Culture: Trauma in the Pathological Public Sphere', *October*, vol. 80, Spring, 1997.

Shaw, Christopher and Malcolm Chase (eds), *The Imagined Past: History and Nostalgia*, Manchester, Manchester University Press, 1989.

Sheldon, Deborah, *Practical Advice for Australian Widows*, Melbourne, Mandarin, 1996.

Smith, Mary, 'War Widows: The Forgotten Vicitms of War', *Journal of the Australian War Memorial*, no. 5, October 1984.

Soloman, Zahava, Mark Waysman, Gaby Levy, Batia Fried, Mario Mikulincher, Rami Benbenishty, Victor Florian and Avi Bleich, 'From Front Line to Home Front: A Study of Secondary Traumatization, *Family Process*, no. 31, September 1992.

Stewart, Susan, *On Longing: Narratives of the Miniature, the Gigantic, the Souvenir, the Collection*, Baltimore, Johns Hopkins University Press, 1985.

Summerfield, Penny, *Reconstructing Women's Wartime Lives: Discourse and Subjectivity in Oral Histories of the Second World War*, Manchester, Manchester University Press, 1998.

Swain, Shurlee with Renate Howe, *Single Mothers and Their Children: Disposal, Punishment and Survival in Australia*, Cambridge, Cambridge University Press, 1995.

Tal, Kali, *Worlds of Hurt: Reading the Literature of Trauma*, Cambridge, Cambridge University Press, 1996.

Tansley, Tangea, *For Women Who Grieve: Twelve Steps to Life after Your Partner*, Melbourne, Lothian, 1995.

Tennant, Christopher, Jeffrey H. Steiner and Helen Temperly, 'Memories of Vietnam: Post-Traumatic Stress Disorders in Australian Veterans', *Australian and New Zealand Journal of Psychiatry*, vol. 24, no. 1, March 1990.

Thomas, L. Eugene, Robert C. Di Giulio, Nancy W. Sheehan, 'Identity, Loss and Psychological Crisis in Widowhood: A Reevaluation', *International Journal of Aging and Human Development*, vol. 26, no. 3, 1988.

Thomson, Alistair, *Anzac Memories: Living with the Legend*, Melbourne, Oxford University Press, 1994.

Thorpe Clark, Mavis, *No Mean Destiny: The Story of the War Widows' Guild of Australia, 1945–1985*, Melbourne, Hyland House, 1986.

Walker, David and Stephen Garton (eds), *Ageing: Australian Cultural History*, no. 14, 1995.

Walsh, Andrea S., *Women's Film and Female Experience, 1940–1950*, New York, Praeger, 1984.

Wheeler, Wendy, 'After Grief: What Kind of Inhuman Selves?', *New Formations*, vol. 25, Summer, 1995.

Wilkinson, Sue and Celia Kitzinger (eds), *Women and Health: Feminist Perspectives*, London, Taylor and Francis, 1994.

Wilson, John P. and Beverley Raphael (eds), *International Handbook of Traumatic Stress Syndrome*, New York, Plenum Press, 1993.

Wilson, John P., Zev Harel and Boaz Kahana (eds), *Human Adaptation to Extreme Stress: From Holocaust to Vietnam*, New York, Plenum Press, 1988.

Unpublished theses

Boxshall, Glenn, 'The Development and Evaluation of the Vietnam Veterans Counselling Service, Country Outreach Programme, Master of Social Work, University of Melbourne, 1993.

Gilman, Sandy, '"Widowhood Remembered" – An Analysis of the Oral Testimony of War Widows as an Illustration of the Human Conse-quences of the Second World War', BA Hons, Department of History, University of Melbourne, 1989.

Guthrie, Desma Jean, 'Widows and Welfare in Victoria in the 1920s and 1930s', MA, University of Melbourne, 1984.

Index